SAS® For Dummies®

D0472473

SAS Tasks and Associated Procedures

Data Tasks: For Data Access, Data Manipulation, and Filtering

SAS Task	SAS Procedures Used	SAS Task	SAS Procedures Used
Filter and Query (subset, join, compute new columns)	SQL	Rank Data	RANK
Import Data (text and Excel)	DATA step	Sort Data	SORT
Import SAS Information Map	DATA step	Split Columns	TRANSPOSE
Append Table	SQL	Stack Columns	TRANSPOSE
Compare Data	COMPARE	Transpose	TRANSPOSE
Create Format	FORMAT	Download SAS Data to PC (available from http://support.sas.com)	SQL; DATA step
Data Set Attributes	DATASETS	Upload Data to SAS Server (available from http://support.sas.com)	SQL; DATA step
List Data	PRINT	Delete Data Sets and Formats	SQL
Random Sample	SURVEYSELECT	Assign Library (in Tools menu)	LIBNAME statement
Standardize Data	STANDARD		

Describe Tasks: For Simple Tabular Reports

SAS Task	SAS Procedures Used	SAS Task	SAS Procedures Used
List Data	PRINT	Summary Tables (cross-tabulation)	TABULATE
Summary Statistics	MEANS, UNIVARIATE	One-Way Frequencies	FREQ
Distribution Analysis	UNIVARIATE	Table Analysis	FREQ
Characterize Data	CONTENTS, UNIVARIATE, FREQ		

Graph Tasks: For Creating Charts and Plots

SAS Task	SAS Procedures Used	SAS Task	SAS Procedures Used
Bar Chart	GCHART	Contour Chart	GCONTOUR
Line Plot	GPLOT	Box Plot	GPLOT
Pie Chart	GCHART	Map Chart	GMAP
Scatter Plot	GPLOT, G3D	Create Map Feature Table (for use with Map Chart)	GPROJECT
Area Chart	GCHART	Radar Chart	GRADAR
Bubble Plot	GCHART	Surface Plot	G3D
Bar-Line Chart	GBARLINE	Interactive Graphics (download from http://support.sas.com)	SQL
Donut Chart	GCHART		

SAS® For Dummies®

Cheat Sheet

Analysis Tasks: For Statistical Analysis, Modeling, Forecasting, and Measuring

SAS Task	SAS Procedures Used	SAS Task	SAS Procedures Used
t Test	TTEST	CDF Plots	CAPABILITY
One-Way ANOVA	ANOVA	Mean and Range Chart	SHEWHART
Nonparametric One-Way ANOVA	NPAR1WAY	Mean and Standard Deviation Chart	SHEWHART
Linear Models	GLM	Individual Measurements Chart	SHEWHART
Mixed Models	MIXED	Box Chart	SHEWHART
Linear Regression	REG	p Chart	SHEWHART
Nonlinear Regression	NLIN	np Chart	SHEWHART
Logistic Regression	LOGISTIC	u Chart	SHEWHART
Generalized Linear Models	GENMOD	c Chart	SHEWHART
Correlations	CORR	Pareto Chart	PARETO
Canonical Correlations	CANCORR	Prepare Time Series Data	EXPAND
Principal Components	PRINCOMP	Basic Forecasting	FORECAST
Factor Analysis	FACTOR	ARIMA Model and Forecasting	ARIMA
Cluster Analysis	CLUSTER, FASTCLUS, TREE	Regression Analysis with Autoregressive Errors	AUTOREG
Discriminant Analysis	DISCRIM	Regression Analysis of Panel Data	TSCSREG
Life Tables	LIFETEST	Create Time Series Data	TIMESERIES
Proportional Hazards	PHREG	Forecast Studio Create Project (SAS Add-In for Microsoft Office)	HPF
Histograms	CAPABILITY	Forecast Studio Open Project (SAS Add-In for Microsoft Office)	HPF
Probability Plots	CAPABILITY	Forecast Studio Override Values (SAS Add-In for Microsoft Office; download from http://support.sas.com)	HPF
P-P Plots	CAPABILITY	Model Scoring	DATA step
Q-Q Plots	CAPABILITY		

For Dummies: Bestselling Book Series for Beginners

by Stephen McDaniel and Chris Hemedinger

Wiley Publishing, Inc.

SAS® For Dummies®

Published by
Wiley Publishing, Inc.
111 River Street
Hoboken, NJ 07030-5774
www.wiley.com

WILEY

About the Authors

Stephen McDaniel works at Yahoo! in Sunnyvale, CA, and is the Senior Manager of User Empowerment–Business Intelligence and Analytics. He is a strategic advisor and mentor for the business units in Yahoo! Search Marketing, helping business users to harness the potential of their data assets for planning and decision-making. As a member of Strategic Data Systems, he works closely with the data warehousing, business intelligence, and analytic teams on behalf of the business units to provide user-centric vision and guidance to their efforts. You can reach him at www.stephenmcdaniel.us. Previously, Stephen was the senior manager in charge of the SAS Enterprise Guide and the SAS Add-In for Microsoft Office development teams at SAS. Stephen has been a SAS user for more than 17 years and has experience at over 50 companies as a statistician, statistical programmer, product manager, and manager of data warehousing and business intelligence.

Chris Hemedinger is a senior software manager in the Business Intelligence Clients division at SAS. Chris began his career at SAS in 1993 as a technical writer, creating such hits as *SAS Companion for the OS/2 Environment* (remember OS/2?) and *SAS Companion for the Microsoft Windows Environment*. In 1997, he became involved in a prototype project to make SAS easier to use for non-programmers, and that project evolved into the hugely popular SAS Enterprise Guide, a product that Chris has worked with ever since.

Dedications

Stephen McDaniel: I want to thank my wonderful wife Eileen for her love, patience, support, help, reviews, and encouragement throughout the writing process!

Chris Hemedinger: For my beautiful wife Gail: for her patience and for our three daughters (even though they would never tolerate my chapters as acceptable bedtime-story material, despite my coaxing).

Authors' Acknowledgments

They said it couldn't be done. They said that it wasn't possible to cover a broad and complex topic like SAS in a *For Dummies* book.

"They" (whoever they are) obviously were not aware of the fantastic help that we had on this project, so it turns out that "they" were wrong.

We, the humble authors, could not have planned and completed this book without the tremendous help of our editors at Wiley and at SAS Press. From Wiley, we relied on Jodi Jensen, Katie Feltman, Teresa Artman, and James Russell. At SAS Press, Judy Whatley served as our acquisitions editor, traffic cop, and cheerleader.

We also had great technical and content feedback from our panel of reviewers: Marilyn Adams at SAS, Sarah Hayford at Duke, Eileen McDaniel at UNC-CH, Tonya Balan at SAS, David Bailey at SAS, Ted Meleky at SAS, and I-Kong Fu at SAS.

In the area of moral support, we thank Gail Kramer (our boss) and David Rieder (Stephen's friend) for their encouragement. We would also like to thank all of the people who helped us in SAS R&D and the SAS Enterprise Excellence Center for providing the demo servers for some of these chapters. Demos used from the EEC were created by Ken Matz, Justin Choy, and Renato Luppi of SAS. Stephen would also like to thank Rick Styll and I-Kong Fu for their support throughout the process.

—*Stephen and Chris*

I also want to thank a few of the many friends I have made over the years in my career: David Vangeison, Huifang Wang, Rajiv Ramarajan, Brian Casto, Joe Carter, Brenda Wolfe, David Duling, Michael Leonard, and Pat Maher from SAS; Alan Churchill of Savian; Bala Ganesh and PJ Haselton from Loudcloud; John Rotherham, Ken Kane, and Dave Jesky from Brio; Lynn Polingo, Gene Lim, and Anthony Edmonds from TAP Pharmaceuticals; Jim Esinhart and Ferrell Drewry from PharmaResearch; Mike Wisniewski, Paul Jarrett, and John Jones from Glaxo; and Meimei Ma, Steve Wright, and Sid White from Quintiles. Thanks to all of you for helping me, encouraging me, and supporting me throughout the years!

—*Stephen McDaniel*

Publisher's Acknowledgments

We're proud of this book; please send us your comments through our online registration form located at www.dummies.com/register/.

Some of the people who helped bring this book to market include the following:

Acquisitions, Editorial, and Media Development

Project Editor: Jodi Jensen

Senior Acquisitions Editor: Katie Feltman

Development Editor: James Russell

Senior Copy Editor: Teresa Artman

Technical Editor: SAS, Inc.

Editorial Manager: Jodi Jensen

Media Development and Quality Assurance: Angela Denny, Kate Jenkins, Steven Kudirka, Kit Malone

Media Development Coordinator: Jenny Swisher

Media Project Supervisor: Laura Moss-Hollister

Editorial Assistant: Amanda Foxworth

Senior Editorial Assistant: Cherie Case

Cartoons: Rich Tennant (www.the5thwave.com)

Composition Services

Project Coordinator: Patrick Redmond

Layout and Graphics: Claudia Bell, Joyce Haughey, Barbara Moore, Heather Ryan

Proofreaders: Aptara

Indexer: Aptara

Anniversary Logo Design: Richard Pacifico

Publishing and Editorial for Technology Dummies

Richard Swadley, Vice President and Executive Group Publisher

Andy Cummings, Vice President and Publisher

Mary Bednarek, Executive Acquisitions Director

Mary C. Corder, Editorial Director

Publishing for Consumer Dummies

Diane Graves Steele, Vice President and Publisher

Joyce Pepple, Acquisitions Director

Composition Services

Gerry Fahey, Vice President of Production Services

Debbie Stailey, Director of Composition Services

Contents at a Glance

Table of Contents

Introduction

*U*nless you live as a hermit, chances are good that your life is touched by SAS almost every day.

Have you ever received an offer for a credit card in the mail? The bank might have used SAS to select you for the particular offer you received. Remember a recent news article that cited demographic trends in the United States? The Census Bureau uses SAS to crunch its numbers. Were you tempted to buy that new gadget in a big-name retail store? The corporate office might have used SAS to calculate the best price to set for that specific item in that specific week.

The rate you pay for life insurance, the analysis behind pharmaceutical drug trials, the quality of parts used to assemble your automobile — all of these are determined by people who use SAS. You don't see SAS directly from day to day — but, like gravity, it's an invisible force that affects your life.

This book offers a prolonged glimpse into the multifaceted world of SAS software. Read on to discover how people use SAS to influence the world around you. Perhaps you'll see how to grab the reins yourself and use SAS to affect your own sphere of influence.

About This Book

Even though this book is titled *SAS For Dummies*, you absolutely need some smarts to get solid results using SAS. However, the overarching message of this book is that you don't need to be an expert at using software. You just need to know what questions to ask, what data is needed to provide an answer, and how to interpret the results.

This book covers a variety of SAS products. We take a high-level look at some and dive deeply into those that you're most likely to use. The amazing fact is that SAS offers hundreds of software products covering dozens of industries and disciplines. No single person could possibly use them all and still have time for essential activities, such as sleep and personal hygiene. (Hmm, maybe that explains the smell around here.)

And, hey! Here's something else cool about this book: You don't have to read it from stem to stern. Feel free to skip around, reading the sections that cover what you need to know.

This book does *not* address two popular SAS topics:

- **Learning the SAS programming language:** SAS software has been around for more than 30 years, and you can find plenty of books about SAS programming. Indeed, one goal of this book is to show you how much you can do with SAS without having to become a SAS programmer — unless you really want to.

- **Life at SAS Institute Inc., the makers of SAS software:** SAS, the company (along with its founder Jim Goodnight) has had more than its 15 minutes of fame on TV shows (such as *60 Minutes* and *Oprah*) plus a big dose of coverage in business magazines (such as *Fortune* and *Forbes*). The stories are overwhelmingly positive (not featuring anyone trying to blot out the camera view with his palm). SAS is famous for being a great place to work. Because we, the authors, hold (or have held) day jobs at SAS — and we really like those jobs — that's all we'll say about that.

Foolish Assumptions

To better manage the task of writing this book, we had to begin with some assumptions about you, the reader. Here they are:

- SAS software runs on many different types of computer systems, but the majority of people experience it from Microsoft Windows. So, the examples provided are presented as if you're using a PC. We assume that you know your way around a PC, clicking the mouse, selecting menus, and so on.

- As we stated earlier, we don't assume that you are a SAS programmer or that you even aspire to be one. However, if you are or if you do, you can still find this book useful to round off your SAS knowledge.

What Not to Read

Occasionally, you'll see some sidebar topics or Technical Stuff icons in the margin that indicate an historical or a technical side point. You can skip those if you want to, but reading them will give you that extra edge when SAS comes up in the discussion at the next cocktail party you attend. Study up and impress your friends!

Conventions Used in This Book

This book contains lots of descriptive information about SAS software. Because a picture is worth — well, you know — this book has lots of figures of the software in action. (_Action_ is a relative term; after all, this _is_ business and analytical software, not _World of Warcraft._)

- You'll find plenty of step-by-step instructions to accomplish specific tasks. You can follow along with these if you have the software handy; otherwise, you can use your imagination and pretend how much fun it is.

- When we show a URL, filename, path, data set, or code within regular text, we set it off in a monofont type, `like this`.

- When we want you to type something, we bold the characters you type (such as, **type this**).

- If you get the munchies while reading this book, it's because most of the examples refer to data with a candy theme.

- The data files discussed in the book actually ship with _SAS Enterprise Guide,_ which is a SAS application that features prominently in this book.

Icons Used in This Book

All the information in this book is special; we would not have included it otherwise. But some information that we provide is more special than the rest. To draw attention to its "specialness," we tagged it with some eye-catching little icons:

The Tip icon calls out a sentence or two that might prove to be a real time-saver in your work. (You're welcome.)

Got a mind like a steel sieve? Well, you might want to reserve some space in your memory banks for the content next to the Remember icon. We use these as a way to emphasize important points or concepts.

Hear the voice in your head yelling "Danger Will Robinson! Danger!"? Well, there is little danger really, as long as you heed the advice shown near the Warning icon.

This book contains many little gems of technical information. You can still use SAS if you don't read and understand this stuff, just like you can still enjoy watching hockey if you don't know what "icing" means. But, as any fan will tell you, it's more fun knowing what it all means.

How This Book Is Organized

Yes, this book *is* organized; the chapters don't simply appear in random order. There are six major parts, each of which includes some relatively self-contained chapters. Don't feel like you need to read them in order though. Please, make yourself at home and read whichever chapters interest you the most. (Really, it's okay; we won't be offended.)

Part 1: Welcome to SAS!

SAS, meet reader. Reader, meet SAS. In Part I, you get to know each other in this overview of what SAS software is about and what it can do for you. You'll find an introduction to SAS Enterprise Guide and some examples for getting quick results without having to be an expert.

Part 11: Gathering Data and Presenting Information

Data is everywhere, but information is scarce. Part II shows how you can use SAS to take data and turn it into information you can use. And even better, you can see how to turn it into information that others will use and thank you for. You'll find out how to build basic reports and graphs that actually convey useful information.

Part 111: Impressing Your Boss with Your SAS Business Intelligence

Part III is a whirlwind tour through the concepts of statistics and analytics. You get an overview of the basics, as well as some examples of how those are applied to help you understand and predict behavior, as represented in data. Correlations, causality, forecasting — those topics and others are discussed here.

Part IV: Enhancing and Sharing Your SAS Masterpieces

Part IV could be titled "SAS: It's Everywhere You Want to Be" or "SAS: It's Not Just for Programmers Anymore." You'll see how you can use SAS from your desktop, on the Web, in Microsoft Excel, and even in Microsoft PowerPoint!

Part V: Getting SAS Ready to Rock and Roll

Part V provides the high-level view of how to install and configure SAS software. You might come away with an enhanced appreciation for whomever performs that task for you. This part also covers the concept of data collection and preparation — the repeatable process for making data available for analysis. And for the SAS programmers in the audience, you can find a candid overview of SAS Enterprise Guide, your new friend.

Part VI: The Part of Tens

Part VI is where we stored the nuggets of knowledge that you can count on both hands (or feet!). Even if you already consider yourself a SAS expert (maybe your Mom gave you this book for Christmas), we promise that you will discover something new here. Check out Part VI for ten productivity tips for SAS Enterprise Guide users, ten "must-know" items for SAS administrators, and links to more resources.

Where to Go from Here

After you read through this book, you might crave more details about specific areas that we cover. (Or maybe those cravings are related to the candy-themed examples.) The best starting place for more information is the SAS support Web site at http://support.sas.com.

If this book transforms you into a card-carrying SAS user, your next step might be to seek out others like you. That will be easy because millions of people all around the globe use SAS. And do you know what? They like to get together every so often in SAS user groups. User group meetings and conferences provide a great way to learn more from your peers about how to use SAS in practical and creative ways. Again, user group information is available from SAS at http://support.sas.com.

Part I
Welcome to SAS!

The 5th Wave   By Rich Tennant

"We're not sure what it is. Rob cobbled it together from paper clips and stuff in the mail room, but <u>MAN</u> wait till you see how it analyzes data."

In this part . . .

What exactly is SAS anyway? Is it really a Scandinavian airline (wrong "SAS"), or do those letters mean something else?

In this part, you discover how to see the world for what it is: a huge bucket of data. And we show you how you can use SAS software to pull some of that data together and draw useful information from it. We introduce you to some of the basic tools that will become your companions as you begin your journey toward SAS savvyness.

Chapter 1

Touring the Wonderful World of SAS

*O*ne of the questions newcomers ask most frequently about SAS is "What does the name mean?" After all, those capital letters usually indicate an acronym, right? Today, SAS just refers to the name of a company. If you've been around the world of data analysis for a while, however, you may also be familiar with the old meaning of the abbreviation, *Statistical Analysis System*.

SAS software was initially developed by a bunch of really smart and inquisitive people at North Carolina State University (NCSU) in the late 1960s and early 1970s. Some of these people are still at SAS (the company) as owners or executives: Jim Goodnight (the current company president), John Sall, and Herb Kirk (the first SAS user). Most of these SAS software pioneers were trained as statisticians or mathematicians and developed the SAS language to specifically help analyze a variety of scientific experiments being conducted at NCSU and other research universities.

Over time, the software became as important as the experiments it was being used to analyze. In 1976, several people brave enough to leave the cozy life of academia for the then unknown world of software started the company today known as SAS. The first few years were a bit rough; but before long, word of this software and its capabilities began to spread, revenues increased, and the company began to grow.

This chapter is an overview of the power and flexibility of SAS for a wide range of applications and industries. In particular, SAS has expanded from being just for experts to meeting the needs of a wide range of users in almost every industry and country in the world. SAS has come a long way, changing from just a programming language to a wide range of applications tailored to various business and scientific needs.

SAS — Isn't That Just for Gurus?

You might assume that you need to be a statistician or math guru to use SAS, but that's happily not the case. In the last few years, SAS has made significant investment in taking the unparalleled analytical and data management capabilities developed over 30 years and making them available to almost anyone with a problem to solve in business, science, or government. With new products such as SAS Enterprise Guide and the SAS Add-In for Microsoft Office, SAS has never been more accessible or flexible. These products provide user-friendly interfaces and wizards to maximize the heavy-duty capabilities that SAS has long provided to gurus!

Most of this book is dedicated to simple-to-learn principles that are full of possibilities and limited only by your situation and imagination. SAS offers so much potential that this book just scratches the surface and hopefully gets you up to speed on the basics.

Data, Data Everywhere — But Not Where I Need It!

The glamorous side of business intelligence and data analysis is all the gee-whiz reports, graphs, and impressive statistics you can present. (It must be true because my p-value says so! And don't worry if you don't know what a *p-value* is right now. That will come later.) The surprising secret of actually arriving at good results for decision-making is the huge amount of time that many people spend accessing, organizing, and preparing their data for a particular analysis. In visiting more than 50 major companies in our various work experiences, we've found that the common theme is the massive amount of resource and rework time spent on the data preparation aspect of business analytics.

As mentioned earlier in this chapter, the first developers of SAS were doing real-world research projects and faced these very same data preparation and analysis issues. Consequently, they developed products that allow seamless access to over 100 data sources on almost every computing platform currently in use. This capability was way ahead of its time back then and is still hands-down the best we have used. These data access products — SAS/ACCESS products — run on your SAS server. They allow fast, seamless access to disparate data sources for your analysis (see Figure 1-1).

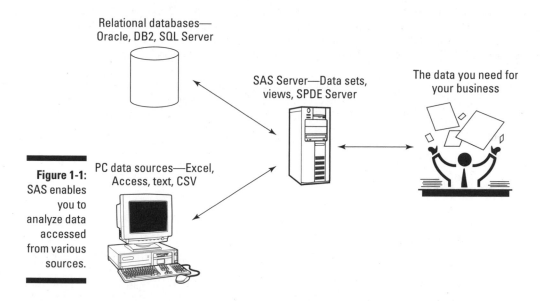

Relational databases— Oracle, DB2, SQL Server

SAS Server—Data sets, views, SPDE Server

The data you need for your business

PC data sources—Excel, Access, text, CSV

Figure 1-1: SAS enables you to analyze data accessed from various sources.

One real-life data preparation story

At one prominent aerospace company, Six Sigma black-belts reported that 85 percent of their time is spent collecting, cleaning, and preparing their data for the business tasks at hand. Even worse, they realize this work is duplicated across various departments. They all end up doing the same preparation work with a given data source, such as data describing all products currently sold, their predecessor products, and the dates that products were discontinued.

This data resides on different platforms in various formats with a wide array of data rules. Staff work with older data in text files on a mainframe computer, data from an acquired subsidiary in Oracle on UNIX, data in DB2 from a new ERP system (Enterprise Resource Planning system — SAP in this case) on a Windows server, or data in a spreadsheet on someone's PC. When each team brings this data together for its own projects, they often arrive at different results. Upper management wonders why teams can never agree on even basic metrics and the analyses needed to run the business. . . .

SAS can get to the data, but that's only the beginning. SAS also has excellent tools to enable centralized management of your data. Applications such as SAS Enterprise Guide have a wide array of data access, query, and management capabilities that enable you to slay your data-management dragons in a flexible and effective manner.

SAS also offers the SAS Data Integration Server, which enables your power users to effectively access, manage, and aggregate your data. The SAS Data Integration Server focuses around the types of problems commonly connected to data warehousing and data quality. Using the SAS Data Integration Server allows you to have one integrated view of your data that is built on common rules and assumptions. The value here is in avoiding different answers to the same question by ensuring that everyone has access to a user-friendly, consistent data store. You find out more about this topic in Chapter 16.

Data Summaries and Reporting

If you've worked with traditional business intelligence tools from other software vendors, you might be familiar with data summarization and reporting. These tasks are critical to your ability to pull value from the data and knowledge inherent in your organization. Unfortunately, this immediate need for data is often the only area that people focus on when they ask for information to answer a particular question. If you can take a broader, long-term approach to your data management, reporting, and analysis needs, however, you can save money and time while yielding superior results.

One example to illustrate this point is a report of accounts past due. You could generate this information in Microsoft Excel and copy and paste subsets of the data to send to various sales teams. This is a very manual process. Or, you could design a report that can be easily updated with the latest data. This report can use subsets for accounts for each sales team and link to order details for each overdue account to show exactly what was in the overdue order. Also imagine if this report could be delivered automatically over the Web, by e-mail, or directly into Microsoft Office. Now it is a much more flexible and powerful asset — all available from one SAS report!

Why summarize data?

Elsewhere in this chapter we give an example of reducing a 50-million–row table to just a few rows. Imagine, then, that you want to present that data, summarized in three forms: a pie chart, a listing, and a bar chart. By explicitly summarizing the large data source once (collapsing the 50 million rows down to 100 or so rows) and then creating the pie chart, listing, and bar chart from the summarized form, you get a much quicker generation of your results for your analyses.

Some simple forms of data summaries include sums, averages, medians, ranges, counts (sometimes called *frequencies*), and percentages. If you're interested in determining total sales by region, for example, the data source you have with this information might be a 50-million–row table. By using the summary functions of SAS, you can collapse this data to a small number of rows — one row per region, for example. Many functions in SAS automatically summarize the data for you. A pie chart of the sales by region would also automatically collapse the data to just a few rows before charting it.

SAS has a variety of powerful techniques to summarize your data, from basic counts, means, medians, minimum values, and maximum values, to sophisticated algorithms that allow you not just to aggregate the data but actually find relevant confidence intervals around the aggregations you request.

The Secret Sauce: Analytics to Optimize the Present and Predict the Future

If you were familiar with SAS before you started reading this chapter, you may be aware that SAS was made famous by its analytic capabilities. And you may be wondering whether you can easily use the analytic capabilities that SAS offers. Even if they are easy to use, can they really make a difference in your business? We can almost absolutely, positively guarantee that the answer will be *Yes*! (Okay, legalese time. This is not some binding guarantee. Your results and mileage can vary, but we're 99.999% sure.)

Almost every analytic technique, statistic, and test is designed to help better identify the true state of something by analyzing limited information. Here are some examples of where analytics can come in handy:

- ✔ Did the Western sales region really have a better average sales number than the Eastern region?

- ✔ Do customers who buy our gum spend more money at retailers than customers who don't?

- ✔ What are the projected sales over the next year of CinnaPecans if I lower their price by 10 percent?

- ✔ Which customer demographic factors are useful in predicting customers' receptiveness to a direct marketing solicitation?

To answer any of these questions effectively, you first need access to data that is of high quality, familiar to you, and properly organized so that you can apply the appropriate analytic technique for the question at hand. Even after you apply the appropriate analytic technique, you need an integrated way to evaluate the success of the technique and a method of presenting (reporting) the results so that even managers (like us) can understand.

Table 1-1 offers a high level view of some of the analytic capabilities from SAS, their potential applications, and where you can go to in this book to find out more about the technique.

Table 1-1	Example Applications of SAS Analytics	
Real World Example	**Statistical Technique**	**Chapter**
An engineer wants to predict the mean time until failure for a new LED television based on 15 test models	Survival Analysis	Chapter 9
A manager wants to know the impact on projected sales next year if she doubles marketing spending	Forecasting	Chapter 9
A clinician wants to know the effect on patient response of doubling the dose of a new drug	Mixed Models	Chapter 8
A sales manager wants to know the projected profitability of a new customer based on the customer's demographic profile	Data Mining	Chapter 9
A taste tester wants to know if people really prefer Fizzy Cola over Foamy Cola	Categorical Data Analysis	Chapter 9

Real World Example	Statistical Technique	Chapter
A procurement team wants to test whether the new super strong titanium bolts meet the specified strength specs for its new jet	Quality Control	Chapter 9
A sales promotion manager at OmniLoMart and her team want to know projected sales by country, store, and even SKU for the next week	High Performance Forecasting	Chapter 9
A hospital wants to predict patient stay length based on physician and nurse comments captured in the patient database	Text Mining	Chapter 9

Sharing the SAS Wealth

SAS has gone above and beyond its traditional market in the last few years to add an impressive array of tools and delivery mechanisms to make the lives of business analysts, managers, and executives easier and more productive. The following list describes just a few of the tools SAS offers you:

✔ **OLAP (On-Line Analytic Processing):** Frequently referred to by lay people as *pivot tables*, provides a mechanism for large volumes of data to be summarized in advance and presented to users via customized tools specifically designed to make exploring this data easy and fast. With OLAP, you can take a very large table, such as a sales history table for a large retailer, and predefine certain categories and metrics of interest that are run on a nightly basis. This results in a greatly collapsed data size with data stored in a specific format that enables very fast creation of summaries and exploration. Figure 1-2 illustrates a view of such a sales table before and after using it in OLAP.

✔ **SAS Add-In for Microsoft Office:** Provides you with direct access to SAS reports, data engines, data management, reporting, and analytic tasks seamlessly from Microsoft Excel, Word, and PowerPoint. The add-in allows you to avoid the commonly discussed concern of using Excel for your analytic needs, often called *spreadsheet hell*. Spreadsheet hell is the issue of using a simplistic yet user-friendly tool like Excel for complex data processing that really should be done with a better tool. SAS is well suited to perform this type of processing through the SAS add-in. When you use the SAS add-in, SAS content and data sources are centrally maintained and can be dynamically synchronized with your SAS server to ensure that all analysts in your company are accessing "one version of the truth." A simple example is illustrated in Figure 1-3: a centrally created and maintained SAS forecast analysis that is dynamically streamed and easily updated by end users from PowerPoint.

✔ **SAS Information Delivery Portal and SAS Web Report Studio:** Allow for simplified delivery of content over the Web and intuitive reporting for almost any level of user. Users access a centrally maintained view of their data to quickly create powerful and insightful reports that can be easily shared throughout the organization. Figure 1-4 illustrates just one of the many report formats that you can create in a matter of minutes with SAS Web Report Studio.

Figure 1-2:
Sales data
in standard
table form
and then in
OLAP form.

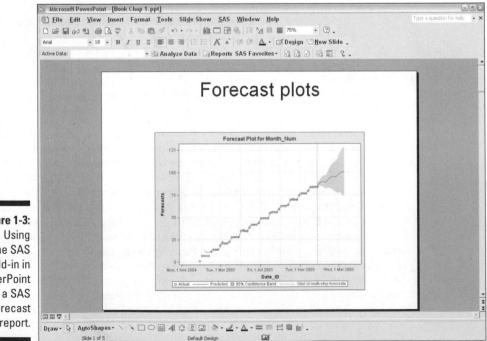

Figure 1-3:
Using
the SAS
add-in in
PowerPoint
for a SAS
Forecast
report.

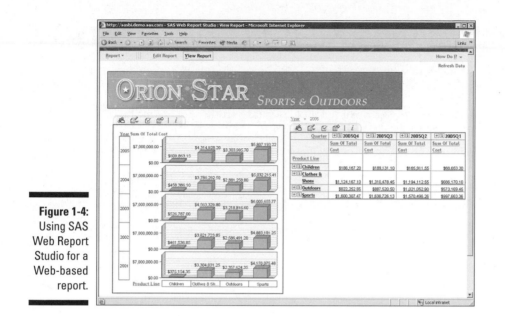

Figure 1-4:
Using SAS
Web Report
Studio for a
Web-based
report.

What the IT Department Needs to Know

The ease of use and the powerful analytical applications of SAS are great for the end user and number crunchers, but SAS is friendly to your IT folks as well. The good news for IT professionals is that SAS 9 provides you with a centralized approach for deploying software, managing security, managing user environments, creating content, distributing content, and controlling user access to data.

By using standard software packaging tools, administrators can prepackage the distribution of SAS software. Using SAS Management Console to maintain metadata in the SAS Metadata Server (also known as the Open Metadata Repository), you can configure servers, server options, users, and user groups, manage data sources, and manage content available to users.

SAS Information Map Studio enables you to create dynamic data views based on administrator-defined Information Maps. These Information Maps hide the complexity and danger of accessing complex data schemas by presenting users with administrator-defined business views of the data. Based on user selections, SQL is dynamically created to provide them with just the data they need for their report.

More details that IT folks may be interested in reviewing are covered in Chapters 4 (data access), 15 (setting up SAS), 16 (data warehousing), 17 (SAS programming with the new world of SAS), and 19 (administrator tips).

Checking Out Real-World Success Stories

As users and employees of SAS, we have personally seen many real-world SAS success stories. From forecasting to data warehousing to data mining to business intelligence, SAS can meet just about any need you can imagine. To read a wide array of detailed SAS case studies, use your favorite Web browser and go to www.sas.com/success.

Chapter 2

Your Connection to SAS: Using SAS Enterprise Guide

In This Chapter

▶ Seeing how SAS made its way to the PC

▶ Checking out your data access options

▶ Summarizing and otherwise compiling your data

▶ Reporting on-the-spot

SAS has been around for a long time and has often been considered the province of math or programming experts. About ten years ago, Dr. Goodnight (cofounder and CEO since the company was created in 1976) thought that this image needed to change. To accomplish the image change, SAS needed a new interface that was both user friendly and capable of delivering SAS power without programming. Thus, SAS Enterprise Guide was born.

SAS Enterprise Guide was the first application from SAS developed just for Microsoft Windows users to allow them to access, query, summarize, analyze, and publish results from their SAS server running almost anywhere. SAS servers can run from your PC, a Windows server, a UNIX server, or even on a good old mainframe (with no funny-looking punch cards required!). And because SAS Enterprise Guide can run from a Windows desktop (for ease of use), yet interact with SAS on any computing platform, it is one of the most powerful user interfaces on the planet.

In this chapter, you see how to use this marvelous interface to the broad capabilities of SAS.

Using SAS Enterprise Guide, the Swiss Army Knife of SAS

When you look across the wide array of capabilities that SAS Enterprise Guide comprises, we can confidently call it the Swiss army knife of SAS. Just like a Swiss army knife, SAS Enterprise Guide is handy in lots of situations and offers a surprising array of options in a simple-to-learn package.

SAS Enterprise Guide is included with PC SAS. PC SAS is a local copy of SAS for your PC that works like your own personal SAS server. A modified version of SAS Enterprise Guide with a restricted copy of PC SAS is the basis for the SAS Learning Edition. (The release of SAS Enterprise Guide used in the SAS Learning Edition is typically one or two versions behind the latest version of SAS Enterprise Guide.) Many companies also license desktop-based versions of SAS Enterprise Guide to allow their users to work with remote Windows, UNIX, or mainframe SAS servers. Whichever configuration of SAS you use with SAS Enterprise Guide, most of the functionality is the same; the difference is whether the processing is mainly performed on your PC or on a remote computer.

We recommend that you find out what version of SAS Enterprise Guide you're working with because it underwent major revisions in the 3.0 release, first available in 2004. If you are using the 2.1 release or earlier, you'll find that the general user interface and workflow capabilities are very different from what we show in this book. Many of the core capabilities are in the earlier releases, but we show the 4.1 release (first available in early 2006), which is fairly similar to the 3.0 release. If you're using either 3.0 or 4.1, you should have little trouble following along with this book.

Using SAS Enterprise Guide for the first time

When you first install and use SAS Enterprise Guide, the interface looks something like what you see in Figure 2-1. This is the default, out-of-the-box view.

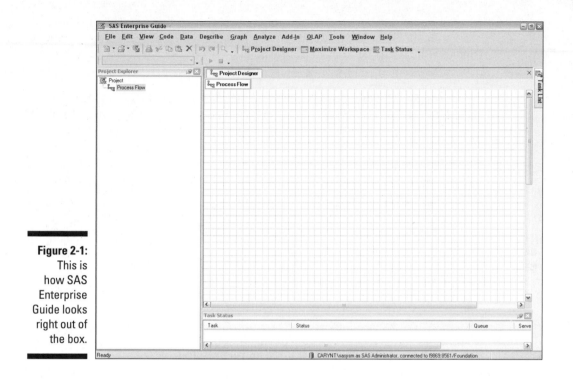

Figure 2-1:
This is
how SAS
Enterprise
Guide looks
right out of
the box.

The interface shows you some familiar elements:

- ✔ **A menu bar**
- ✔ **Toolbars**
- ✔ **Workflow presentation:** Two panes — the tree-like Project Explorer and the work flow-oriented Process Flow — show your workflow from two different perspectives. More than one Process Flow can exist in a project; the Project Designer is the overall "container" for all of them.
- ✔ **Task List:** This feature offers quick access to almost all tasks and functions.
- ✔ **Task Status pane:** This pane shows the status of work submitted to your SAS server.

Although the default view is a good general-purpose layout, we walk you through our preferred customizations to the interface. When you get ready to make SAS Enterprise Guide your own, you have a huge array of options for how to manage your workspace. You can

✔ **Toggle toolbars.** Turn toolbars on and off by choosing View➪Toolbars and selecting from the list in the resulting dialog box. You can turn them all on and lay them out in no more than two rows. We use all of them frequently.

✔ **Customize the workspace.** Dock, pin, or turn on and off the interface panes so that you maximize the Process Flow and workspace viewing area.

✔ **Choose app settings.** Set a wide array of options for overall application behaviors by choosing Tools➪Options and making selections from the Options dialog box. For example, you can choose to control the following things:

- What you see in the Project Explorer and the Process Flow

- Your default output type (HTML, RTF, PDF, text, and/or SAS Report formats)

- Whether you view your report output embedded inside SAS Enterprise Guide or external to SAS Enterprise Guide by launching the relevant application with the report

- How data is browsed

- How user-written SAS code is managed and displayed

- How and whether your security credentials are cached

- What metadata server and SAS server you are using

Changing what you see on-screen

For this book, we changed the following areas for all screenshots to simplify what new users need to view while providing the minimum set of functionality for most scenarios. Start SAS Enterprise Guide and follow these steps to set your interface to look like the screenshots you see in this book:

1. Launch SAS Enterprise Guide from the Start menu.

SAS Enterprise Guide appears, displaying the Welcome to SAS Enterprise Guide dialog box, as shown in Figure 2-2.

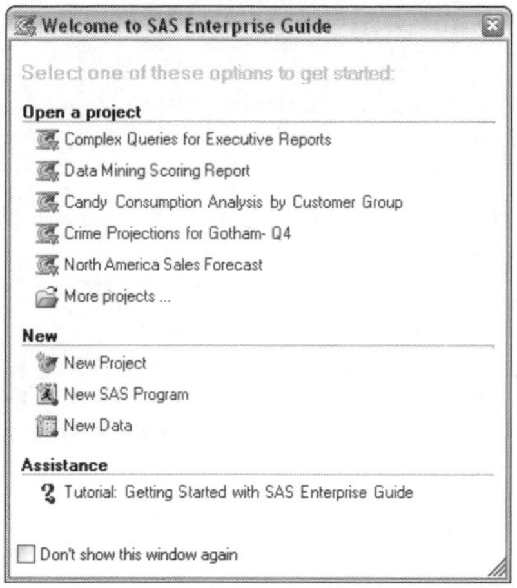

Figure 2-2:
The
Welcome
to SAS
Enterprise
Guide dialog
box offers
several
options.

> ◆ Welcome to SAS Enterprise Guide   ✕
>
> Select one of these options to get started:
>
> **Open a project**
>
> 🎬 Complex Queries for Executive Reports
> 🎬 Data Mining Scoring Report
> 🎬 Candy Consumption Analysis by Customer Group
> 🎬 Crime Projections for Gotham- Q4
> 🎬 North America Sales Forecast
> 📂 More projects ...
>
> **New**
>
> 🗐 New Project
> 🗐 New SAS Program
> 🗐 New Data
>
> **Assistance**
>
> ? Tutorial: Getting Started with SAS Enterprise Guide
>
> ☐ Don't show this window again

From this dialog box, you can choose to

- Open a recently used project
- Open a project located by searching your computer drives or SAS server
- Create a new project
- Run the Getting Started with SAS Enterprise Guide tutorial

Our favorite choice is the Don't Show This Window Again check box! You can always open or create new projects from the File menu.

2. **Choose Tools⇨Options from the main menu bar.**

   The Options dialog box appears.

3. **If your SAS server is version 9.1.3 Service Pack 4 or later, deselect HTML under Result Formats type and select SAS Report.**

   This selection might not affect most activities in this book, but the reporting section (see Chapter 6) requires this change. If you make this change to SAS Report and your SAS version is earlier than Service Pack 4, SAS Enterprise Guide automatically reverts to HTML output.

4. **In the Results General section, select Replace Without Prompting.**

   This enables you to rerun SAS Tasks without being prompted about whether you want to replace the last report created.

5. **Select Persist for User under Security: Credentials Persistence.**

   I make this selection so that you only need to enter your password once — that is, until your password changes on the source. Click OK to close the Options dialog.

6. **Hover over the Task List pane, which is unpinned and on the far right side of the application (refer to Figure 2-1).**

   The Task List pane expands.

7. **Click the pushpin at the upper right of the Task List pane to pin it.**

   When you pin it, the pane stays open regardless of whether you hover over it.

8. **Click the pushpin again to unpin it.**

   The Task List pane docks on the far right.

   The Task List re-expands if you hover the mouse over the docked icon. After you use and then move away from the re-expanded pane, it docks itself again.

   You can pin or unpin other panes, such as Task Status or Project Explorer, based on your preferences.

   Leave everything else in the default state.

You can arrange your workspace differently at any time. If you don't like your changes and want to revert back to the default layout, choose Tools⇨Options⇨ General and click the Reset Docking Windows button.

Accessing and Managing Data

After setting up the application workspace, you're probably anxious to see SAS Enterprise Guide in action. A primary role of SAS Enterprise Guide is to give you access to and control over your business data. For example, you can open SAS data sources or import most any type of commonly used data format for use in SAS Enterprise Guide. SAS Enterprise Guide has a truly wide array of data access and management options, and this section provides a brief glimpse into accessing and managing data with SAS Enterprise Guide.

Opening SAS data sets

SAS data sets are the building block of many reports and analyses in SAS. A SAS data set is the standard data storage format for data created with SAS. The great thing about SAS data sets is that they are fast to open and analyze relative to other data storage methods, such as text files, comma separated values (CSV) files, Excel spreadsheets, and even relational databases like Oracle or DB2. By default, the output data created by your activities in SAS Enterprise Guide are SAS data sets.

To open a data set and create a project from scratch, follow these steps:

1. **Launch SAS Enterprise Guide from the Start menu.**

2. **Click New Project.**

   The Welcome dialog box closes, and the new project appears with a blank Process Flow pane.

3. **Choose File⇨Open⇨Data.**

   The Open Data From dialog box appears. Your choices are

      • **Local Computer:** Clicking this icon allows you to browse your local computer resources, such as Windows Explorer, to select a data source.

      • **SAS Server:** Clicking this icon takes you to predefined data libraries defined on your SAS server to select a server based data source.

4. **Click the Local Computer icon.**

   The file types that SAS Enterprise Guide can open appear in a standard Windows Open dialog box. If you want to examine only SAS data files, click the Files of Type drop-down list, as shown in Figure 2-3, and choose SAS Files.

We're working with a sample SAS data set named Candy_Sales_
Summary that comes with SAS Enterprise Guide. Our copy of this
data set is at

```
C:\Program Files\SAS\Enterprise Guide 4\Sample\Data\
            Candy_Sales_Summary.sas7bdat
```

If you want to follow along with this example, you may have to browse to
a different location to find this file on your system.

Figure 2-3:
The Open
dialog box
displaying
only SAS
data sets.

5. Click the Open button.

The data set opens in your project and appears in the data grid, as
shown in Figure 2-4. You can easily browse the data by using the
vertical and horizontal scroll bars.

Keep this data set open and continue to the next section to find out how to
filter data in the data set.

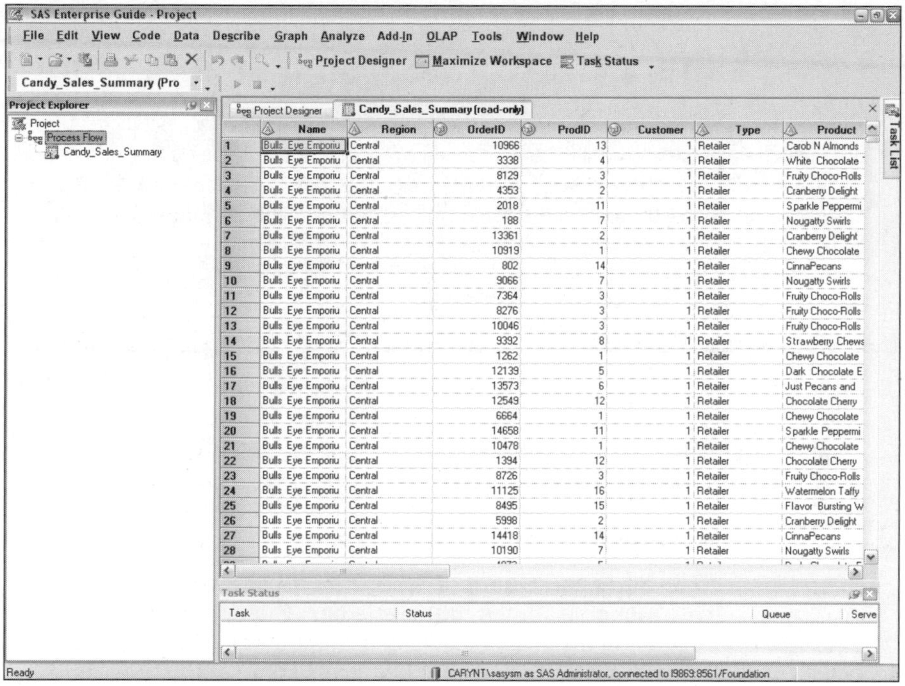

Figure 2-4:
The Candy Sales Summary data set browse view via the data grid.

Filtering SAS data

One of the most frequently used features of SAS Enterprise Guide is the Filter and Query task. After you open a data set, this task makes it easy to filter the data to analyze just the records that interest you. Filtering data can be as simple as organizing customer data based on country or the patients in a trial based on year of birth. Filtering can be based on one or many conditions, using "and" or "or" logic, and can even utilize complex formulas in the conditions. A complex condition could be "all patients born in 1968 with a mean blood sugar reading on their first three visits greater than 100 or a history of diabetes with at least two hospitalizations required."

What's a SAS Task? Sounds like work!

SAS Tasks in SAS Enterprise Guide are the wizards and dialog boxes that make your life easier. They logically present you with a variety of choices to enable you to perform the activity requested by you just the way you want it. When you click Run, the task automatically generates and submits to your SAS server the SAS code needed to perform the actions you requested. Some people use SAS Tasks and the preview code button from the tasks to teach themselves SAS programming. However, if you don't care about learning programming in SAS, you don't ever need to look at the code!

Using the Candy_Sales_Summary data set you opened in the preceding set of steps, follow these steps to filter the data for records from the fiscal year 2003:

1. **Choose Data⇨Filter and Query.**

   The Filter and Query task appears, as shown in Figure 2-5. Notice that the task title shown in the title bar (Query) doesn't exactly match the option name you chose from the Data menu (Filter and Query.) A quick glance at this task dialog box gives some indication of how much you can do from this one task. You can compute new data columns, add parameters for dynamic filtering, apply filters, preview the results before running the task, and sort output data.

2. **Choose your variables:**

   a. *Select all the variables from the Candy_Sales_Summary data set for the filtered data set.*

   b. *Click and drag the Candy_Sales_Summary data set symbol to the blank space on the Select Data tab labeled* Drop a column here to add it to the query *to add it to the query.*

   All the variables in the Candy_Sales_Summary data set appear in the Select Data space, as shown in Figure 2-6. By default, no variables are added automatically to your query (no variables are in the Select Data space) because you might have a very wide data set that you want to reduce to just a few variables. This setting and many other defaults are configurable via the Data⇨Options dialog box, which is also accessible via the Options button in the Filter and Query task.

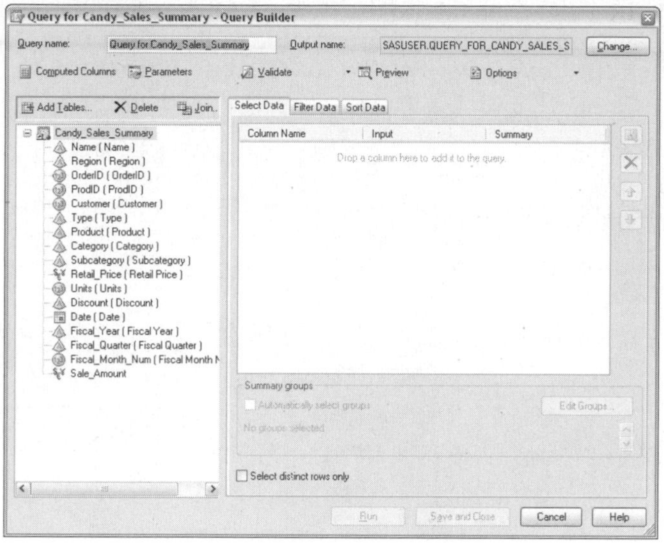

Figure 2-5:
The Filter and Query task dialog box when first opened.

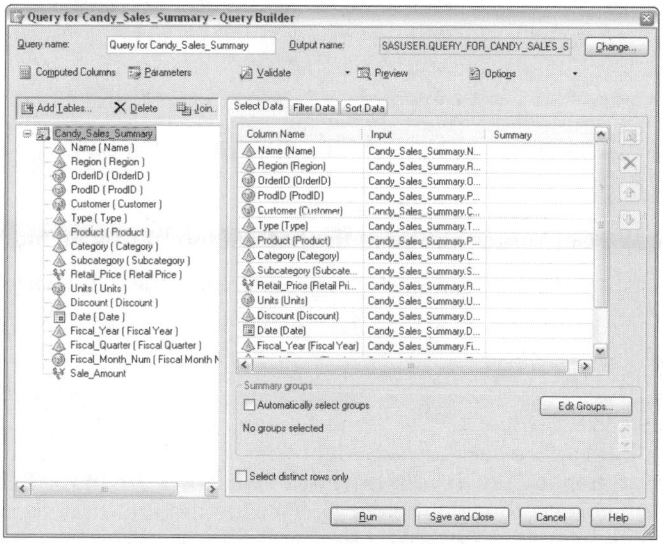

Figure 2-6:
The Filter and Query task Select Data variables selected.

3. **Click the Filter Data tab (to the right of the Select Data tab), and then click and drag the Fiscal_Year variable to the blank Filter Data space labeled** *(Optional) Drop a Variable Here* **to filter the data.**

   The Edit Filter dialog box for variable Fiscal_Year appears, as shown in Figure 2-7.

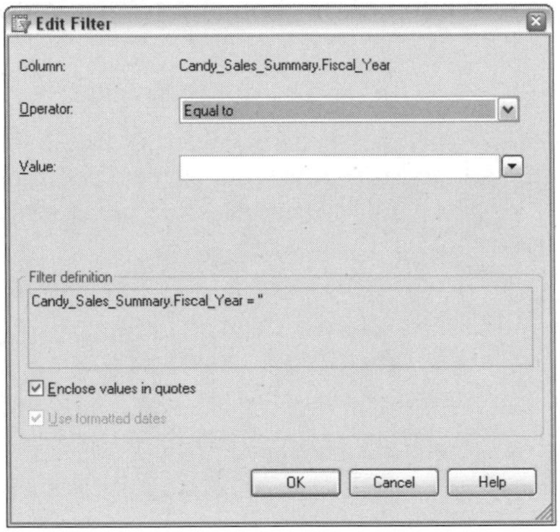

Figure 2-7:
The Edit
Filter
dialog box.

4. **Click the down arrow of the Value drop-down list box.**

   The Values selection dialog box appears.

5. **Click the Get Values button at the bottom left of this dialog box.**

   The distinct values for Fiscal_Year appear, as shown in Figure 2-8.

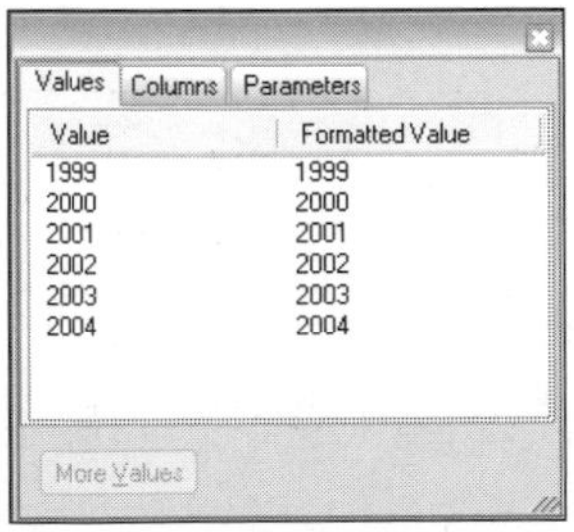

Figure 2-8:
A listing of
distinct
values for
variable
Fiscal_Year.

6. Click 2003 to return to the Edit Filter dialog box.

The left side of the dialog shows the "raw" data value and the right side shows the formatted data value. In this case, they are the same. A variable such as gender could have an *M* on the left "raw" value side and a value of *Male* on the right formatted side. You can click anywhere on the value row to select the desired value.

7. Click OK to close the Edit Filter dialog box and return to the main Filter and Query task.

8. Click the Run button to close the Filter and Query task.

SAS Enterprise Guide automatically generates the SAS code needed to fulfill your request and submits it to your SAS server. The filtered data set, which the task titles as *QUERY_FOR_CANDY_SALES_SUMMA_0001*, opens in the data grid, as shown in Figure 2-9.

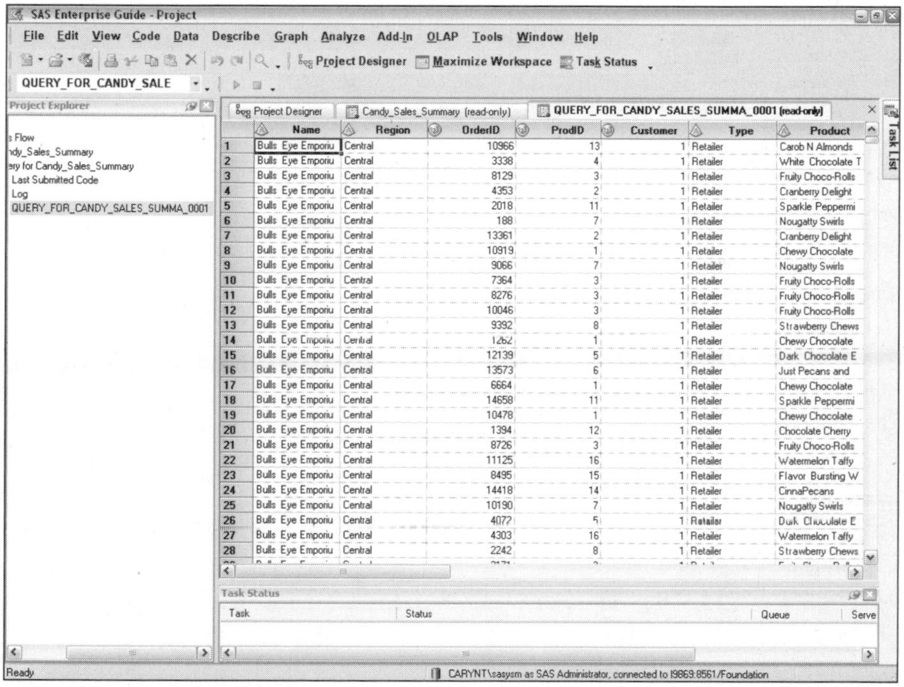

Figure 2-9:
The Candy Sales Summary data set filtered for fiscal year 2003.

9. **Click the Project Designer toolbar button to view the Process Flow built in this example.**

   SAS Enterprise Guide keeps an up-to-date process flow view of the data set opened, the query task built from it, and the resulting data set created when the query ran, as shown in Figure 2-10. This information is also visible to the left in a tree format via the Project Explorer. Each view can be useful in quickly navigating your project. Double-clicking any of the items in the process flow automatically reopens the item.

You have opened a data set, viewed it, filtered it based on fiscal year 2003, and created a new data set with just the 2003 data in it. The Process Flow shows you this visually at a high level.

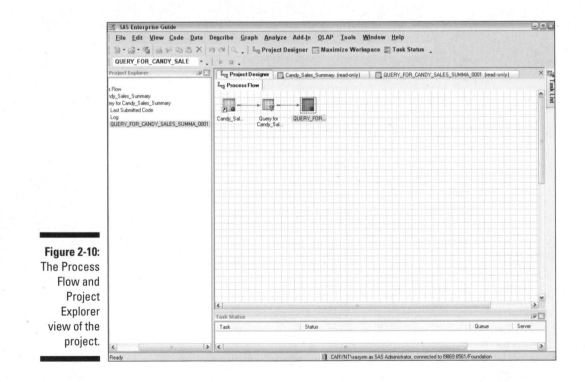

Figure 2-10:
The Process Flow and Project Explorer view of the project.

Visualizing Success with Charts

The extensive charting capabilities of SAS Enterprise Guide give you the power to add new levels of insight to your reports and analyses. Different types of data and questions are best displayed with different types of charts, and SAS Enterprise Guide offers 13 major types and 60 subtypes of charts. This section provides a brief glimpse into graphing with SAS Enterprise Guide. To find out more about working with charts and graphs in SAS, see Chapter 7.

Bar charts are one of the most common and useful chart types. In this example, you see how to chart sales by region, quarter, and product category in one easy-to-read and interpret chart. To create this chart, follow these steps:

1. **To use the Candy_Sales_Summary data set you've already opened and filtered, choose Graph⇨Bar Chart from the main menu in SAS Enterprise Guide**

   The Bar Chart task appears with the bar chart subtypes in the opening panel. The task automatically uses the last active data source, which in this case is the result of the query.

2. **Click the Grouped/Stacked Vertical Bar chart type.**

   Notice the task tip near the bottom part of the task. Most tasks have this context-sensitive help available at all times, as shown in Figure 2-11.

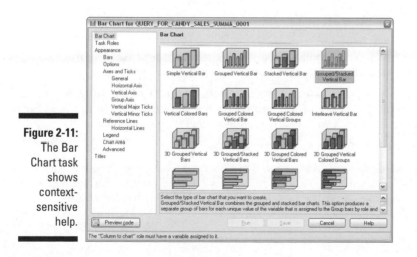

Figure 2-11: The Bar Chart task shows context-sensitive help.

3. **In the panel on the left, click Task Roles.**

4. **Click Fiscal_Quarter and drag it to the Column to Chart role in the Task Roles pane.**

   Assigning variables to roles is part of the process of specifying the work the application will do once you click Run.

5. **Repeat Step 4 to assign Region to the Group Bars By role, Category to the Stack role, and Sale_Amount to the Sum Of role, as shown in Figure 2-12.**

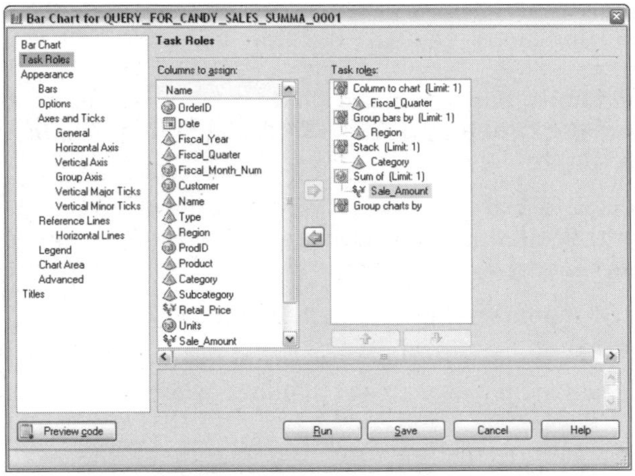

Figure 2-12: The Bar Chart task showing the assigned roles.

Most tasks have a similar structure to the bar chart task. The roles and options available vary according to the individual task.

6. **Click Titles in the panel on the left, deselect the Use Default text box to turn off the default title, and then type the following in the Text for Section: Graph:** 2003 Sales by Region, Quarter, and Category.

7. **Click the Run button to run the Bar Chart task.**

   The task dialog box closes and SAS Enterprise Guide instructs the SAS server to execute the submitted SAS code based on your requested specifications. After the code is executed, the graph opens in SAS

Enterprise Guide, as shown in Figure 2-13. With this bar chart, you can see the importance of each region in overall sales, the differences in sales trends by quarter by region, and the contribution of each product category to overall sales.

To make it easier to see the entire graph without the rest of the project workspace visible, click the Maximize Workspace toolbar icon, as shown here in the margin. When you finish viewing the output in the maximized mode, click the same toolbar icon to go back to the standard project view.

You can also access the Maximize Workspace feature by clicking Ctrl+M. This feature works when you display any report view, data view, or Process Flow view.

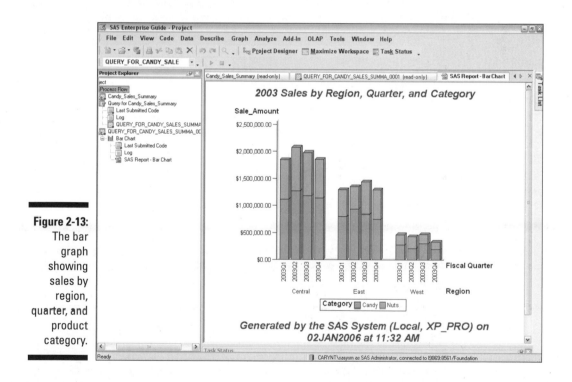

Figure 2-13:
The bar graph showing sales by region, quarter, and product category.

Creating Reports for Even the Crankiest Manager

When most software products refer to *reporting*, they mainly focus on bringing in data to a pretty layout or cross-tabular report and controlling the layout, page numbering, and other appearance options such as formatting. SAS Enterprise Guide certainly lets you do this type of work, but it also gives you many other options. SAS Enterprise Guide has an impressive array of SAS Tasks to help you make just the right presentation consisting of simple counts, descriptive statistics, complex cross-tabulations, graphs, and even advanced analytics and forecasting — all in one report! In this section, you see how to create a moderately complex cross-tabulation report and then enrich it to make a composite report featuring some of your graphs and the summary table.

Creating a summary table report

Summary table reports are a great way to summarize data by categories or by groups. Summaries could include average sales amount, number of units sold, or maximum sales discount. Categories could be year, quarter, region, or product line. To create a summary table report of regional sales summary by subcategory and product, follow these steps:

1. **Choose Describe⇨Summary Tables.**

   The Summary Tables task appears.

2. **For Task Roles, click and drag the following items to their appropriate destinations as shown in the following table:**

Drag This	Here
Region	Pages
Fiscal_Quarter, Subcategory, and Product	Classification Variables
Sale_Amount	Analysis Variables

   Figure 2-14 shows the roles assigned in the Summary Tables task.

   Region is added automatically to the Classification Variables role because a Pages role is considered a classification of the report.

3. **Set the following layout:**

a. *In the panel on the left, click Summary Tables.*

b. *In the Summary Tables pane that opens, drag the variable Fiscal_Quarter to the top of the variable identifier* N *box.*

c. *Drag Product to the left side of the row identifier box* ALL.

d. *Drag Subcategory to the left side of the* Product *box.*

e. *Drag Sale_Amount to the top of the table area just below* N.

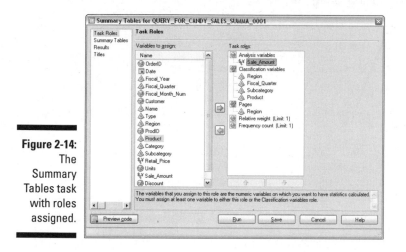

Figure 2-14:
The
Summary
Tables task
with roles
assigned.

Figure 2-15 shows the layout you just created.

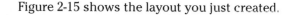

Figure 2-15:
The
Summary
Tables pane
with table
layout.

4. **From the Available Statistics box on the bottom left of the Summary Tables pane, scroll down the statistics list to Sum; then drag and drop the statistic Sum over the variable identifier N.**

   The cell where the statistic N was displayed changes to Sum.

5. **Right-click the variable statistic Sum; then select Data Value Properties from the contextual menu.**

6. **From the Data Value Properties dialog box that appears, click the Format tab and set the following:**

   • Currency, from the Categories scrollable list

   • DOLLARw.d, from the Formats scrollable list

   • Overall width to 12 in the Attributes area

7. **Click OK.**

   Figure 2-16 shows the completed Format tab of the Data Value Properties dialog box.

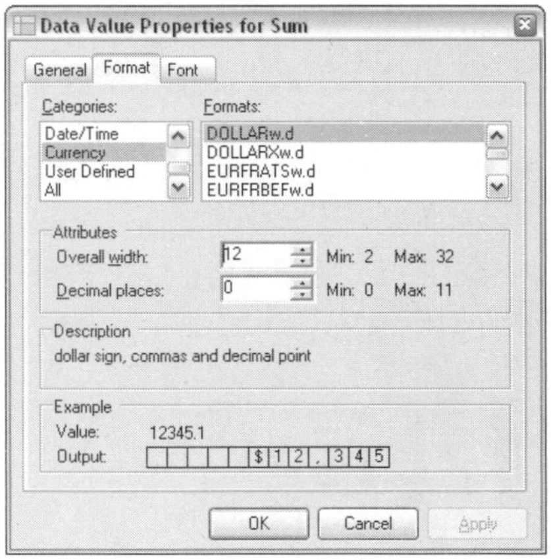

Figure 2-16:
The Data Value Properties dialog box with specified formatting.

8. **Right-click the identifier All and choose Remove Cells from the contextual menu.**

   Figure 2-17 shows the completed Summary Tables pane.

9. **Right-click the row identifier Subcategory in the Preview pane and choose Heading Properties from the contextual menu.**

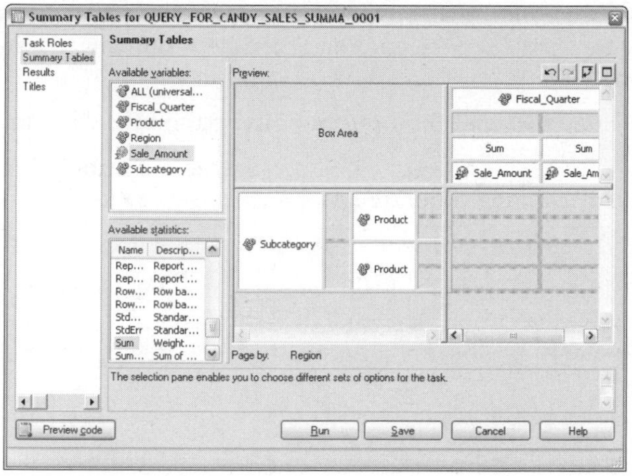

Figure 2-17:
The
completed
Summary
Tables pane.

10. **From the Heading Properties for Subcategory dialog box that appears, click the General tab, as shown in Figure 2-18, and delete the text in the Label field. Do the same for the row identifier Product and for statistic identifier Sum. Click OK.**

Figure 2-18:
Heading
properties
for a
categorical
variable.

11. **Back in the Summary Tables pane, click Titles in the left panel.**

12. **Click the Use Default text box to turn off the default title and enter the following for Text for Section:** Regional Sales Summary by Subcategory and Product.

13. **Click the Run button at the bottom of the pane to close and run the Summary Tables task.**

    The summary table is generated and opens automatically, as shown in Figure 2-19.

The regional sales summary provides a concise summary of sales by product. The summary tables task makes it easy to create a wide array of summary reports using a highly flexible layout pane that includes the most commonly used statistics.

Figure 2-19:
The completed Regional Sales Summary report.

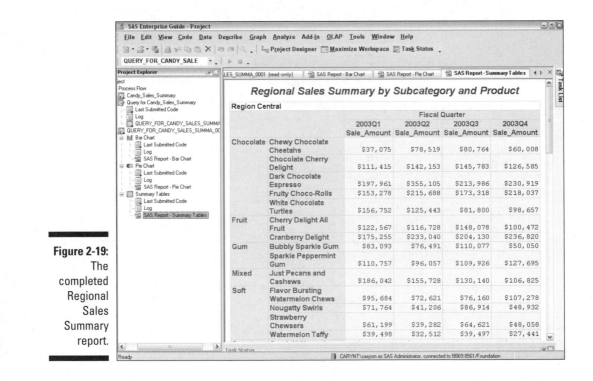

Enriching a summary table report with graphs

A composite report enables you to combine output from multiple tasks on one report for easy viewing and printing. Viewing data from a variety of perspectives on one composite report often makes it easier for decision makers to arrive at an effective conclusion. To create a composite report using the summary table and the charts created earlier in this chapter, follow these steps:

1. **Click the Project Designer toolbar button to view Process Flow.**

2. **Right-click the SAS Report - Summary Tables icon and choose Create Report from the contextual menu.**

   A copy of the Summary Tables report is created in the project and automatically opens, as shown in Figure 2-20. Read on to see how to turn it into a composite report by including results from more than one task. This report is linked to the original tasks it is based on. It is *dynamic,* meaning that it will always update if you rerun the tasks.

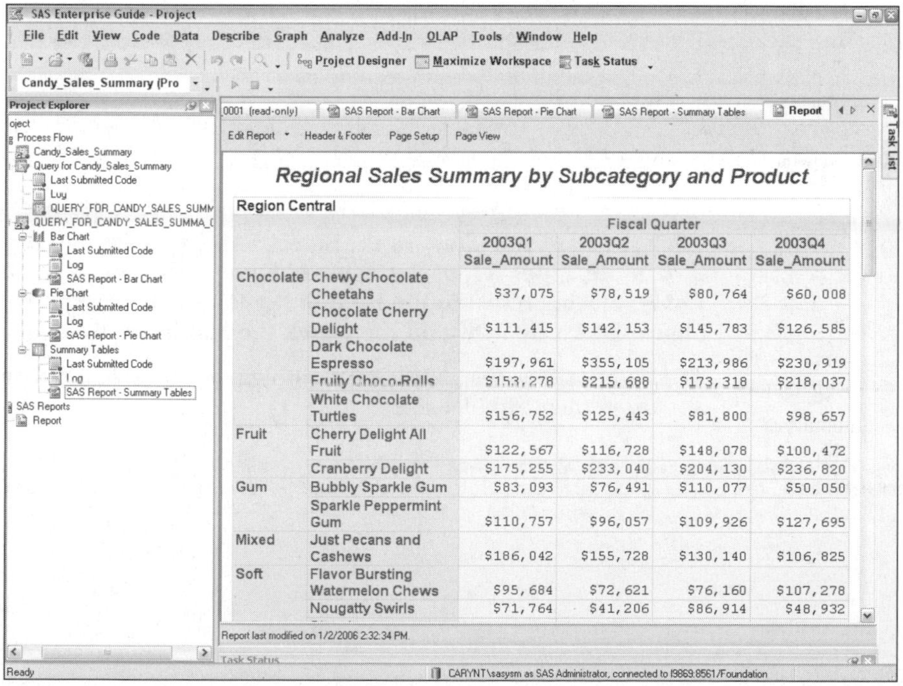

Figure 2-20: The composite report editor showing the Summary Tables.

3. **Click the Edit Report button at the top of the report window.**

4. **In the Edit Report Contents dialog box, click the Summary Tables box in the Report Layout view at the right of the dialog box; then move Summary Tables down in the report view by dragging down to the cell below where it is currently displayed, as shown in Figure 2-21.**

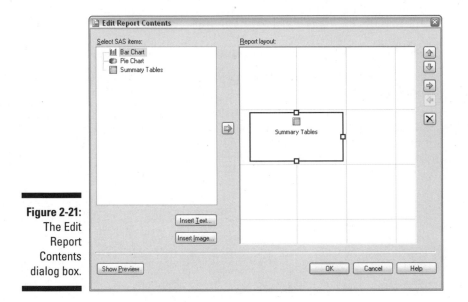

Figure 2-21:
The Edit
Report
Contents
dialog box.

5. **Click the Bar Chart item in the Select SAS Items list and drag it to the box in the upper left of the Report Layout. Repeat this for the Pie Chart, placing it just to the right of the Bar Chart, as shown in Figure 2-22. Click OK and then click the Maximize Workspace icon.**

   The composite report appears, as shown in Figure 2-23. All charts appear in their original sizes.

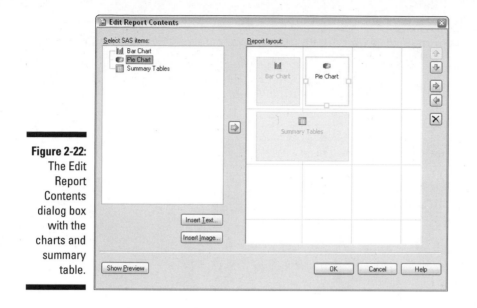

Figure 2-22:
The Edit Report Contents dialog box with the charts and summary table.

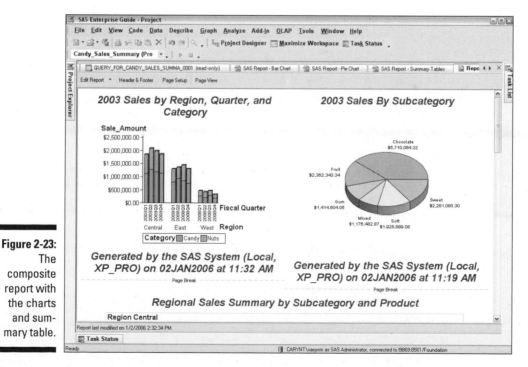

Figure 2-23:
The composite report with the charts and summary table.

6. **Clean up the report view by removing the chart footnotes:**

   a. *Click the Header & Footer button at the top of the report window.*

   b. *In the Header & Footer dialog box that appears, click the Titles & Footnotes tab and deselect the Footnote check boxes for Bar Chart and Pie Chart, as shown in Figure 2-24.*

   c. *Click OK.*

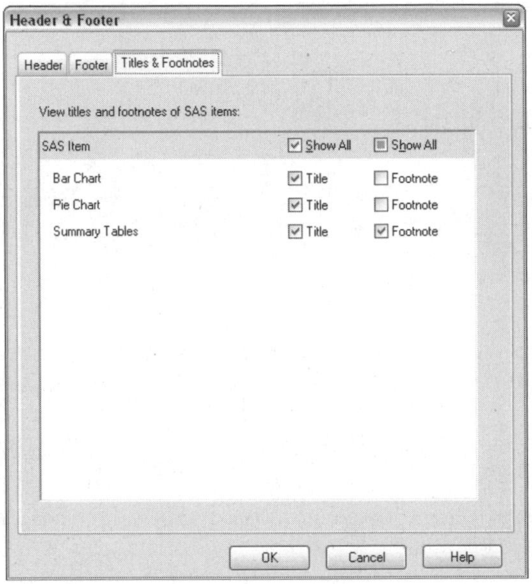

Figure 2-24:
Remove
footnotes on
the Titles &
Footnotes
tab.

The composite report updates. You can print this report; before doing that, however, choose File⇨Print Preview to ensure that the layout is what you want, as shown in Figure 2-25. You can easily page through the report using your Page Up and Page Down keys. Click the Close button from the Print preview dialog box to return to the project.

7. **To save your work, choose File⇨Save Project As.**

   In the Save Project To dialog box that appears, you can choose

- **Local Computer:** Enables you to save this project to your local computer drives.

- **SAS Server:** Takes you to predefined file storage locations defined on your SAS server.

8. **Click the Local Computer Icon.**

   The default location for saving SAS Enterprise Guide projects on your computer appears in the Save As dialog box.

9. **(Optional) If you've followed along with the examples in this chapter and want to save this project as-is, name this project** SAS for Dummies Chapter 2, **as shown in Figure 2-26, and click Save.**

   You can exit SAS Enterprise Guide by choosing File⇨Exit.

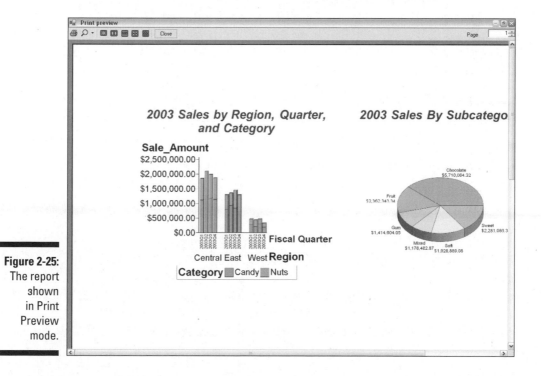

Figure 2-25:
The report shown in Print Preview mode.

The next time you want to use the project you just saved, you can open it by selecting it from the recently used projects listed at the bottom of the File menu. Recently used projects are also listed at the Welcome Screen when you restart SAS Enterprise Guide — unless you turned off that screen as suggested earlier in this chapter!

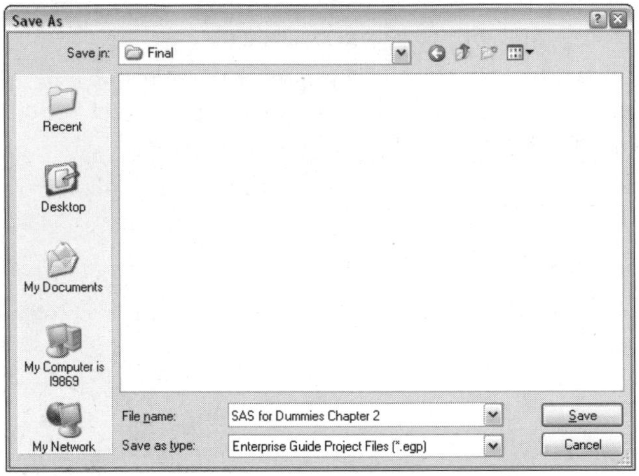

Figure 2-26:
The project
Save As
dialog box.

Chapter 3

Six-Minute Abs: Getting Miraculous Results with SAS

*O*ne of the cornerstones of the progress made in the 20th century was a great gain in economic efficiency and capacity. Americans, in particular, have been obsessed with making things faster, quicker, cheaper, or bigger. One of my favorite examples was a recent comedic movie in which a character had big plans to strike it rich with a product named Six-Minute Abs. He stated that this would provide the same workout as the one touted by the Seven-Minute Abs folks but in just six minutes — thus saving you a minute a day!

SAS Enterprise Guide is the Six-Minute Abs of SAS, only much better! Stephen has used SAS since the late 1980s and has been a senior programmer and senior statistician using SAS the old-fashioned way: programming in the SAS language. Mastering SAS Enterprise Guide, though, has made it possible for even a SAS programming guru like Stephen to be far more productive in accessing, managing, analyzing, graphing, and reporting in his daily work life.

In this chapter, you see more of the awesome capabilities SAS Enterprise Guide offers.

Where Is My Data Set Coming from and Where Is It Going?

SAS uses server *libraries*, which are the logical assignment of actual folders on your computer or server to simple but meaningful library names, such as WORK or SASUSER. Depending on your SAS configuration, you might use the WORK or SASUSER library by default because these are typically available by default on SAS servers.

For example, WORK is a special temporary library automatically assigned by the SAS server. WORK data exists only for your current SAS session and goes away when you close your SAS Enterprise Guide session. Data you place in the WORK library is not available if you close SAS and later reopen it!

If your data is required for a future SAS Enterprise Guide session, do not use the WORK library. You would have to rerun your analysis to re-create it each time. Re-creating isn't an issue for a table that takes just a few seconds to re-create. If a table results from a long-running task, however, you don't want to waste your time re-creating it unless the source data is constantly being updated and you want those updates every time you work on them.

Another automatic SAS library is SASUSER. Unlike WORK, SASUSER is a permanent library. Any data placed in SASUSER during your current session stays there until you overwrite or delete it.

Some organizations turn on a special option to prevent writing back to SASUSER, often because they have other standards in place about where your personal data and work project are placed. Other organizations don't even use SASUSER because of security concerns about shared data that may be restricted due to privacy and confidentiality policies.

You — or your administrator — will likely create numerous other libraries specific to your organization and needs. Some of these might be *read-only* (you can't save data sets there), and others can allow you to write to them. Depending on your SAS configuration, you may be using the WORK or SASUSER library by default.

Organizations can create user- or administrator-created libraries that provide access to relational databases such as Oracle, Teradata, DB2, or SQL Server. These libraries let you seamlessly transfer data in to and out of these systems at will. This is critical for companies because their key corporate data is often stored in these systems.

Querying Your Way to Success

Of the many capabilities that SAS Enterprise Guide offers via SAS tasks, the Filter and Query task is one of the most important for use across a wide array of users and applications. With the Filter and Query task, you can

- ✔ Join data from separate data tables
- ✔ Filter data
- ✔ Sort data
- ✔ Create computed columns
- ✔ Summarize data
- ✔ Add dynamic run-time prompts so you can select exactly which filter criteria to apply
- ✔ Create basic listings
- ✔ Create output data sets from the selections made in the task

As you can see, the Filter and Query task encompasses a broad area of functionality. The capability to access tables in a database, join them together, and filter the results is often the first step in reporting or analysis. A simple example would be joining a sales history table with a products table to obtain a detailed sales and product table. You can also filter the sales data to a particular year and the products to a certain product line. Additionally, you may have several computed columns that compute the net sale price for each transaction based on the discount given and the full retail price.

When you master the basics of the Filter and Query task, your success at accessing the data you need will know no limits! The following example touches on some of these features. For more in-depth coverage on working with your data, see Chapter 5.

What's all this talk of joining?

Joining data is like getting married — bringing together two separate entities and making them one — except that joining data is a lot quicker and cheaper. When you have relevant data for a report or analysis in more than one table, you can merge that data by matching rows based on the columns they have in common so that all the relevant information is in one table. Examples of columns commonly used to join data tables are customer ID, date, product ID or name, and location. Figure 3-1 shows a simple example of joining two tables. Here, the Students table is joined with the Grades table by column Student_ID so that you have a unified table of student information and their grades.

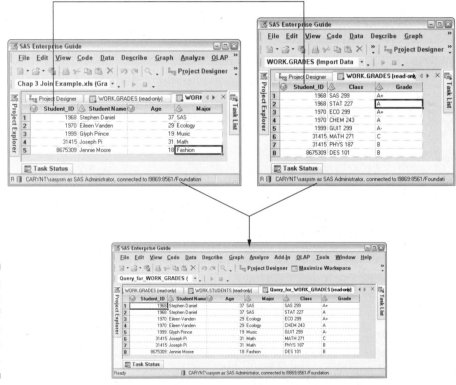

Figure 3-1: Here is an example of a simple two-table join.

Joining data from multiple tables

To examine the power of the query task, follow these steps to see how you can join data sources:

1. **Launch SAS Enterprise Guide and create a new project.**

   If you need a refresher on how to create a new project, see Chapter 2.

2. **Choose File⇨Open⇨Data and click the Local Computer Icon.**

3. **From the sample data provided with SAS Enterprise Guide, open the following data sets (which you can find by choosing File⇨Open⇨Data to open the Open Data From dialog box):**

   - Candy_Customers
   - Candy_Products
   - Candy_Sales_History
   - Candy_Time_Periods

   Just as you can in Windows Explorer, you can select multiple items in an open dialog box by pressing Ctrl+click (to select individual, non-contiguous items), or Shift+click at the beginning and end of a list of files (to select a contiguous block).

   All the data sets open in your project; the last one opened appears in the data grid, as shown in Figure 3-2.

4. **Choose Data⇨Filter and Query.**

   The query task appears with the last active table in use — in this case, Candy_Time_Periods.

5. **Click the Add Tables button in the upper-left quarter of the task.**

   The Open Data dialog box appears, as shown in Figure 3-3.

6. **Click Project as the data source location for this query.**

   In this example, you open all four tables used in the project before beginning to create the query.

   Another option is to open only the Candy_Time_Periods table in Step 3 and then add the other tables by using the Add Tables button in the Filter and Query dialog box. When you add tables to the query this way, they are added to the project for you.

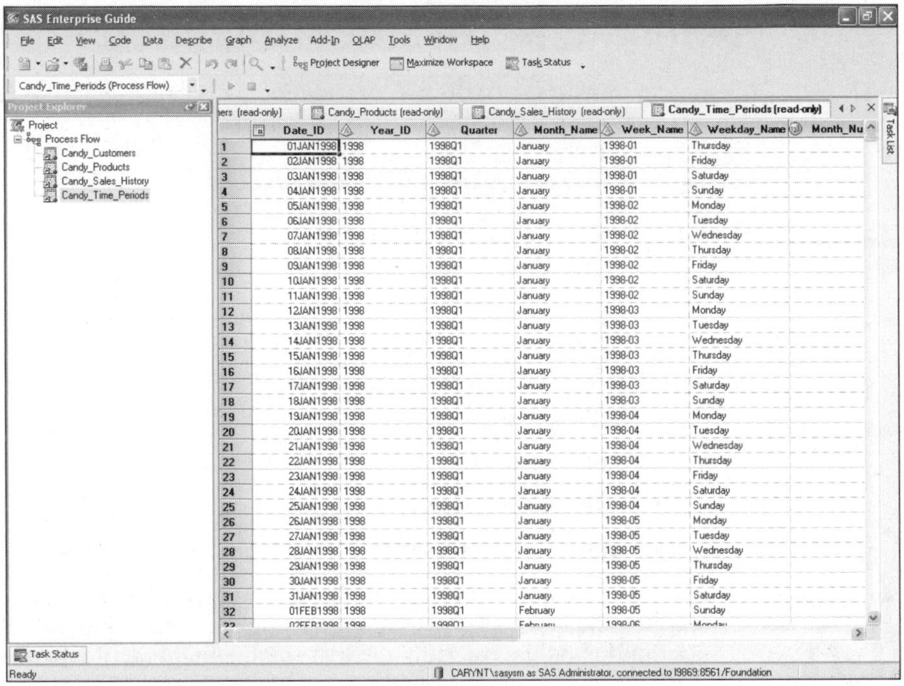

Figure 3-2:
Browsing
the candy
data set via
the data
grid.

Figure 3-3:
The Open
Data dialog
box from the
Add Tables
selection.

7. **From the Add From Project dialog box that appears, select the first three tables (as shown in Figure 3-4) and click OK.**

Figure 3-4:
The Add
From
Project
dialog box.

You might have noticed that Candy_Time_Periods appears in this dialog box even though you already have it in the query (refer to Step 4). In case you were wondering why it appears, it's because a special type of query (called a Cartesian Product) actually joins the same table back to itself! However, unless you understand what a Cartesian Product is and you're certain that you need it, do not ever use the same table twice. You can end up with a very large table that's not what you're expecting!

After clicking OK, you receive a warning message, as shown in Figure 3-5; but don't worry about this right now. The warning message is informing you that you have some work to do in the next window that appears.

Figure 3-5:
For now,
don't worry
about this
suitable join
warning
message.

Query for Candy_Time_Periods - Query Builder

A suitable join could not be determined for the new table. You will need to join the tables manually.

OK

8. Click OK to dismiss the warning message.

The Tables and Joins dialog box appears, and Candy_Products is automatically joined to Candy_Sales_History via column ProdID. SAS Enterprise Guide automatically joins tables by columns with identical names because SAS Enterprise Guide assumes that identically named columns in different tables contain the same information. The connecting lines between the tables show the columns that will be used to join the various tables. You can exercise some control over the joins:

- If you don't like the auto-join feature, you can turn it off from the Options menu for SAS Enterprise Guide.

- You can easily delete joins by clicking the join connectors between the tables and pressing the Delete key.

9. To add joins that weren't automatically determined based on identical column names, perform the following:

   a. Click the CustID column from the Candy_Customers table and drag and drop it over the Customer column in the Candy_Sales_History table.

   b. Do the same with the Date_ID column from the Candy_Time_Periods table to the Date column in the Candy_Sales_History table.

Your dialog box should be similar to Figure 3-6.

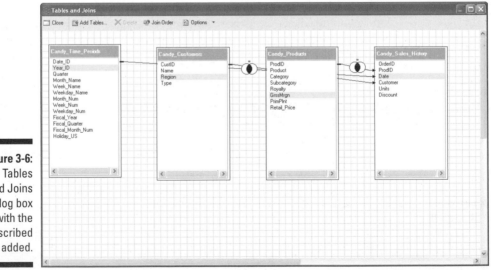

Figure 3-6:
The Tables and Joins dialog box with the described joins added.

10. Click the Close button in the upper-left corner to close the Tables and Joins dialog box.

Now you are back to the main dialog box for the Filter and Query task. The table join details just added are a vital step that you should always perform when you build a new query with multiple tables. If you neglect this step with multiple tables in a query and one of them unjoins the others, the application warns you about possible performance issues before it runs the query.

You can also rearrange the table layout for easier reference in the Tables and Joins dialog box. Typically, you have one central table that the other tables join with. Putting the central table in the middle (often called the *fact table*) and the supporting tables around it (often called *dimension tables*) can make your join much simpler to understand at a glance.

11. From the main dialog box of the Filter and Query task, select the variables that will be in the output table created by the query.

For this example, click and drag the following variables to the blank space on the Select Data tab labeled *Drop a column here to add it to the query*:

- Quarter, from Candy_Time_Periods
- Name and Region, from Candy_Customers
- Product and Retail_Price, from Candy_Products
- Units and Discount, from Candy_Sales_History

When you're finished, the task looks like Figure 3-7.

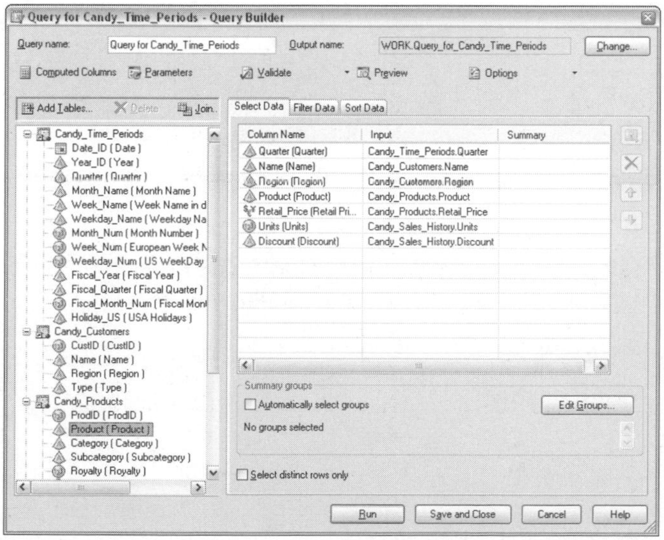

Figure 3-7:
The Filter and Query task with the specified variables selected.

[Screenshot of Query Builder dialog box]

12. **(Optional) To make the variable names in the output data set more meaningful, you can rename them. Here's how to rename the variable Name to Customer Name, in this example:**

    a. *Double-click the variable Name in the Select Data pane.*

    The Properties dialog box opens.

    b. *Type **Customer Name** in the Alias text box and then click OK.*

13. **(Optional) To make the name of the output data set more meaningful, rename it. Here's how to rename the output data set to Quarterly_Sales_Summary, in this example:**

    a. *In the upper-right corner of the Filter and Query task window, click the Change button (beside the Output Name field). You can see this button in the upper-right corner of Figure 3-7.*

    The Save As dialog box opens.

    b. *In the File Name field, enter the new data set name **Quarterly_Sales_Summary**, as shown in Figure 3-8.*

    c. *Click Save.*

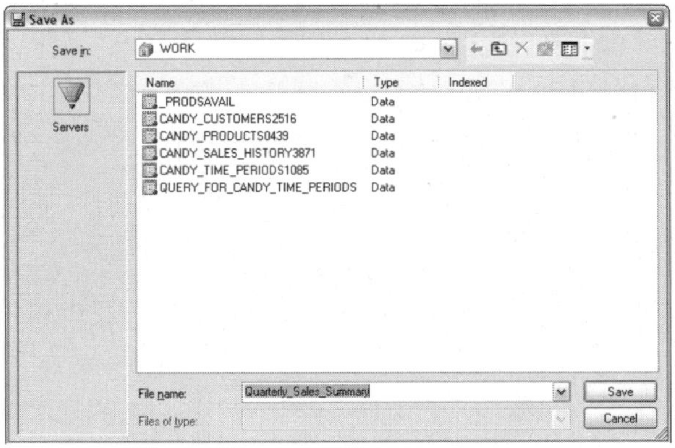

Figure 3-8:
Rename a
data set
here.

After your join is set the way you want it, you can create computed columns with your data, which is discussed in the following section.

Creating computed columns

One of the most powerful features the Filter and Query task offers is the capability to create computed columns based on your current needs. Computed columns allow you to create new variables from your data. For example, you can use a computed column to calculate net sales based on the gross sales and returns columns in your source data.

For the running example used here, you want to review the net sales amount for each record. The net sales amount can be expressed as

```
Net_Sale_Amount = Retail_Price × Units × (1-Discount)
```

To create the computed column Net_Sale_Amount (the right side of the preceding expression), do the following:

1. **Click the Computed Columns icon in the upper-left corner of the Filter and Query task.**

   The Computed Columns dialog box appears.

2. **Choose New⇨Build Expression.**

   The Advanced Expression Editor window opens, as shown in Figure 3-9.

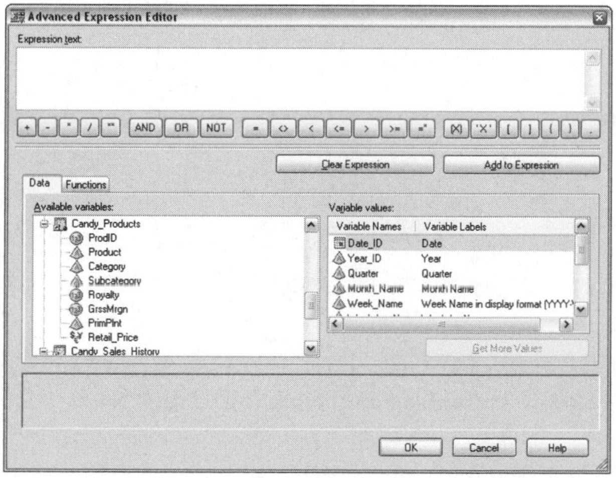

Figure 3-9:
The
Advanced
Expression
Editor awaits
your input.

3. **In the Available Variables pane at the bottom left, click the Candy_ Products data set symbol to fetch the list of variables in that table.**

4. **In the Variable Values pane on the right**

    a. Scroll to the bottom of the pane.

    b. Click the variable Retail_Price.

    c. Click the Add to Expression button (at the top right of the dialog box).

    Candy_Product.Retail_Price appears in the Expression Text field.

5. **Click the single asterisk (*) multiplication button just below the Expression Text field (third button from the left).**

    The multiplier symbol is added to the Expression Text field (see the result in Figure 3-10).

    At any time, you can click inside the Expression Text field and manually type or edit. You can also use the standard Windows copy and paste functions to rearrange your expression.

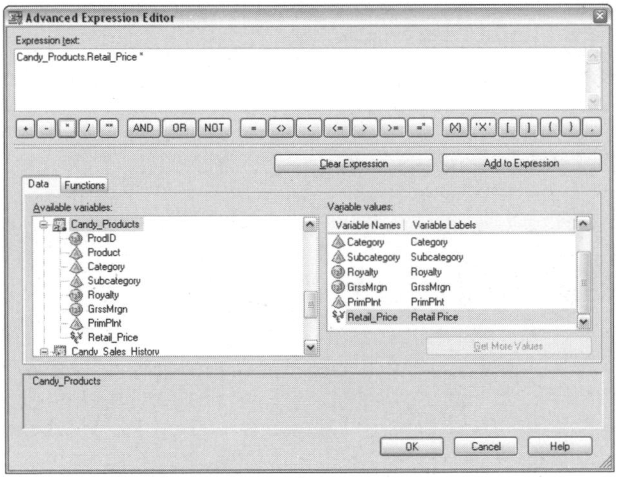

Figure 3-10:
The
Advanced
Expression
Editor with
the net sales
amount
calculation
partially
complete.

6. **In the Available Variables pane, click the Candy_Sales_History data set symbol.**

7. **In the Variable Values pane**

    a. Double-click on Units to add it to the expression.

    b. Click the multiplier symbol (*).

    c. Click once in the Expression Text box and type (1-.

d. From the Variable Values pane, add the Discount variable by double-clicking it.

e. Type a closing parenthesis [ )]at the end of the expression in the Expression Text box.

See Figure 3-11 for the completed calculation.

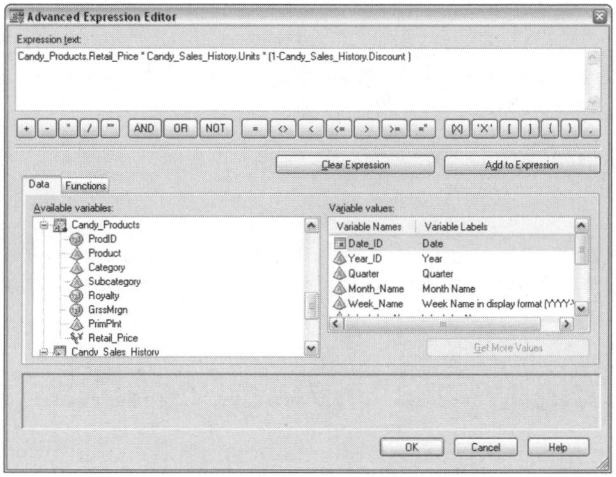

Figure 3-11: The Advanced Expression Editor with the completed net sales amount calculation.

(Advanced Expression Editor dialog box)

Expression text:

Candy_Products.Retail_Price * Candy_Sales_History.Units * (1-Candy_Sales_History.Discount)

8. Click OK.

You are now back at the Computed Columns dialog box, which lists all computed columns for the current query. The newly created computed column name defaults to a standard name: in this case, Calculation1, followed by Calculation2 if Calculation1 exists, and so on.

9. The name Calculation1 is not very intuitive, so you can rename it by clicking the just-created Calculation1 from the Computed Columns dialog box. Click the Rename button, and then follow these steps to give the column a practical name that you can remember:

*a. Type **Net_Sale_Amount,** press Enter, and then click Close.*

b. From the Select Data pane of the Filter and Query task, click the computed column Net_Sale_Amount.

c. Click the Properties button to the right of the Select Data Pane.

The Properties dialog box opens, as shown in Figure 3-12.

*d. In the Alias text box, type **Net_Sale_Amount** to replace the initial name Calculation1.*

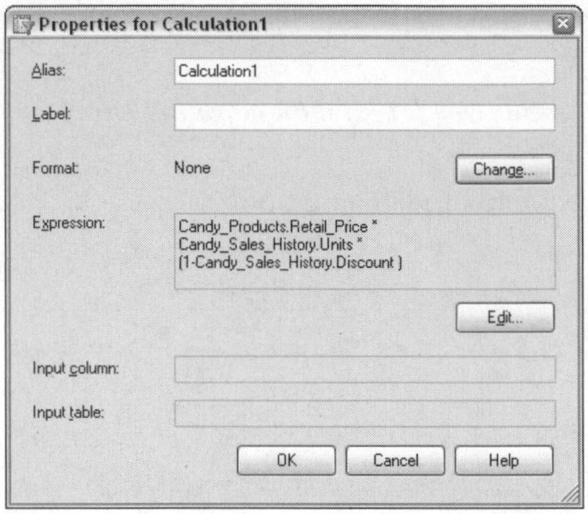

Figure 3-12:
The variable
Properties
dialog
box for
Calculation1.

You may notice that the computed column has no format. But don't worry. In the following section, you find out how to format your computed columns.

Formatting your computed columns

Formats are an important concept to understand if you want to get the most out of your SAS reports and analyses. Data is typically stored as either a character (for example, *New*) or numeric (for example, *18701*) value. A format can change data in many ways, from shortening how your data is represented, to changing the use of commas and decimal points for numbers, to recoding values from system codes to human intelligible words. Table 3-1 shows examples of the many formats available in SAS.

Table 3-1		Formats Available in SAS	
Raw Storage Value	**Format Applied**	**What You See**	**What This Format Means**
New	$1.	N	The dollar sign means that this is a character variable and the 1 shows the variable with just the first character.
New	$3.	New	Shows the variable with the first three characters.

Raw Storage Value	Format Applied	What You See	What This Format Means
New	$20.	New	Shows the variable with the first three characters; because there are only three characters, this is all you see.
New	$QUOTE5.	"New"	Allows five spaces of output and automatically double quotes the raw value.
New	$MyTrans.	New York City	User-defined format that acts as a look-up for abbreviated city names; in this case, New translates to New York City; Ne2 might translate to New Haven, and so on
18701.5	5.	18702	Simplest numeric format; it adds no commas to your number.
18701.5	8.2	18701.50	Allows eight spaces of length and two decimal places to show more detail.
18701.5	4.	19E3	Allows only four spaces, so SAS shows a rounded version in scientific notation; 19 X 10^3 or 19,000 is the closest value it can display with the format specified.
18701.5	Best8.	18701.5	Best is a special SAS format that tries to use the precision in your data to determine the appropriate detail to display.
18701.5	Comma8.1	18,701.5	Adds a comma as the thousands separator and the decimal point with one level of precision.
18701.5	CommaX8.1	18.701,5	Adds decimal points as the thousands separator and commas with one level of precision (for European partners).

(continued)

Table 3-1 *(continued)*

Raw Storage Value	Format Applied	What You See	What This Format Means
18701.5	Dollar10.2	$18,701.50	Uses standard American currency formatting with the dollar sign, commas as thousands separator, and decimal points.
18701.5	Dollar8.2	18701.50	SAS strips out the dollar sign and the comma to show the numeric amount when not enough space exists to show full currency default.
18701.5	MMDDYY10.	03/15/2011	One of the many date formats; this one translates the number in the variable to the number of days from January 1st, 1960 and formats it as month/day/year.
18701.5	MMDDYY8.	03/15/11	Same as last one, but uses two-digit year.
18701.5	ENGDFDWN8.	Tuesday	English word for the day of the week for this date.
18701.5	MMDDYY10.	01JAN60:05:11:42	One of the many date time formats; translates the number in the variable to the number of seconds from January 1st, 1960 and formats it as month, day, year, hours, minutes, and seconds. This format assumes your data is in seconds, not days.

SAS enables you to format data values in the storage table (SAS data set) as an associated attribute of the column. This default format is usually sufficient if someone already did this for you. If you need to see both the formatted and unformatted output, or if the data has not already been formatted for you, SAS allows you to format a column in a particular task for a particular application. Follow these steps to format a column of data in SAS:

1. **From the Computed Columns dialog box, click the Change button next to the Format status.**

   The Formats dialog box opens, as shown in Figure 3-13.

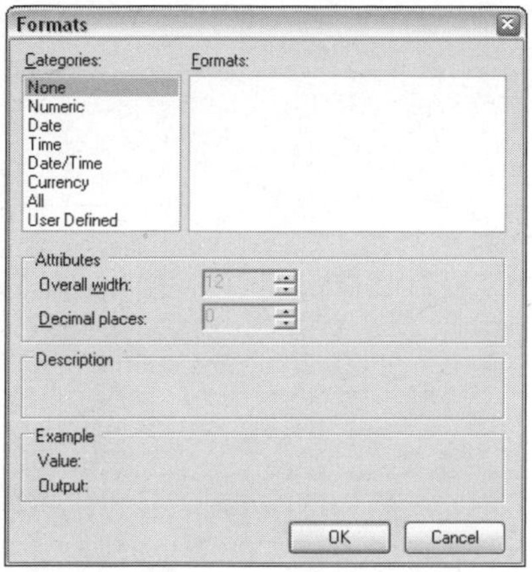

Figure 3-13:
The Formats
dialog box
with no
format
specified.

2. Apply a US Dollar currency format to the Net_Sale_Amount column.

   a. Click Currency in the Categories scroll box.

   b. Click DOLLARw.d in the Formats scroll box.

   c. Change the Overall Width from 6 to 12, as shown in Figure 3-14.

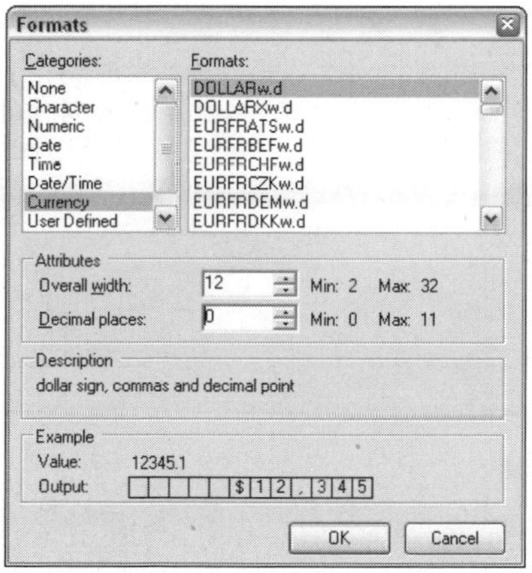

Figure 3-14:
The Formats
dialog box
with the
DOLLAR12.0
format
specified.

3. Click OK twice.

   You are now back at the Filter and Query task.

4. Click Run.

   Within a few seconds, the newly created data set
   Quarterly_Sales_Summary automatically opens, as shown in Figure 3-15.

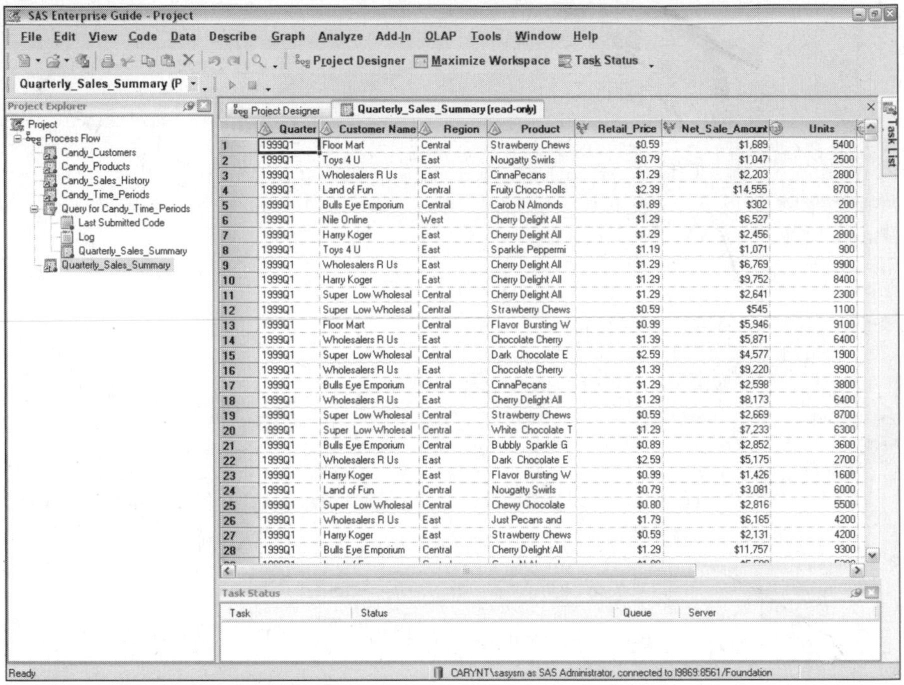

Figure 3-15:
The newly
created
quarterly
sales
summary
data set.

The computed column Net_Sale_Amount appears as dollars with no decimal point, but this doesn't mean that the detailed precision of the calculations has been lost. This is simply a function of the currently applied format. If you add up all the Net_Sale_Amount records, the column would be calculated based on the precise values.

Summarizing the Data

SAS Enterprise Guide presents you with many task choices to summarize and aggregate your data. Table 3-2 presents you with choices by task. As you can see, almost any summary statistic you can imagine is available.

Table 3-2		The Many Ways to Summarize Data in SAS				
Task	Menu	Output Data Set Option?	Printable Report Option?	Statistics Available	Optional Graphs?	Notes
Filter and Query	Data	Yes — default behavior	Yes — optional	Sum, Average, Count, Distinct Count, N, Max, Min, Range, Number Missing, Variance, Standard Error, about 20 others	No	Statistics are calculated for each distinct value of your summary group. If your data source is a relational data-base, the calculations are performed on the database before being sent to your SAS Server session.
Rank	Data	Yes — default behavior	No	Ranked order of records, percentile ranks of records, decile ranking of records, quartile ranking of records, ntiles ranking of records, percentages, six advanced ranking methods	No	A specialized task for creating output data sets that have ranked a variable with one of the specified methods for further analysis, reporting, or graphing.

(continued)

Table 3-2 (continued)

Task	Menu	Output Data Set Option?	Printable Report Option?	Statistics Available	Optional Graphs?	Notes
List Data	Describe	No	Yes — default behavior	Totals and subtotals	No	Most limited task in terms of statistics available.
Summary Statistics	Describe	Yes — optional behavior	Yes — default behavior, can be suppressed	Mean, Standard Deviation, Standard Error, Variance, Minimum, Maximum, Range, Sum, Weighted Sum, N, N Missing, Median, Quartiles, Percentiles, 5 Advanced Statistics	Yes — histograms and box and whisker plots	One of the easier to use general purpose summary tasks. This task offers some of the most common statistics for quick review.
Distribution Analysis	Describe	Yes — optional behavior	Yes — default behavior, can be suppressed	Mean, Standard Deviation, Standard Error, Variance, Minimum, Maximum, Range, Sum, Weighted Sum, N, N Missing,	Yes — histograms, probability, quantiles, box and whisker, and stem and leaf plots	A specialized task for graphically and statistically checking the fit of a variable to a user-specified statistical distribution. This task is often used to determine if data needs to be standardized to fit a specified distribution prior to further statistical analysis.

Task	Menu	Output Data Set Option?	Printable Report Option?	Statistics Available	Optional Graphs?	Notes
				Median, Quartiles, Percentiles, Many Advanced Statistics specifically for the purpose of checking goodness of fit with various statistical distributions- Normal, Lognormal, Exponential, Weibull, Beta, Gamma, and Kernel		
Characterize Data	Describe	Yes — default behavior, can be suppressed	Yes — default behavior, can be suppressed	Count, N, N Missing, Total, Minimum, Mean, Median, Maximum, Standard Mean	Yes — default behavior, can be suppressed, bar charts	A specialized wizard that analyzes every variable in a data set or every data set in a library and prints a concise report and analysis of every variable for quick data review.
Summary Tables	Describe	Yes — optional behavior	Yes — default behavior	Mean, Standard Deviation, Standard Error, Variance, Minimum,	No	A task focused on creating multi-dimensional tabular reports. One of the most complex tasks to master in SAS Enterprise Guide.

(continued)

Table 3-2 (continued)

Task	Menu	Output Data Set Option?	Printable Report Option?	Statistics Available	Optional Graphs?	Notes
				Maximum, Range, Sum, Weighted Sum, N, N Missing, Median, Quartiles, Percentiles, Other Advanced and Table Statistics		
One Way Frequencies	Describe	Yes — optional behavior	Yes — default behavior, can be suppressed	Frequencies, percentages of total, cumulative percentages, Chi-square and binomial proportions tests	Yes — horizontal and vertical bar charts	A specialized task specifically for creating one-way frequency (incidence) tables of your data.
Table Analysis	Describe	Yes — optional behavior	Yes — default behavior, can be suppressed	Frequencies, percentages of total, cumulative percentages, many table statistics such as Chi-square,	No	A specialized task specifically for creating n-way frequency (incidence) tables of your data. Has a plethora of statistical options available.

Task	Menu	Output Data Set Option?	Printable Report Option?	Statistics Available	Optional Graphs?	Notes
				exact p-values, CMH, Jonck-heere-Terpstra, Cochran-Armitage, and various scores		
Various graph tasks	Graph	No	Yes — default behavior	Frequency, Cumulative Frequency, Percentage, Cumulative Percentage, Mean, Sum, Median, Percentiles depending on chart type	N/A	The graph tasks automatically aggregate your data for the graph type selected. They typically provide you with several statistical choices dependent on the chart type in use.

With many customers of SAS Enterprise Guide, the most commonly used task for summarizing data is the Summary Statistics task. In the following two examples, you use this task and a few others to create some useful summaries of the Quarterly_Sales_Summary data you created in the preceding section.

With SAS, you can easily summarize every variable in a data set or summarize only specific numeric variables. The following steps use the Query_Sales_Summary example to show you how to summarize every variable in a data set:

1. **Choose Describe⇨Characterize Data.**

   The Characterize Data task wizard appears showing Quarterly_Sales_Summary as the input data source, as shown in Figure 3-16.

   Click Add to use additional data sets as inputs to the task. This task is able to summarize one or more data sets at once in one concise report.

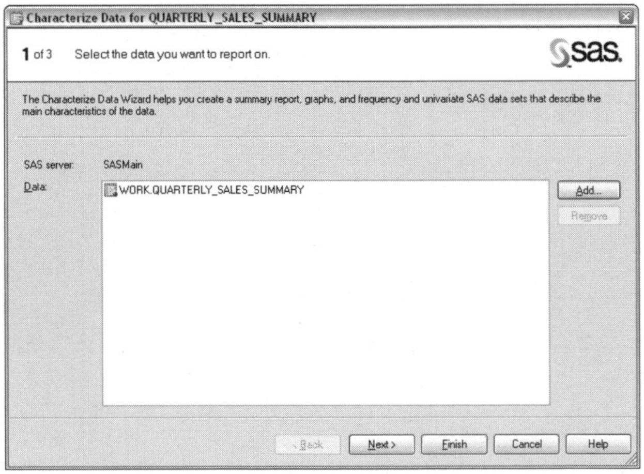

Figure 3-16:
The Characterize Data wizard.

2. **Click Next.**

3. **Clear the option for generating SAS Data Sets.**

4. **Click Finish.**

   The task runs, and the summary report opens in a few seconds, as shown in Figure 3-17.

Summary of Categorical Variables for WORK.QUARTERLY_SALES_SUMMARY

Limited to the 30 Most Frequent Distinct Values per Variable

Variable	Label	Value	Frequency Count	Percent of Total Frequency
Customer Name	Name	Harry Koger	1911	12.7400
		Bulls Eye Emporium	1898	12.6533
		Land of Fun	1898	12.6533
		Super Low Wholesaler	1896	12.6400
		Toys 4 U	1887	12.5800
		Floor Mart	1886	12.5733
		Nile Online	1839	12.2600
		Wholesalers R Us	1785	11.9000
Product	Product	Sparkle Peppermint Gum	986	6.5733
		Cherry Delight All Fruit	979	6.5267
		Bubbly Sparkle Gum	976	6.5067
		Nougatty Swirls	976	6.5067
		Just Pecans and Cashews	957	6.3800
		Flavor Bursting Watermelon Chews	953	6.3533
		Carob N Almonds	933	6.2200
		Fruity Choco-Rolls	931	6.2067
		Chocolate Cherry Delight	929	6.1933
		Dark Chocolate Espresso	928	6.1867
		Chewy Chocolate Cheetahs	926	6.1733
		Cranberry Delight	916	6.1067
		Watermelon Taffy	916	6.1067
		Strawberry Chewsers	909	6.0600

Figure 3-17:
The Characterize Data wizard report.

The report automatically creates sections based on the various data types for each variable in the data set: character, numeric, currency, and date. These are presented in frequency count and numeric variable summary tables for each variable. This is one of the quickest ways to summarize many variables.

Here's something to keep in mind when you use the Characterize Data task: Because it analyzes every record and every variable, if you have very large tables or have selected many tables, the task may be fairly time-consuming to run.

Summarizing specific numeric variables

As mentioned at the beginning of this section, SAS also lets you focus on only the variables you need to evaluate from a data set instead of summarizing every variable. Follow these steps to summarize specific numeric variables in the Net_Sale_Amount data set:

1. **Choose Describe⇨Summary Statistics.**

   The Summary Statistics wizard appears.

2. **From the Task Roles pane, click and drag Net_Sale_Amount to the Analysis Variables role and then drag Region to the Classification Variables role, as shown in Figure 3-18.**

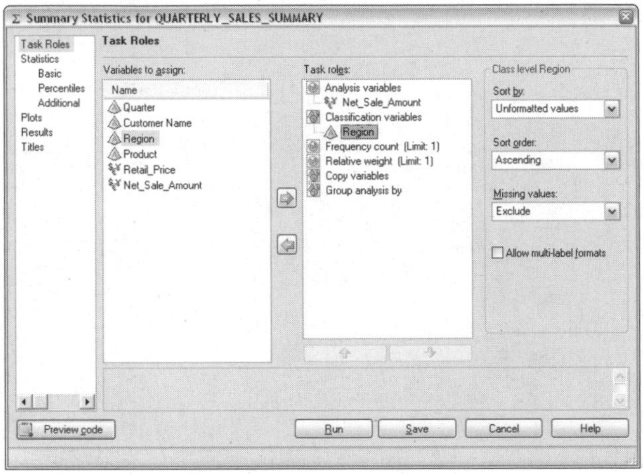

Figure 3-18:
The Task
Roles pane
of the
Summary
Statistics
task.

3. **From the far left, select the Percentiles pane and then select the Median Statistic check box.**

4. **Select the Plots pane; then select the Histogram and Box and Whisker plots.**

5. **Click Run.**

   The analysis runs, and the summary report opens in a few seconds.

6. **To view the box and whisker graph, scroll down to the bottom of the report, as shown in Figure 3-19.**

   In addition to the box and whisker plot, Figure 3-19 also shows the group statistic box for the Central Region. You can see this by moving your mouse cursor to hover over the Central Region box part of the chart. This box gives you detailed statistics for a group while viewing the graph. Hovering over the outlying dots displays the individual values for these records (these are commonly referred to as *outliers*). Many graph types in SAS Enterprise Guide have this type of mouse hover detail information box. For more details on graph types and their use, refer to Chapter 7.

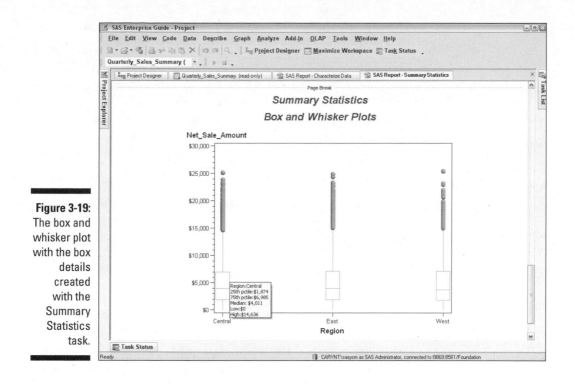

Figure 3-19:
The box and whisker plot with the box details created with the Summary Statistics task.

Building a Forecast

SAS Enterprise Guide adds the capability to create forecasts to your arsenal of reports and presentations. Although forecasting is probably one of the easiest areas of statistical analyses to understand, it's also one of the easiest to oversimplify, resulting in answers that are just plain wrong. To ensure that you have a solid grasp of forecasting principles, be sure to see Chapter 9.

Forecasting can take on several levels of complexity. For example

- ✔ Using the data on the historic variable of interest as the sole predictor based on the historic trend of just this variable (net sales for candy)

- ✔ Adding additional variables of relevance and their historic impact on the variable of interest (marketing spent and monthly weather conditions)

The Basic Forecasting task uses the simple single variable approach to obtain a forecast for your variable of interest. Follow these steps using the SAS Enterprise Guide sample data set beer_sales_minimal (found in the same sample data location as the candy data sets earlier in this chapter):

1. **Open the beer_sales_minimal data set, as shown in Figure 3-20.**

   Notice all the results from the work earlier in this chapter displayed in the Project Explorer pane. The beer_sales_minimal data set has several years of monthly beer sales data for a fictional company.

2. **Choose Analyze⇨Time Series⇨Basic Forecasting.**

   The Basic Forecasting task appears, as shown in Figure 3-21. Note that the task automatically added the date variable — SaleDate — to the Time ID Variable role. It also created the new task specific variable NewTimeID, which you can ignore in this example.

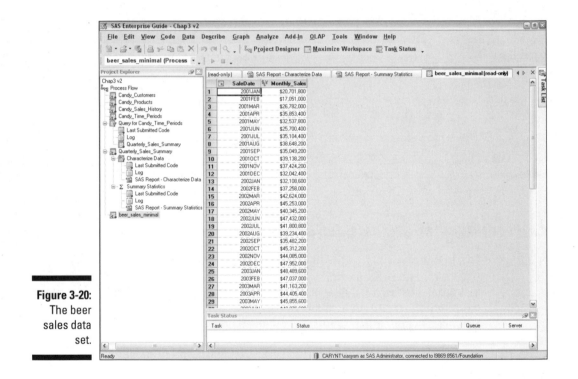

Figure 3-20:
The beer sales data set.

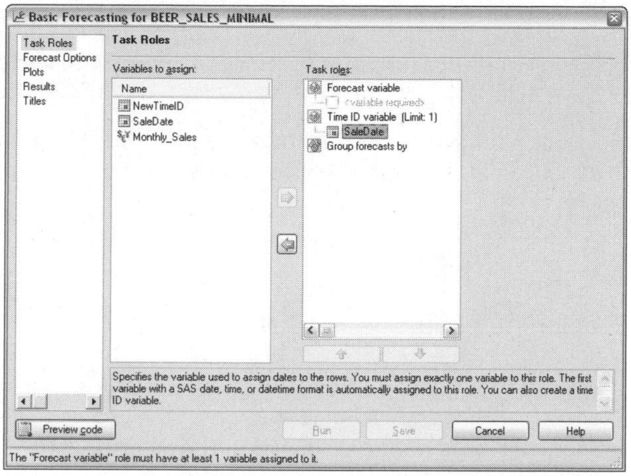

Figure 3-21:
The Basic
Forecasting
task using
the beer
sales data
set.

3. **Click and drag Monthly_Sales from Variables to Assign to the Forecast Variable role.**

4. **In the left panel, select the Forecast Options pane and then**

    a. *Change the drop-down selection for Forecasting method from Stepwise Autoregressive to Winters Additive Method.*

    b. *Change the drop-down selection for Time interval between observations from Number of Units to Monthly.*

    c. *Change the drop-down selection for Seasonal cycle length from Number of Intervals to Three Months.*

    See Figure 3-22 for all the settings in this step. For further details on forecasting, see Chapter 9.

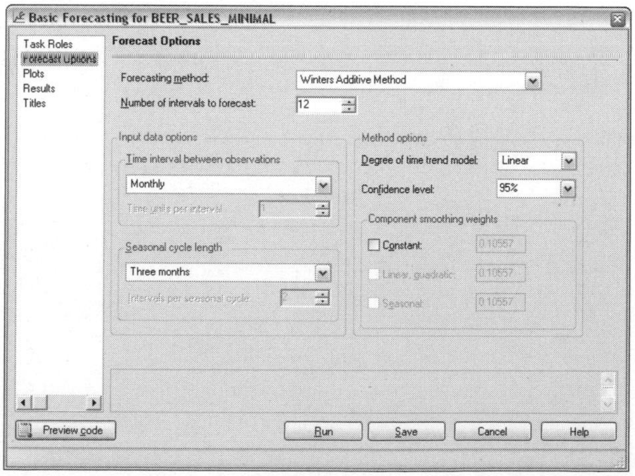

Figure 3-22:
The Basic
Forecasting
task
Forecast
Options
settings
with
changes
made.

5. **Click Run.**

   The forecast runs, and the forecast plot opens in a few seconds, as shown in Figure 3-23.

6. **To save the work you performed in this chapter, choose File⇨Save Project As and then save your work to either your local computer or your SAS server.**

Figure 3-23 shows you several things:

✔ Historic values for sales (the dashed line to the left of 2006)

✔ Model results applied to the historic data and projected into 2006 (the solid line)

✔ 95% confidence intervals just for the predicted year of 2006 (the lines above and below the solid line for 2006)

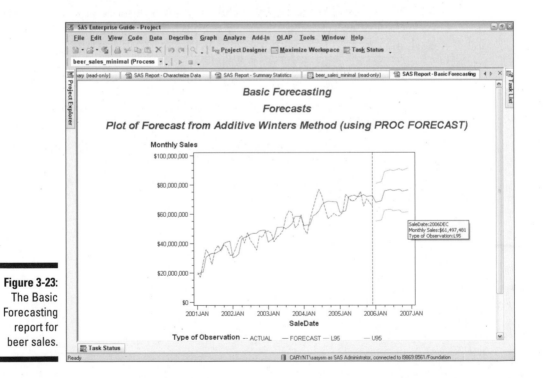

Figure 3-23:
The Basic Forecasting report for beer sales.

You can quickly see that the model appears to match up with the historic data pretty well. However, because you use only historic sales as a predictor of future sales, you can see that the confidence intervals are pretty wide for the 2006 forecasts (from $55 million to $81 million for 2006/01.) This implies that other variables can likely be added to the forecast to improve the accuracy — things such as average high temperature and marketing dollars spent. Still, you can obtain some insight into what next year might look like. After all, this is just the basic forecast, which is far more than you get with many other business intelligence tools.

Part II
Gathering Data and Presenting Information

The 5th Wave
By Rich Tennant

"Well, shoot! This eggplant chart is just as confusing as the butternut squash chart and the gourd chart. Can't you just make a pie chart like everyone else?"

In this part . . .

In this part, you see how you can pick up spare data that you find from almost anywhere and make it usable in SAS. After you have a hold on the data, you can begin "massaging" it. That might sound like a treat, especially from the data's point of view, but really it's all about getting data into a usable form that is suitable for analysis and reports.

Every data source has a story that it's itching to tell. Simple listings, summarizations, and cross-tab reports begin to tease that story apart. And graphs? Well, when done right, graphs can make your data sing.

Chapter 4

Accessing Data: Oh, the Choices!

• •

• •

*T*he fact that SAS can meet just about any of your reporting and analysis needs is of little use if you can't quickly and efficiently access your data wherever it exists. SAS has the broadest set of data access options available from any business intelligence or analytic product. Whether your data is in Microsoft Excel spreadsheets, relational databases, or legacy locations such as mainframe text files, you can access and use it as a source for your data reports and analyses.

SAS offers two approaches to accessing data:

▸ Opening a local data file or connecting to a data source from your local PC and moving it to your SAS server

▸ Accessing the data source directly from your SAS server

Using your local PC as a conduit to opening your data is more convenient than accessing the data directly from the server; but it is also a slower method and not intended for accessing large data sources. *Large* is a relative term, but any source with more than 10,000 records (also referred to as *rows, observations, or data points*) of data can probably be considered large for this purpose. Thus, using SAS server connections to your data sources is much more efficient than accessing data from your PC and is therefore the preferred way to access data sources that you frequently use. In this chapter, we present you with your data access options and points to consider with each one.

Data storage and SAS Enterprise Guide projects

SAS Enterprise Guide offers many ways to access your relevant data. As a rule, you never embed and store data in your SAS Enterprise Guide project. Instead, SAS Enterprise Guide stores the needed information on how to connect to your data source in the future. Any data changed using the native table editor in SAS Enterprise Guide is immediately written to the data table source, assuming that you have write permissions to the data source.

Microsoft Excel, Microsoft Access, and Text Files: Accessing the Data Hidden on Your PC

Using applications like Excel and Access to manage important data is common in almost every organization, regardless of whether the IT department approves such activities. For many valid reasons, IT groups frown on the use of these products to manage important data:

- **Undocumented data management methods.** People often build various rules into their local spreadsheets or databases that can vary significantly from those in the corporate systems, resulting in different results when using various sources.

- **Systems may not be backed up on a regular basis.** Although your local PC may be backed up, do you keep an audit of the transactions?

- **Isolation from central naming schemes.** For example, one Excel spreadsheet might define net profit very differently than another.

- **Concerns about privacy and security.** Excel passwords are notoriously easy to break; don't delude yourself into thinking that they secure your spreadsheet.

Errors can occur quite easily within applications such as Excel and Access. These applications lack the centrally maintained, automated data integrity checking commonly available in relational databases.

Despite the potential problems just listed, users often have valid reasons for maintaining their own personal databases. For example, you can start and complete some short-term projects more quickly with Excel or Access. You also may decide to use Excel as a staging area before loading the final results of a subset of the overall project into the centralized, corporate system. The good news is that SAS can easily access, manage, and analyze the data from these sources at will. Here are the locally stored PC file types that SAS Enterprise Guide can import:

- SAS data sets on your PC
- SAS views of data on your PC
- Microsoft Excel worksheets
- Microsoft Access tables
- dBase tables
- Lotus 1-2-3
- Paradox database tables
- Text files (fixed width, tab delimited, and comma delimited)
- HTML documents

SAS Enterprise Guide leverages the vendor-specific data providers automatically installed with your relevant data source application (for example, Excel or Access) for each data source to optimize the accuracy of your data import. For example, if you use the local import functionality of SAS Enterprise Guide with an Excel spreadsheet, Microsoft Excel native capabilities are automatically called to acquire the appropriate translation method for converting the data into SAS data sets.

SAS Enterprise Guide translates your data like this:

1. The spreadsheet (we assume you're using Excel) is converted into a specially delimited text file (typically consisting of columns of data separated by commas called a *comma-delimited* file).

2. SAS Enterprise Guide copies this text file to your SAS server.

3. SAS imports your data based on definitions extracted in the process (from Excel, in this scenario).

The conversion and copying processes can be slow when using large sources, so consider how large your data is before using this method. As mentioned earlier, *large* is a relative term, but anything with more than 10,000 rows is pretty large for our purposes. If you don't fully understand all this, don't worry: It just works!

Importing an Excel workbook

Importing data from most applications is easy and quite similar regardless of the type of document you're importing from. For this reason, we won't waste pages discussing how to import each file type; instead, this section shows you how to import from one of the most popular spreadsheet formats: Microsoft Excel. If you want to play around with other file formats later, SAS Enterprise Guide includes many sample files in the sample directory (typically `C:\Program Files\SAS\Enterprise Guide 4\Sample\Data` if your install used the standard directory for installation) for you to try importing. The sample files include Access databases and text files. The process for importing other file types is similar to the process outlined in this section with slightly different functionality depending on the file type.

Without further ado, here's an example of importing data from a local Excel spreadsheet for use with SAS:

1. **Choose File⇨Import Data.**

    The Open Data dialog box appears, as shown in Figure 4-1.

Figure 4-1:
Start
importing
data here.

Open Data

Open data from one of the following locations:

Local Computer   SAS Servers

2. **Click the Local Computer icon.**

    A standard Windows Open dialog box appears.

3. **Navigate to the SAS Enterprise Guide sample data folder (`C:\ Program Files\SAS\Enterprise Guide 4\Sample\Data`), select the `SupplyInfo.xls` file, and then click Open.**

    As mentioned at the beginning of this section, many sample files are available for you to try out importing from this directory, including Access databases and text files. Feel free to try these later; the process is similar with slightly different functionality, depending on the file type.

    The Open Tables dialog box appears, as shown in Figure 4-2. This shows you the worksheets available in the Excel workbook file. You can select one or more tables from this dialog box.

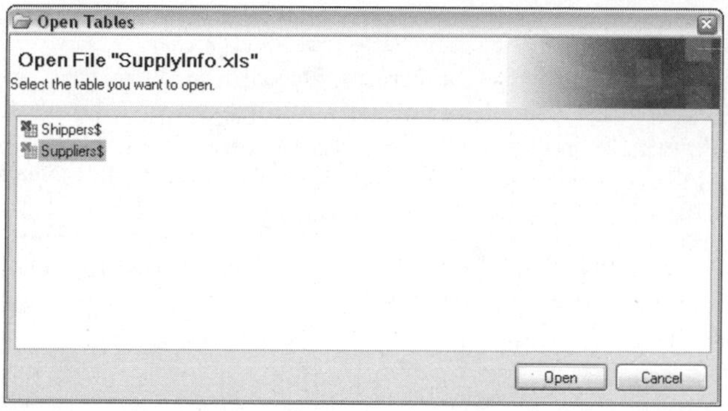

Figure 4-2:
Choose files
from the
Open Tables
dialog box.

4. **For this example, select the Suppliers$ table and then click Open.**

The Import Data dialog box appears, as shown in Figure 4-3. This dialog box is where you can tweak the default import instructions that SAS Enterprise Guide uses, such as whether the data file has a header row with column names and whether to import all data rows.

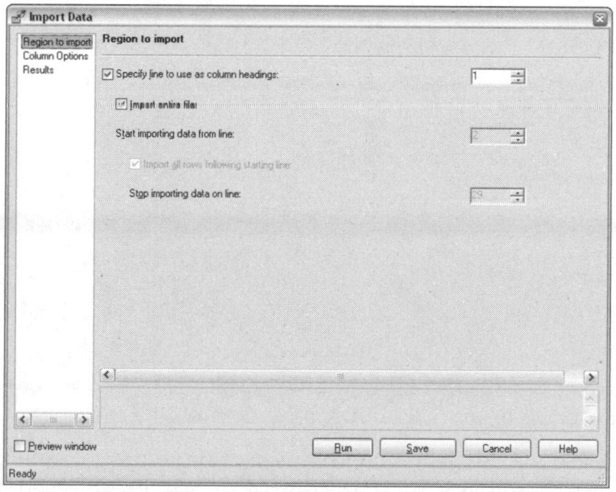

Figure 4-3:
Start
tweaking
import
instructions
here.

Spending time upfront to get your data right saves you headaches later on. For example, properly formatting your data prevents you from having to tweak this later in your work.

You can generally keep the defaults for the first pane, Region to Import. The defaults work fine for this example.

Note these options:

- **Specify Line to Use as Column Headings:** When you import text files without a starting line with column names, be sure to turn off this option. You then have to name manually all the columns in the column options pane, or your column names will be generic, such as Column1, Column2, and Column3.

- **Preview Window:** Enable this check box (bottom-left corner in this dialog box) to preview how your selections affect your imported data.

5. Select Column Options.

The Column Options pane that appears (see Figure 4-4) is where you typically spend most of your time tweaking import definitions. The Include in Output selector is useful when you are paring down large data files with unneeded variables. For this example, you don't need to adjust any of the SAS Enterprise Guide selected details.

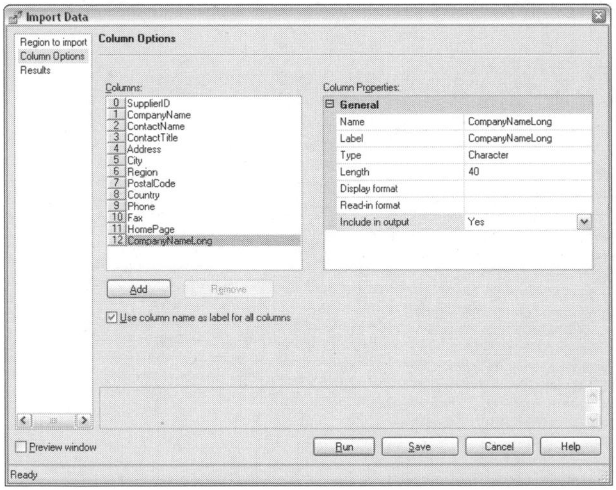

Figure 4-4:
Tweak more import instructions here.

6. Select the Preview Window check box.

By previewing the import after you set all details, you can see the SAS code being submitted to import your data, the data in a shortened format, and the log to check for any errors before you run the full import.

7. In the Preview Window that opens, click the Results tab, as shown in Figure 4-5.

The data shown is a subset of the full data that will be fetched when the full import occurs. You can use the data preview as a quick way to determine whether your import options are correct before you commit to importing the entire data file. Click the Close button in the upper right to close the Preview Window and return to the Import Data dialog box.

	ContactName	ContactTitle	Address	City
1	Charlotte Cooper	Purchasing Manager	49 Gilbert St.	London
2	Shelley Burke	Order Administrator	P.O. Box 78934	New Orleans
3	Regina Murphy	Sales Representative	707 Oxford Rd.	Ann Arbor
4	Yoshi Nagase	Marketing Manager	9-8 Sekimai Musashino-shi	Tokyo
5	Antonio del Valle Saavedra	Export Administrator	Calle del Rosal 4	Oviedo
6	Mayumi Ohno	Marketing Representative	92 Setsuko Chuo-ku	Osaka
7	Ian Devling	Marketing Manager	74 Rose St. Moonie Ponds	Melbourne
8	Peter Wilson	Sales Representative	29 King's Way	Manchester
9	Lars Peterson	Sales Agent	Kaloadagatan 13	Goteborg
10	Carlos Diaz	Marketing Manager	Av. das Americanas 12.890	Sao Paulo
11	Petra Winkler	Sales Manager	Tiergartenstraße 5	Berlin
12	Martin Bein	International Marketing Mgr.	Bogenallee 51	Frankfurt
13	Sven Petersen	Coordinator Foreign Markets	Frahmredder 112a	Cuxhaven
14	Elio Rossi	Sales Representative	Viale Dante, 75	Ravenna
15	Beate Vileid	Marketing Manager	Hatlevegen 5	Sandvika
16	Cheryl Saylor	Regional Account Rep.	3400 - 8th Avenue Suite 210	Bend
17	Michael Björn	Sales Representative	Brovallavagen 231	Stockholm
18	Guylene Nodier	Sales Manager	203, Rue des Francs-Bourgeois	Paris
19	Robb Merchant	Wholesale Account Agent	Order Processing Dept. 2100 Paul Revere Blvd.	Boston
20	Chandra Leka	Owner	471 Serangoon Loop, Suite #402	Singapore

Figure 4-5: Previewing the data import.

8. Before running the Import Data task, click Results from the far-left panel.

You can change the destination of the imported data set here. If you want the data for just the session you are using, select the WORK library. Otherwise, use one of the permanent libraries at your site to keep the imported data around for use by other people or in other sessions.

The default data set name is IMPW, which is an abbreviation of IMPort Wizard.

9. Click Run.

The data set import occurs, and the resulting data set opens automatically in SAS Enterprise Guide. The data looks much like Figure 4-5, except that it is now a node in the project and all data is available for further use.

OLE! Accessing Your Data with OLE DB and ODBC

As we mention earlier in this chapter, SAS Enterprise Guide takes full advantage of the varied data sources accessible from a PC. The last section discussed using SAS to import data from your PC to the SAS server. In this section, you use your local PC-based ODBC and OLE DB data connections to retrieve the data from your PC and seamlessly send the data to the SAS server.

Two common methods for connecting to local and remote data sources are ODBC and its Microsoft-built successor, OLE DB:

- **ODBC (Open Database Connectivity):** This method is a standard means for accessing data from multiple data sources from a variety of software products.

- **OLE DB (Object Linking and Embedding for Databases):** This newer technology from Microsoft attempts to extend ODBC capabilities to various non-relational databases and spreadsheet formats that otherwise could not be accessed with ODBC.

Both technologies are commonly used to access various databases such as Oracle, DB2, or SQL server. If an ODBC driver or OLE DB provider is available for your data source, SAS can access it and use it via SAS Enterprise Guide. Hundreds of data sources are accessible via these two technologies.

SAS Enterprise Guide provides the capability to use local ODBC or OLE DB connections for convenience in accessing smaller or infrequently accessed data sources. When you use native SAS Enterprise Guide access to these data sources (instead of SAS server-based SAS/ACCESS to ODBC or SAS/ACCESS to OLE DB), importing processes can be much slower than reasonable for very large data sources. The reason for this is simple: SAS Enterprise Guide first reads the data table results from your database to your PC and then must transfer the data table to your SAS server as a data set to allow your SAS analysis to occur. Therefore, we recommend limiting use of this functionality to tables that are small — say 10,000 rows or less. Although using very large tables will work, you could wait a long time (for example, one million rows on Stephen's work laptop took three minutes). The warning dialog box shown in Figure 4-6 reminds you of this limitation.

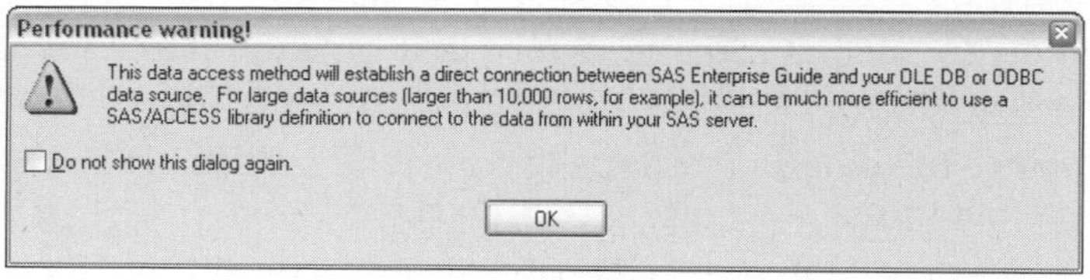

Figure 4-6:
You can
ignore this
warning for
smaller data
sources.

> **Performance warning!**
>
> ⚠ This data access method will establish a direct connection between SAS Enterprise Guide and your OLE DB or ODBC data source. For large data sources (larger than 10,000 rows, for example), it can be much more efficient to use a SAS/ACCESS library definition to connect to the data from within your SAS server.
>
> ☐ Do not show this dialog again.
>
> OK

Importing an Access database table with ODBC

ODBC data sources can be local files or remote databases on other PC's or servers. ODBC drivers that you configure to access various data sources provide an easy and consistent way to access the desired data through one configuration to multiple applications, including SAS. In this example, we use the sample Access database to demonstrate how you access an ODBC data source. One advantage of using ODBC over the import method is that data column and format definitions are more precise and make this easier than importing.

1. **Choose File⇨Open⇨ODBC.**

   The Performance Warning dialog box appears (refer to Figure 4-6). If you don't want to see this warning notice in the future, click the Do Not Show This Dialog Again check box.

2. **Click OK to dismiss the Performance Warning dialog box.**

   The Select Data Source dialog box appears, as shown in Figure 4-7.

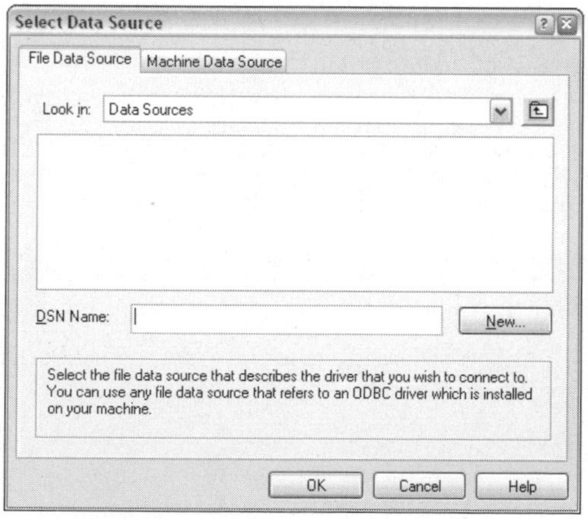

Figure 4-7:
The ODBC
Select Data
Source
dialog box.

> **Select Data Source**
>
> File Data Source | Machine Data Source
>
> Look in: Data Sources
>
> DSN Name: [ ]   New...
>
> Select the file data source that describes the driver that you wish to connect to. You can use any file data source that refers to an ODBC driver which is installed on your machine.
>
> OK   Cancel   Help

3. **Click New to define a new ODBC data source.**

4. **In the Create Data Source Wizard that appears, select Microsoft Access Driver (*.mdb) as your driver type and then click Next.**

5. **For the file data source, type in a meaningful name, such as** SAS Dummies Example.

6. **Click Next and then click Finish.**

   The ODBC Microsoft Access Setup dialog box appears, as shown in Figure 4-8.

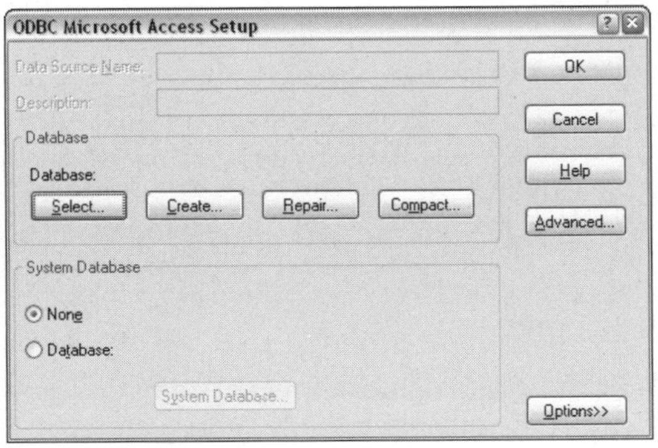

Figure 4-8:
The ODBC
Microsoft
Access
Setup dialog
box.

7. **Click Select.**

8. **From the Select Database dialog box that appears, navigate to and click the file that you want; then confirm your selection by clicking OK.**

   For the purpose of this example, navigate to the supplied sample data directory supplied by SAS Enterprise Guide and click the stdreg.mdb file.

9. **Click OK to close the ODBC Microsoft Access Setup dialog box.**

10. **Click OK to close the Select Data Source dialog box.**

    The Open Tables dialog box appears, as shown in Figure 4-9.

11. **Select the tables you want.**

    For this example, select the following check boxes to make a report of course enrollment by instructor:

    • Course

    • Enrollment

    • Instructor

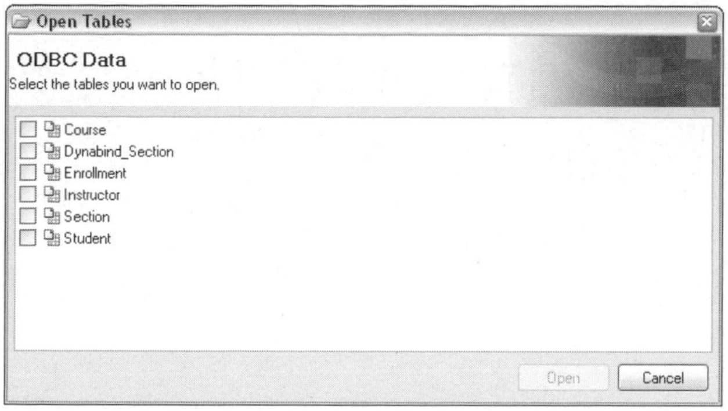

Figure 4-9:
Select
tables here.

12. **Click Open.**

The three tables open in your project, as shown in Figure 4-10. You can use these tables as input to tasks and wizards in your project. When you use them with a task in SAS Enterprise Guide, they are converted into SAS data sets just prior to the analysis task running. You won't be aware of this conversion occurring or see the SAS data set that is created because this conversion happens every time you access one of these tables behind the scenes. The conversion is done for you each time you access one of these tables because your source file can change at any time.

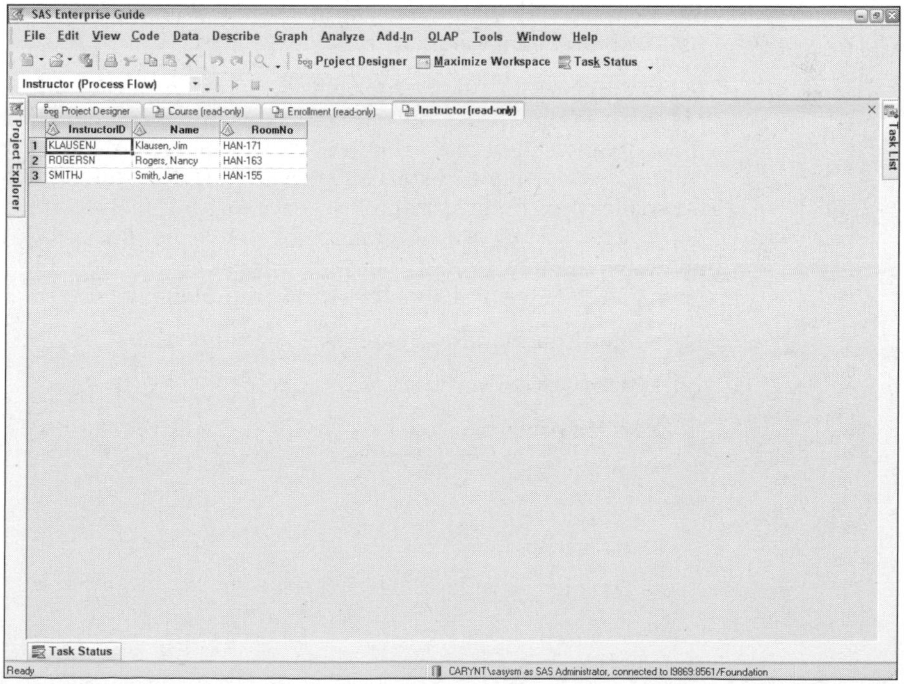

Figure 4-10:
The course,
enrollment,
and
instructor
ODBC data
sources.

Importing an Access database table with OLE DB

Importing an Access database table by using OLE DB is very similar to using ODBC except that you use an OLE DB provider to access your data source. To configure an OLE DB data source, consult the documentation included with your OLE DB provider. OLE DB is a newer technology developed by Microsoft that expands on the capabilities of ODBC. Whether you choose OLE DB or ODBC to access your data is not a critical point in this chapter. Use the one that is available for your data; even better, use whichever one is already installed on your PC!

More ways to access data from your PC

In addition to importing data from other databases or spreadsheets or using ODBC or OLE DB to do so, you have a variety of other options available to you for accessing other types of non-database data. Although we don't discuss these processes in-depth in this book (the book would weigh 200 lbs. if we did!), we do want to mention them to you so that you know the options are available. The two main alternative options for accessing data are

✔ **Exchange E-mail:** SAS Enterprise Guide allows you to access Exchange mail server-based e-mail sources, which can be very useful for analyzing and reporting on e-mail received by you or a support team in your organization. Using this function imports the e-mail folder specified into a SAS data set with all the relevant fields about your messages converted to columns in your data set.

✔ **Other Documents:** Another means of adding content to your SAS Enterprise Guide project is to open almost any document type you commonly read or browse and embed a shortcut to it from SAS Enterprise Guide. You can embed external files via File⇨Open⇨Other. Although these files aren't converted to SAS data sets for analysis purposes, they do provide a simple way for you to link to relevant project documentation and presentations from within your project. A few of the file types that you can reference as a shortcut within a project include

   • Microsoft Word documents

   • Microsoft PowerPoint presentations

   • HTML pages

   • Adobe Acrobat files

For more in-depth information on accessing non-database content using SAS Enterprise Guide, refer to the SAS Enterprise Guide help system by choosing Help⇨SAS Enterprise Guide Help.

Server-Based Data: Can You Super-Size That?

Using technologies on the SAS server is by far the fastest and most efficient way to access large data sources. And SAS has a plethora of choices for accessing data from SAS servers. Often, you can ask your SAS administrator to add direct server-based access to key data sources if you don't already have this at your organization. In addition, with products like SAS Enterprise Guide, you can easily add server access libraries to open almost any data source directly from the SAS server. A summary of frequently used data access methods is in Table 4-1.

Table 4-1	Frequently Used Data Access Methods	
Storage Type	*SAS Server Product Required*	*Comments*
SAS data sets	BASE: Always available on any SAS server.	The default storage method of libraries in SAS. This is optimized for very fast reading of data in a sequential fashion. You can easily make a library on your SAS server with the Assign Library Wizard to save data in this format.
Indexed SAS data sets	BASE: Always available on any SAS server.	By indexing SAS data sets, you can achieve much faster retrieval of subsets of a table.
SAS views	BASE: Always available on any SAS server.	Views allow you to make a virtual look-up of a table accessible to SAS so you don't have to copy it and take up additional storage. They are typically slower than direct data set access.

(continued)

Table 4-1 *(continued)*

Storage Type	SAS Server Product Required	Comments
Relational databases	Relevant SAS/ACCESS product. Examples include Oracle, DB2, Teradata, ODBC, and OLE DB.	SAS/ACCESS engines allow SAS to speak with almost any data source in a very efficient way. It is even possible to make multiple connections concurrently to accelerate storage and retrieval to these systems.
SAS OLAP	SAS OLAP server (included with SAS Enterprise BI Server).	A very fast way to access your data in presummarized form. Business analysts seeking unusual trends or quick answers to questions often favor this technology.
Other OLAP servers	Both SAS Enterprise Guide and SAS Web OLAP Viewer for .NET can access SAP BW and SQL Server Analysis Services OLAP data sources.	Use them if you have to, but why deal with the hassle and lower performance when SAS OLAP Server is available?
SAS Scalable Performance Data Engine (SPDE)	SAS Scalable Performance Data Server (SPDS).	By using multiple hard drives to store your large data tables, SAS Scalable Performance Data Engine (SPDE) can greatly accelerate storage and retrieval of very large data sources. Support was recently optimized to leverage several of the most common data warehouse storage structures.
XML Engine	BASE: Always available on any SAS server.	Allows you to read directly from XML data sources; a common format for data exchange among companies and organizations.
Text files like `.txt`, `.csv`, and tab-delimited files	BASE: Always available on any SAS server.	An old way to get data, but still common!

Make like a library and book . . .

A SAS library is like a virtual pointer to your data source, referenced by a simple name. Libraries enable you to change the route used to access your data at any time. As long as you keep the library name, all your SAS processes will still work with the data sourced from the new location. The library map might be a simple access description, like a folder name on a server. Or it might be more complex, like a database connection with required user credentials and specialized data connection software installed on your server.

After you define a library, using any library is seamless from SAS Enterprise Guide if you choose File⇨Open⇨SAS Servers. A sample dialog box is shown in Figure 4-11. To switch libraries, use the up-one-level-folder icon to the right of the Look In box. If you have multiple servers in your environment, you can switch servers by clicking the Servers icon in the left panel of this dialog box.

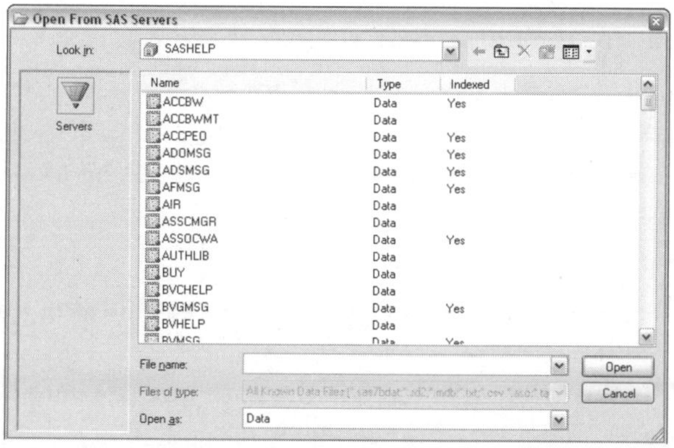

Figure 4-11:
Use the
Open from
SAS
Servers
dialog box
to choose a
library.

A common need among users is the capability to create a library specifically for a current project. SAS Enterprise Guide makes this easy with the Assign Library Wizard. The following example shows this in action:

1. **Choose Tools⇨Assign Library.**

   The Library Wizard dialog box appears, as shown in Figure 4-12.

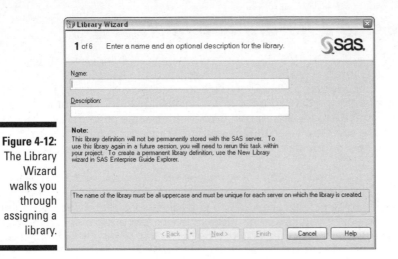

Figure 4-12:
The Library
Wizard
walks you
through
assigning a
library.

2. **Enter a name for the library and click Next.**

   In this example, you can use CHAPTER4 for the name. The Specify Server dialog box appears.

3. **Select the server on which you want this library to be available and then click Next.**

   The Select an Engine dialog box appears.

4. **Type the file path for a directory on your server holding the data of interest and click Next.**

   In Figure 4-13, the location entered in the Path box is where the SAS Enterprise Guide sample data is installed.

Figure 4-13:
Enter the
path to
where your
data is
located.

The default engine is BASE, which is used in this example. You could browse this drop-down list to see the complete set of choices of engine type. Some of these choices come with Base SAS, but others require the appropriate SAS/ACCESS engine or SAS Scalable Performance Data Server (SPDS) on your selected server. Depending on the engine selected, the following screens vary based on the additional information required for that engine's library.

5. **When the Configure options dialog box appears, click Next.**

   Unless you are an advanced user who has referenced the detailed library documentation, you probably won't need to enter any advanced options here.

6. **When the test library dialog box appears (as shown in Figure 4-14), click the Start Test button to verify that your library can be assigned.**

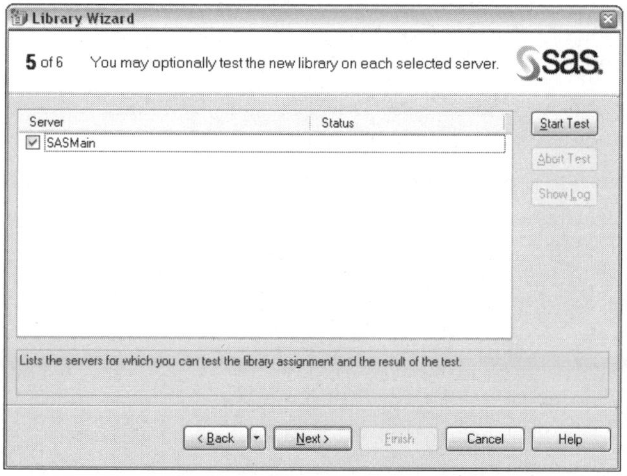

Figure 4-14:
The test library dialog box.

Just because your library can be assigned doesn't mean that you have any data in the library. You can assign empty libraries or libraries already populated with data sources.

7. **Click Next.**

   A confirmation dialog box appears.

8. **Click Finish.**

   The task runs, and the library is assigned.

If you want to use this library for the output SAS data set location of the Excel import task earlier in this chapter, you must update the Process Flow to ensure that the library is assigned before the import data task is run. To achieve this automated processing order, follow these steps:

1. **From the Process Flow pane, single-click and drag from the corner of the Assign Library task to the middle of the Excel spreadsheet.**

   This creates a link, as shown in Figure 4-15.

2. **Edit the Import Data wizard to use the CHAPTER4 library and rerun the import task.**

   Manually connecting the Assign Library task to the Excel import flow ensures that the right order of events occurs the next time you open and run the project.

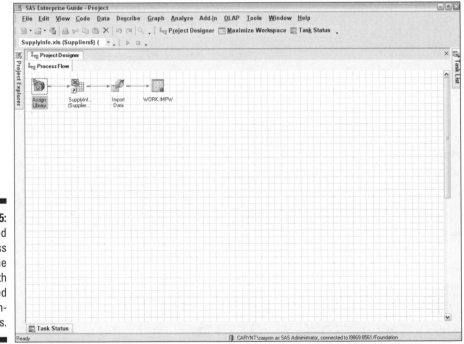

Figure 4-15:
The updated process flow for the project with added dependencies.

Chapter 5

Managing Data: I Can Do That?

*I*f you have only a passing familiarity with SAS, it might bring to mind images of fancy statistics, cool graphs, and complex analyses — things your college professors created to earn their tenure. Rarely do people new to SAS — or to data management in general — think of it as fun or difficult.

One of the reasons why SAS is an unparalleled system for getting work done in so many industries is because of its impressive data management capabilities. People sometimes find that most of their analysis time is spent trying to get their data into a form that lets them perform the needed analysis. At your service, SAS Enterprise Guide offers you frequently used forms of data management, right at your fingertips!

Taking a Quick Look at What You Can Do with Data

Managing your data can include the following tasks:

✔ Filtering your data

✔ Creating new computed columns in your data

- Manually editing data values
- Taking a sample of your data
- Comparing a new version of a data set with a previous version

By putting a little upfront thought into what you want to accomplish, you can simplify the tasks you perform in SAS and have an easier time creating effective projects. Think about these things:

- Results you want to create in your SAS Enterprise Guide project
- Data sources you have at hand
- Steps required to arrive at your results

Based on the data sources at hand and your desired outcome — and with practice — you can mentally sketch out the steps you must take to get to the results you want. You can accomplish many of these steps by using the functionality discussed in this chapter. Let the following sections be your guide.

Queries: Bringing Your Data Together and Making It Sing (Or at Least Hum)

The Filter and Query task in SAS Enterprise Guide provides a tremendous amount of power in one task, available when you choose Data⇨Filter and Query.

This task enables you to

- Join two or more tables into a single output table
- Filter the rows of your input tables
- Select a subset of columns for your output data set
- Create computed columns based on an extensive array of functions
- Recode a column's values
- Sort the output data
- Parameterize your query filter so that you are prompted each time you rerun the query to get just the output data you want in your project

With the Filter and Query task, you can filter candy sales by product type, join the sales table with a sales discount table (to have all the needed columns in one table), create a computed column of net sales based on the original transaction price multiplied by the updates sales discount, sort the sales data by date, and recode the date column to a quarter/year column — all in one task!

The following sections tell you more about each of these activities.

Joining table data

Joining data allows you to combine two or more related tables by specifying the columns that they have in common — often referred to as *keys*. Matching rows are combined, and the new table has the columns specified by you from each source table.

The columns used in a join may be named identically or similarly but must be of an identical type (for example, character or numeric) and typically be the same format (for example, date.) There are four join types between two tables: inner, left, right, and full outer. Joins occur between two columns in two separate tables, but you can have many join specifications in one task, so you could be combining two or more tables at one time.

Joins can be simple (joining data from the sales and product table into one table by the product ID column) or complex (joining sales, product, customer, customer state, and salesperson tables together using multiple columns and join types). Columns used in a join don't have to be included for the output table created, nor do all columns in the tables need to be in the output table.

Figure 5-1 illustrates the use of two data tables and is the basis for the next four figures that illustrate the results of the four most common join types. The circle on the left represents all students. The circle on the right represents all courses. The two tables are joined by the student ID number. Students with no courses are off on the far left (they must be in Cancun partying for the semester). A few courses have no students enrolled — too bad for the underwater basket-weaving instructor! Finally, the intersection of the two circles shows the students enrolled in courses. In reality, this would likely be the majority of the data, but this figure represents it as a rather small section.

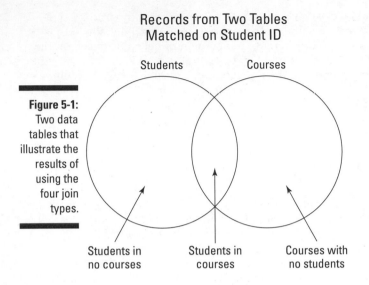

Figure 5-1:
Two data
tables that
illustrate the
results of
using the
four join
types.

The following list describes the four types of joins:

✔ *Inner:* Most of the time, you want matching rows or an inner join, which returns only those rows that have rows with a matching key in each table (see Figure 5-2). With this type of join, rows that have no corresponding matching row are left off the output table.

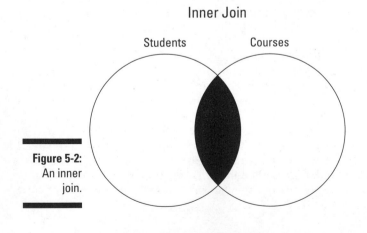

Figure 5-2:
An inner
join.

✔ *Left:* This join returns all rows from the table to the left of the join symbol and all data from the right side table that has a matching key value (see Figure 5-3). An example of a left join is if you need data on all students and the matching courses they have taken.

Left Join

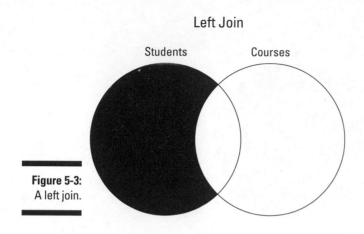

Figure 5-3:
A left join.

▶ *Right:* This join is like a left join except that it is reversed for the right table (see Figure 5-4).

Right Join

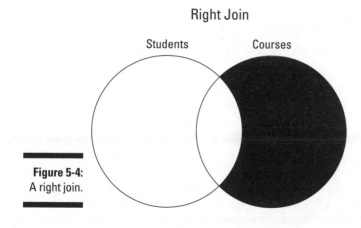

Figure 5-4:
A right join.

▶ *Full outer:* This join returns all rows from both tables regardless of whether a matching row based on the key value is in the other table (see Figure 5-5). The result of this join is all students (including those who never took a course) and all courses (regardless of whether a student ever enrolled.)

Imagine two simple tables:

▶ On the left side of the query is the Student table with join column Student_ID and values of 001, 003, and 004.

▶ On the right side of the query is the Courses table with join column Student_ID and column values of 001, 002, 004, and 005.

Full Outer Join

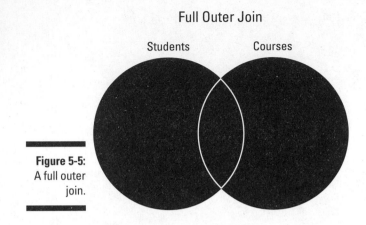

Students   Courses

Here is how the different joins and their results play out:

- *Inner join:* Student_ID row values of 001 and 004 (two rows)
- *Left join:* 001, 003, and 004 (three rows)
- *Right join:* 001, 002, 004, and 005 (four rows)
- *Full outer join:* 001, 002, 003, 004, and 005 (five rows)

To access the join feature, click the Join button in the upper-left main task window. There is no need to use this feature unless your output table requires data from more than one input table.

Filtering table data

Filtering data allows you to reduce the rows returned in your output table based on conditions that you set. Filtering your data can significantly improve your query processing time and greatly speed up the tasks downstream of your data.

Filter conditions can be simple (say, chocolate candy sales) or complex (chocolate candies sales with a discount greater than 30 percent or a total sale amount over $9,000). Columns used in a filter don't have to be selected for the output table.

To use the filter option, click the Filter Data tab in the upper-right main task window; then drag columns to this area from the tables area.

Selecting specific columns of data

Your input tables might contain columns irrelevant to the question at hand. By selecting specific columns of interest, your output table gives you exactly the information needed for your analysis and can greatly decrease your overall processing time.

When you select columns, you can also specify formats for the column, rename the column, or specify an aggregation for certain columns. When you select an aggregation for a column (Sum, for example), the output table automatically includes one row for each unique set of nonaggregated columns. For example, the sum of sales by quarter and region has only one row per unique combination of quarter and region.

To select specific columns of data, drag columns from the tables area to the Select Data tab.

You can specify an aggregation after you add a column to the Select Data tab.

Creating a computed column

Computed columns let you create a column based on either of the following:

✔ A simple expression

```
Net_Sales = Revenue - Expenses
```

✔ A more complex expression

```
Net_Sales = Gross_Sales X (1-Discount) - Expenses -
       Gross_Sales*(1-Sales_Commision)
```

The Expression Builder in SAS Enterprise Guide can help you build and validate your new column. You access Expression Builder by clicking the Computed Columns button in the upper-left main task window and choosing New⇨Build Expression from the Computed Columns dialog box. SAS provides Expression Builder with many powerful functions, including

✔ IF, THEN, and ELSE logic via the CASE statement

✔ Many statistical and financial functions

✔ The capability to look up column values

✔ The capability to utilize data quality functions in SAS

Computed columns are automatically added to your selected columns list.

Recoding a column

The Filter and Query task gives you the capability to rename (or *recode*) data value abbreviations or numeric codes for a couple of handy purposes:

✔ To rename data abbreviations to something understandable by average humans (for example, you can set a gender identifier of 1 to appear as Female)

✔ To collapse a range of values to one category (for example, you can set test scores of 90–100 to appear as an A)

You can achieve the same results in the Computed Columns feature by using the CASE function (IF, THEN, and ELSE logic). The recoding feature is a simplification of using that approach. Recoded columns are added automatically to your selected columns list.

To access the recoding function, click the Computed Columns button in the upper-left main task window and choose New➪Recode a Column from the Computed Columns dialog box.

Sorting data

Sorting data lets you sort your output table by one or more columns. You can sort data in either *ascending* (1, 2, 3; or A, B, C) or *descending* order (9, 8, 7; or Z, Y, X.) Sorting data affects only your output table, not your input table, unless they are the same! Common uses for sorting include quickly finding records occurring on a particular date or finding a particular range of customers in the sorted output table.

Parameterizing the Query Filter

Queries that filter your data in a frequently changing manner can be *parameterized*. This means that each time the query is run, the user is automatically prompted to specify the exact data filter conditions (also called *parameters*) to apply.

For example, a sales report that you frequently run for other people in your company is filtered each time by product and region. You can parameterize the product and region filter condition so that you can select the appropriate values each time you run the report. One time you might select chocolate candy in the West region; the next time you run the report, you might select hard candy in the Central region.

To use the parameterization option, click the Parameters button in the upper-left main task window. Click Add to add a new parameter value. Use this parameter in the Filter Data dialog box.

A parameterized query example

In the following multi-part example, we build a query that combines data from three data tables found in the Sample Data directory supplied with SAS Enterprise Guide:

- ✓ Candy_Customers
- ✓ Candy_Products
- ✓ Candy_Sales_History

In part one of this example query, you join the Candy_Customers, Candy_Products, and Candy_Sales_History tables. The output table includes the region column and a new calculated column — net sales.

In part two, you parameterize the query with the product column. By adding this parameter, the query prompts users each time they run this query to select a particular product for analysis.

In part three, you use the resulting table from this query with the Bar Chart Wizard to create a graphical summary of net sales by region using the user selected product filter.

Example query: Part 1

Follow these steps to join the three sample tables and create an output table that includes a new calculated column:

1. **Click the Candy_Sales_History table in the Process Flow to specify the initial table used in your query.**

2. **Choose Data⇨Filter and Query.**

   The Filter and Query dialog box appears, as shown in Figure 5-6.

3. **On the left side of dialog box, just to the left of the Select Data tab, click the Join button.**

   The Tables and Joins dialog box appears.

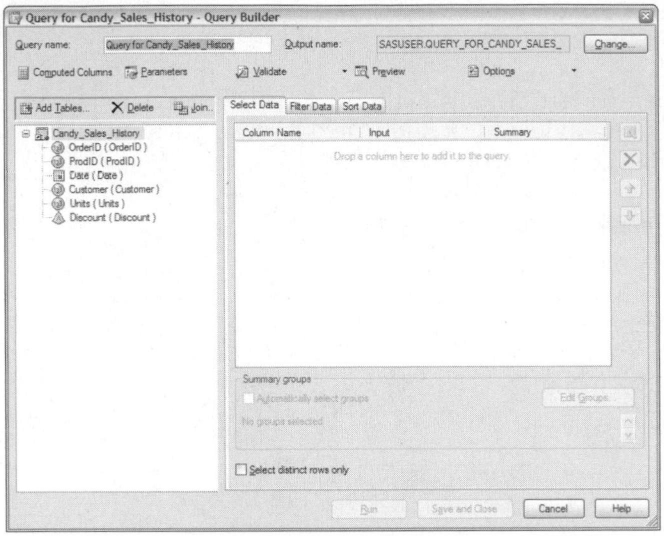

Figure 5-6:
The Filter
and Query
dialog box.

4. **To add the Customers and Products tables to this query, click the Add Tables button at the top of the dialog box.**

   The Open Data dialog box appears.

5. **Select Project as the source for the tables to add.**

   The list of available tables in the project appears.

   If you haven't already added the additional tables to your project, you can add them to your project directly from the Filter and Query task via this dialog box.

6. **Press Ctrl and click the Candy_Products and the Candy_Customers tables; then click OK.**

   A warning message appears stating that a suitable join can't be found. This means that the tables can't automatically be associated by a variable with an exact name match. Click OK to dismiss this warning. See Figure 5-7 for the current state of the Tables and Joins dialog box. Note that ProdID is a variable common to Candy_Sales_History and Candy_Products, so an inner join is added automatically between these two tables by using this column.

7. **Click the Candy_Customers table to select it. Then click and drag it down the screen about half the length of the other two tables.**

   You can see that sales history is now joined to products by the identically named column ProdID.

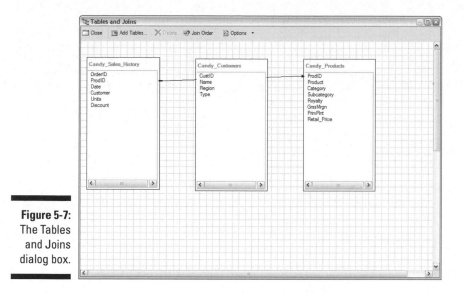

Figure 5-7:
The Tables
and Joins
dialog box.

8. **To join customers to sales history, click the CustID column (in the Candy_Customers table) and drag it on top of the Customer column in the Candy_Sales_History table.**

   The joins between columns in tables default to an inner join. (You can read about inner joins earlier in this chapter.) Figure 5-8 shows this new layout.

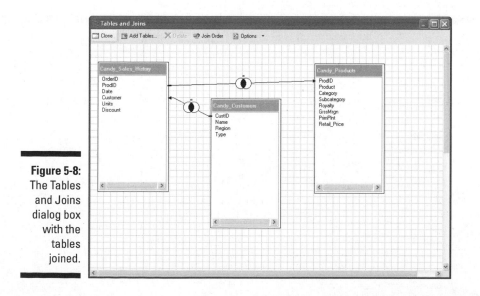

Figure 5-8:
The Tables
and Joins
dialog box
with the
tables
joined.

To change this default join type, double-click the join line at the center of the line.

The symbol in the middle of each join line provides a quick reference to the type of join being used. You can double-click the join line to access the Modify Join dialog box (see Figure 5-9), which presents you with detailed join information and options.

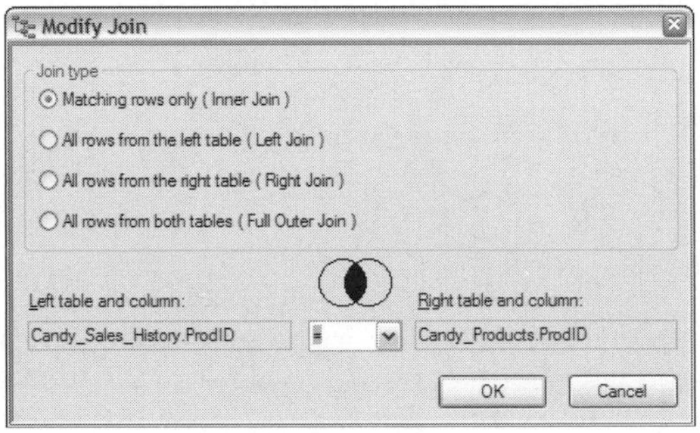

Figure 5-9:
The Modify
Join dialog
box.

9. Click Close to dismiss the Tables and Joins dialog box.

All three tables now appear in the main query dialog box (see Figure 5-10) based on the work you did in the Tables and Joins dialog box.

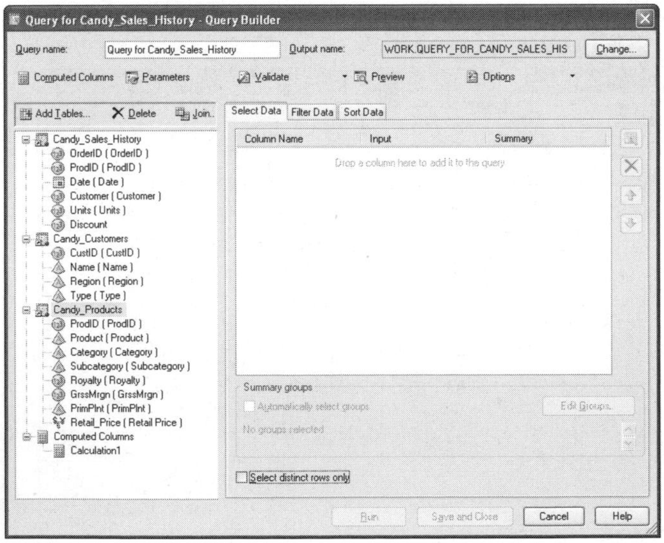

Figure 5-10:
The main
query dialog
box now
listing the
three tables.

10. **Click the Region column from the Candy_Customers table and drag it to the Select Data area.**

    If you want to add all the columns from a particular table, just drag the table name to the Select Data region.

11. **To calculate net sales, follow these steps:**

    a. *Click the Computed Columns button.*

       The Computed Columns dialog box appears.

    b. *Click the New button and choose Build Expression.*

       The Advanced Expression Editor appears, as shown in Figure 5-11.

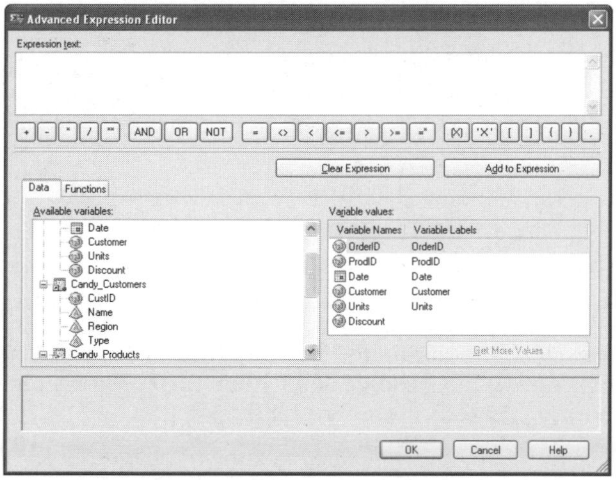

Figure 5-11: You can use the Advanced Expression Editor to create computed columns.

In this example, net sales is calculated as the units sold times the retail price. For example, if an order has 100 units of a product sold at a retail price of $2, the net sale amount for that order is $100 \times \$2$ ($200). And for this example, the general formula to enter in the editor appears as

```
Candy_Sales_History.Units * Candy_Products.
      Retail_Price
```

12. **From the box on the right, Variable Values, double-click Units.**

    Candy_Sales_History.Units appears in the Expression Text at the top of the dialog box.

13. **Click the button showing the asterisk (*) just below the Expression Text box.**

    The multiplier symbol now follows the variable.

14. **Scroll down the bottom-left Available Variables list and click the Candy_Products table.**

    The Variable Values pane updates with the values for the variables in the products table.

15. **From the Variable Values pane, double-click Retail_Price and then click OK.**

    The Advanced Expression Editor closes and the Computed Columns dialog box appears, as shown in Figure 5-12. The column you just created is automatically assigned the default name Calculation1. You can change this and other properties of this column by clicking Edit from this dialog box.

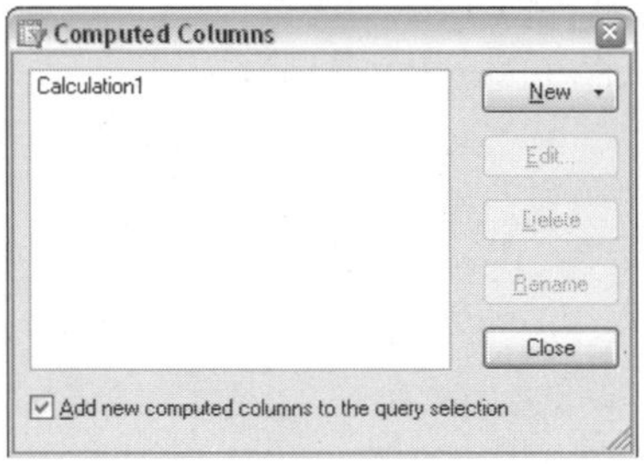

Figure 5-12: The Computed Columns dialog box.

16. **Click OK to close the Computed Columns dialog box and return to the main query dialog box. Then double-click the column Calculation1 to edit the newly created column's attributes.**

    The Properties dialog box appears, as shown in Figure 5-13. The computed column has the default name Calculation1 and the default simple numeric format. This dialog box allows you to customize the column.

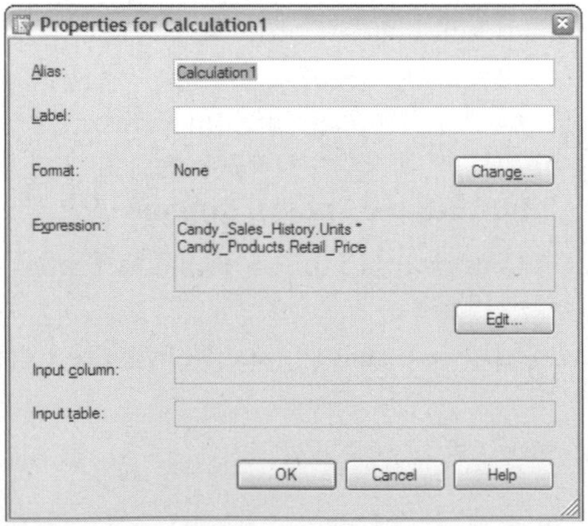

Figure 5-13: The column Properties dialog box.

17. Change the column Alias to a more meaningful name, such as Net_Sales.

18. To change the column format from the default simple numeric format to the appropriate US currency format, do the following:

    a. Click the Format Change button.

      The Formats dialog box appears, as shown in Figure 5-14.

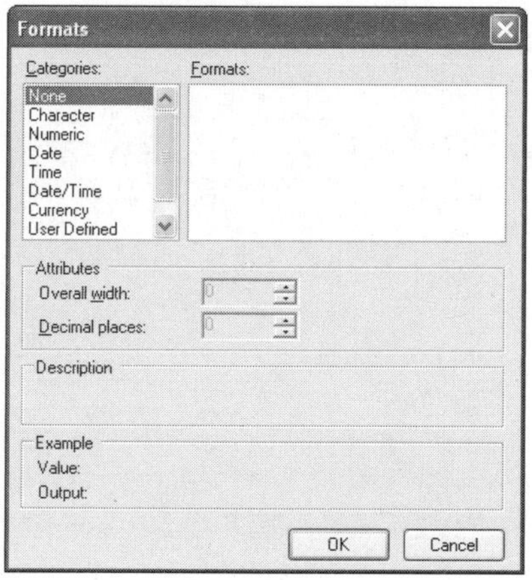

Figure 5-14:
The column
Formats
dialog box.

    b. Select the Currency category and the format DOLLARw.d.

    c. Change the overall width from 6 to 12.

    d. Click OK twice to return to the main query dialog box.

The Advanced Expression Editor, where you specify computed columns, is also available from the column Properties dialog box via the Expression Edit button.

This is the end of Part I of this example. You can click Run to see the table shown in Figure 5-15, or you can continue on in the Filter and Query Task with the next part. If you run the task at this point, but you want to continue with Part II of this query example, reopen the Filter and Query task from the Process Flow by double-clicking it to continue.

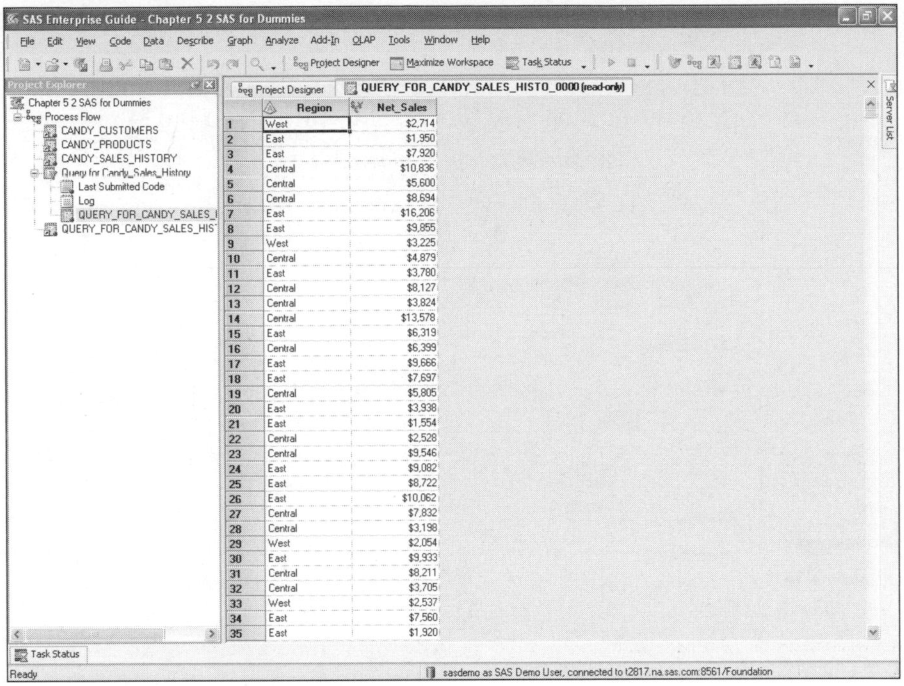

Figure 5-15:
The Filter
and Query
output table.

Example query: Part 11

In this part, you parameterize the query using the product column. By adding this parameter, the query prompts users to select a particular product for analysis each time they run the query.

1. **For the parameterized filter, first create a parameter with the list of products in it.**

   a. *Click the Parameters button near the upper left of the main query builder dialog box.*

   The Parameters dialog box appears.

   b. *Click Add.*

   The Add New Parameter dialog box appears, as shown in Figure 5-16.

2. **In the Display Name box, type** Product; **then click the Data Type and Values tab.**

3. **From the Data Value Type drop-down list, choose A List of Values.**

4. **Click the Load Values drop-down list and choose Project.**

   The Add from Project dialog box appears.

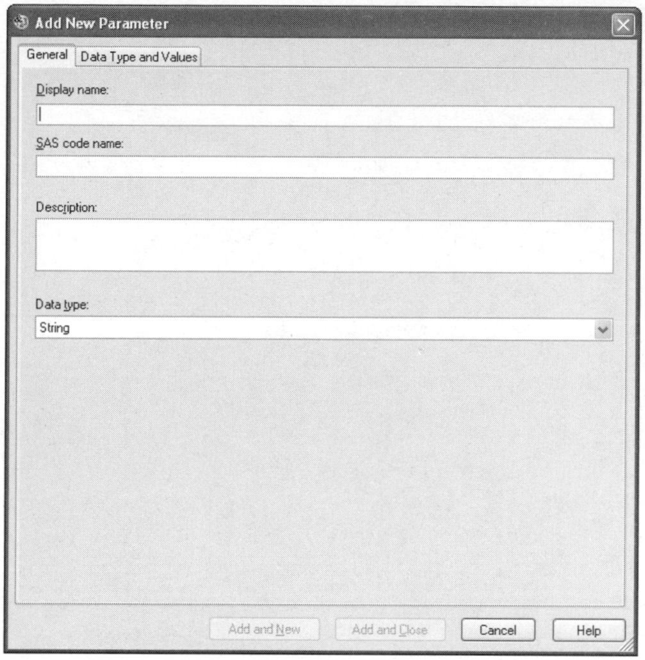

Figure 5-16:
The Add
New
Parameter
dialog box.

5. **Click Candy_Products and then click OK.**

   The Select Column dialog box appears.

6. **Click the Product column and then click OK.**

   The Edit Parameter Definition dialog box opens and a list of distinct values from the Product column appears, as shown in Figure 5-17.

7. **Click Save and Close; then click Close.**

   You return to the main query dialog box.

8. **Click the Filter Data tab and then drag the Product column to the Filter Data area.**

   The Edit Filter dialog box appears.

9. **Click the drop-down arrow beside the Value box.**

10. **Click the Parameter tab, select &Product, and then click OK.**

11. **From the main query dialog box, click Run.**

12. **In the Select Values dialog box that appears, choose the desired product to filter the query for this run and then click Run.**

    We selected Chewy Chocolate Cheetahs for this example. The filtered output data table appears.

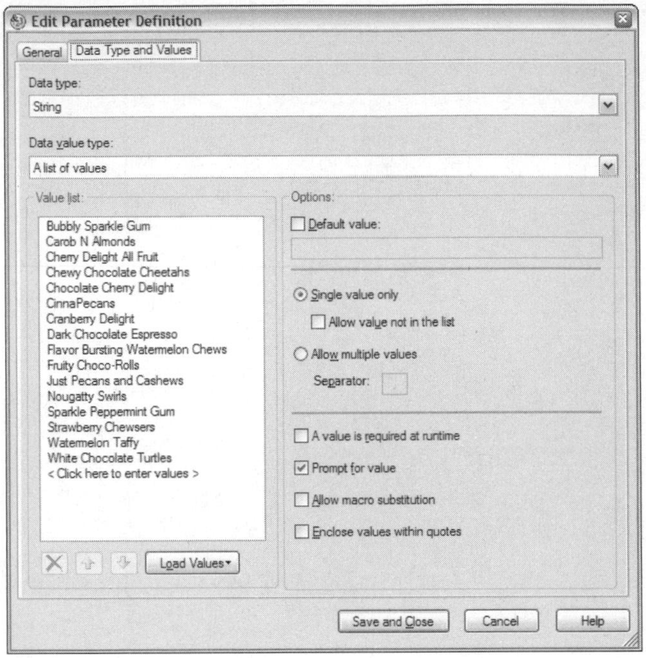

Figure 5-17:
The Edit
Parameter
Definition
dialog box.

This is the end of Part II of this example. You can go have some milk and cookies and revel in the filtered data, or you can continue with Part III.

Query example: Part III

In Part III, you use the resulting table from this query with the Bar Chart Wizard to create a graphical summary of net sales by region:

1. **From the data table view created when you last ran the query, complete this report by creating a bar chart of sales by region; choose Graph⇨Wizards⇨Bar Chart.**

2. **When the Bar Chart Wizard appears, click Next.**

3. **On Step 2 (of 4) of the wizard, change the Bar Height role to Net_Sales; then click Next.**

4. **Change the Color Bars by Value box from All Bars the Same to Bar Category; this colors each bar a separate color. Then Click Next.**

5. **On screen 4 of the wizard, change the Graph title by typing** Net Sales by Region for &Product.

Make sure you use an ampersand before the start of the word *Product*.

The &Product in the graph title is a *macro variable* in the SAS language. This value was set at runtime based on the user selection from the Product parameter used in the query task. These can be very useful for creating meaningful titles and footnotes throughout SAS Enterprise Guide. If you leave off the ampersand, just the word *Product* would be displayed instead.

6. Click Finish.

A graph resembling Figure 5-18 is generated after a few seconds.

If you've been working along with this example, you're now done! You brought together sales data from several data tables with the Filter and Query task, created a new Net Sales computed column, filtered the results to only Chewy Chocolate Cheetahs, and created a nice summary graph of the results. Good work!

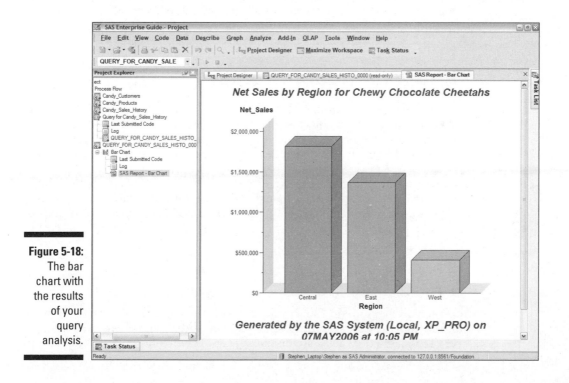

Figure 5-18: The bar chart with the results of your query analysis.

Editing, Sorting, Ranking, Transposing, and Other Data Contortions

In addition to the power of the Filter and Query task, many other data management capabilities are available in SAS Enterprise Guide, such as

- Editing data tables
- Sorting data
- Ranking data values
- Transposing columns and rows
- Sampling large data tables for analysis and graphs
- Comparing new versions of data tables with the previous version

The following sections give you a quick look at the many data management capabilities available in SAS Enterprise Guide.

Editing data table values

SAS Enterprise Guide provides interactive data grid access to your data table and offers basic cell editing capabilities. You access the editing feature by choosing Data⇨Read Only. Changes you type in the data grid are applied to the table immediately. You have the option of printing the data grid.

There is no Undo functionality, so be sure you edit a *copy* of any critical data source. Before overriding the original data table with the edited one, you can compare the two tables with the Compare Data task (explained a little later in the "Comparing data" section).

Appending tables

You can use the Append Table task (choose Data⇨Append Table) to combine multiple tables into one output table. All rows and variables are used from every table, and the tables are combined (or figuratively stacked) one on top of the other.

An example of when you might want to append tables is to combine a sales table that was kept separately for each of the past four quarters (for example,

Sales_Q1, Sales_Q2, Sales_Q3, and Sales_Q4). If you want one table with all records from the four quarters, the Append Table task makes this simple!

Sorting data

You can use the Sort Data task to sort your data by columns from your data source. For example, you can drop unneeded columns or remove duplicate rows. The default behavior is the option to output a data set. You access the Sort Data task by choosing Data⇨Sort Data.

If your input data source and output data location are on the same relational database, use the Filter and Query task instead.

Creating a format

This task allows you to create format *masks* to change how you show data values in your reports. When you use the Create Format task, your SAS format catalog is updated. Formats are a SAS system capability that allows you to store data one way (gender as F and M) and display it another way when used in a report (gender appears as Female and Male when format $Gender is used). Formats can apply to numeric or character columns and are frequently used to minimize the space your data needs for storage (storing a million rows of F or M is much more efficient than the full words.) The SAS format catalog only needs the translation information once, so the words *Female* and *Male* are saved in only one location. For some columns that use formats, the value translation may change over time. So it is easy to quickly modify the value in just one place — the format catalog. A good example of a value translation that might change is a column that tracks customer numbers by purchase amount in the past month (high, medium, or low).

Some other examples of when you might want to use a format include converting numeric or text variables to meaningful text values and specifying ways to present them. For example, you could display the numeric value 419184523 as a Social Security number (419-18-4523) or 9192449876 as a phone number (919-244-9876).

Transposing data

By using the Transpose Data task, you can to turn the data "sideways," with rows transposed to columns. You can group by identifier columns so that one row per unique identifier value appears in the output table. An example of transposing data would be to take a table with one row per quarter for a sales year. To take the four rows (with values for Q1, Q2, Q3, and Q4) and make them just one row with one column per quarter (columns Q1_Sales, Q2_Sales, Q3_Sales, and Q4_Sales), you use the Transpose Data task by choosing Data↷ Transpose Data.

Splitting columns

The Split Columns task is a special case of the Transpose task. A simple example of when you might use this task is to transpose the sales data just mentioned in the transpose task from four rows and two columns (Quarter and Sales) to one row and four columns (one column for each unique quarter).

Stacking columns

The Stack Columns task produces the reverse of Split Columns. Data from many columns is collapsed into one column, with the new number of rows being the same as the number of input columns. If you take the data set created in the Split Columns example (one row of data with a variable for each quarter of sales) and use the Stacked Columns task, you would go back to four rows and two columns with the quarter value in one column and the sales amount in the other column.

Selecting a random sample of data

Use the Random Sample task to select a random sample of your data when analyzing the full data source might be time consuming. This task is very useful when prototyping your project from large data sources. The default behavior is the option to output a data set. A print report option is also available, so you can print a summary of how the sample was performed.

You can sample the following:

 ✔ As a percent of all rows or a fixed number of rows
 ✔ The same amount for each unique or distinct value of a variable

Use the Random Sample task for prototyping your project with smaller data volumes and performing statistical analysis. Be careful, however, not to use this task when you are reporting on actual numbers, such as quarterly sales reports where every row is required to achieve accurate results!

Ranking variables

Rank is a specialized task for creating output data sets that rank a variable with one of the methods for further analysis, reporting, or graphing. Records rank can be determined in twelve different ways. Commonly used methods include smallest to largest (1, 2, 3, . . . n), percentile ranks (1%, 2%, and so on), deciles (first 10%, second 10%, and so on), ntiles (determined by how many groups the data is subdivided into; five groups is called *quintiles*), and normal scores using the statistical normal distribution (see next paragraph for more about normal distribution). From the sales example, you could rank the four rows of sales to see which quarter had the greatest sales (smallest to largest rank of 1) to which quarter had the least sales (rank of 4).

Standardizing data

Many common statistical techniques assume an underlying *normal distribution*. A normal distribution is the most commonly used distribution in statistical analysis; it is often referred to as a "bell-shaped" curve. If your data doesn't meet this assumption, you can transform it to a normal distribution with the Standardize Data task. (See Chapters 8 and 9 to find out how SAS provides the statistics to show whether your selected analysis meets the normal distribution standard.)

Summarizing data set attributes

With the Data Set Attributes task, you can create a detailed report or data set that summarizes the details of a selected data set or table. Information available with this task includes column names, column labels, column type (numeric or character), column format, and various table attributes, such as date created, date modified, and data set label. You might want to use this task to create a printed report of data used in your important analysis, possibly an analysis that may be audited later date by government officials.

Comparing data

The Compare Data task enables you to compare changes between an old version and a new version of a data set. Data differences, such as missing variables, added variables, changes in formats, changes in data values, and added or deleted records are reported in a concise manner.

Deleting data sets and formats

If you have the appropriate security (your system administrator has to give you the capability to delete files from your server), you can use the Delete Data Sets and Formats task to delete unneeded data sets, views, or formats.

Use this feature carefully because there is no undelete capability!

Trying out the data management tasks

In this example, we once again use the sample data table included with SAS Enterprise Guide: Candy_Sales_Summary. This example illustrates some of the most commonly used data management tasks. In this example, you

1. Reduce the data size used by taking a random sample.

2. Collapse the resulting table further by

   • Summarizing sales (via variable Retail_Price) by product and year per row

   • Transposing the summary table so that each product has only one row per product with a column for each year, and then using the Rank task to find the most to least sold product by year

3. Create a report summarizing the products ranked by sales in each year.

In this example, you won't use all the tasks previewed in this chapter. But keep in mind that every task in SAS Enterprise Guide has detailed help to assist you when you're ready to try out a specific task.

Reducing the volume of data

First, use the Random Sample task to reduce the volume of data used in later steps:

1. **Click table Candy_Sales_Summary from the Process Flow.**

2. **Choose Data⇨Random Sample.**

   The Random Sample dialog box appears. Like the filter capabilities of the Filter and Query task, the random sample task reduces the number of rows in your output data. The main difference is that with random sampling, you specify how you want the data *sampled* rather than how you want the data *filtered*.

3. **Add the variables Product, Fiscal_Year, and Retail_Price to the Output Variables role.**

   You use these variables later in the example.

4. **Click the Options pane.**

5. **Change the Sample Size to read 25 percent of rows, a reasonable percentage to sample down to for your initial assessment.**

6. **Click Run.**

   The random sample report appears in a few moments, summarizing the sampling performed and rows output.

In real-world data sizes, this reduction would reduce a 50,000,000-row table to 12,500,000 rows. For subsequent tasks, processing time is greatly reduced. This is an easy way to accelerate your processing time while prototyping your project.

When you finish with the development stage of this example, you can easily change the sample size to 100 percent of rows or simply delete the task from the project.

Transposing the data

In the next part of the data management example, you transpose the data to change from many records per product (one per year) to just one record per product (one column for each year). Then you use the Rank task to find the most successful product for each year:

1. **Transpose the data from the random sample task.**

   The Transpose task expects one row per unique data combination. To achieve this, use the Filter and Query task:

   a. *In Filter and Query, add all three variables (Product, Fiscal_Year, and Retail_Price) to the Select Data area.*

   b. *In the Summary column of the Select Data area, change the Retail_Price column to function SUM.*

   Because you want just one record per year, you will sum all the rows with sales data for a given year.

   c. *Click the Automatically Select Groups option to inform the task to collapse the data by Product and Fiscal_Year.*

   d. *Click Run.*

A data table similar to Figure 5-19 appears, with one row per unique combination of Product and Fiscal_Year.

The values for SUM_OF_Retail_Price in your data will probably be different than what you see in Figure 5-19 because the sum is based on a random sample of observations from the data.

2. **Choose Data⇨Transpose.**

   The Transpose dialog box appears.

3. **Add the following:**

   • SUM_OF_Retail_Price to the Transpose variable role

   • Product to the Group Analysis By role

   • Fiscal_Year to the New Column Names role

4. **Click the Options pane and clear the Use Prefix check box; then click Run.**

   You use the Use Prefix check box when you want to use another column to specify the new column name. You are using the actual year values, so you can uncheck this. A data table similar to Figure 5-20 appears, with one column per year and one row per product.

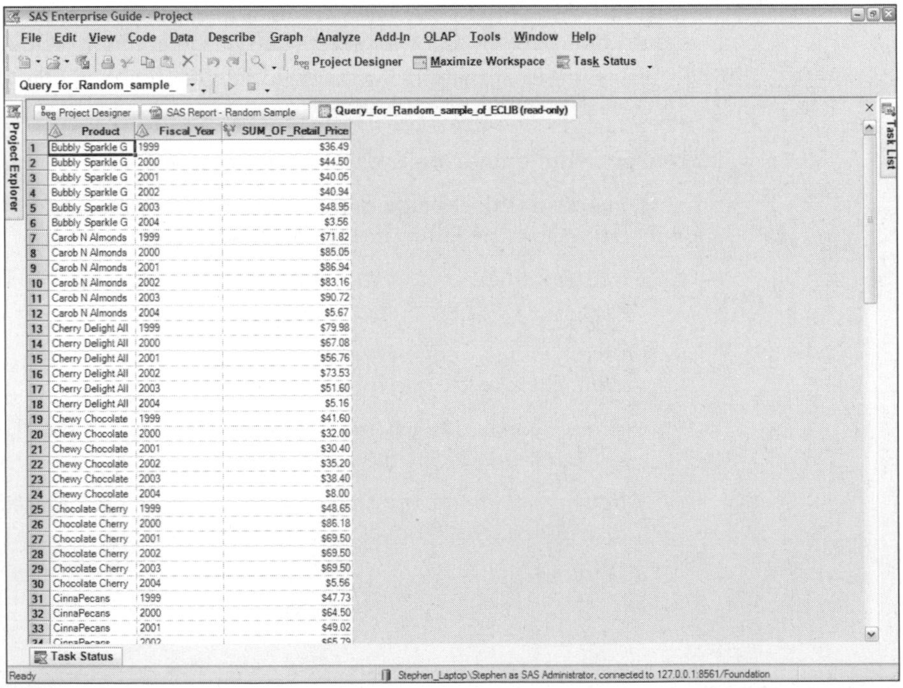

Figure 5-19: The summarized table output from the query task.

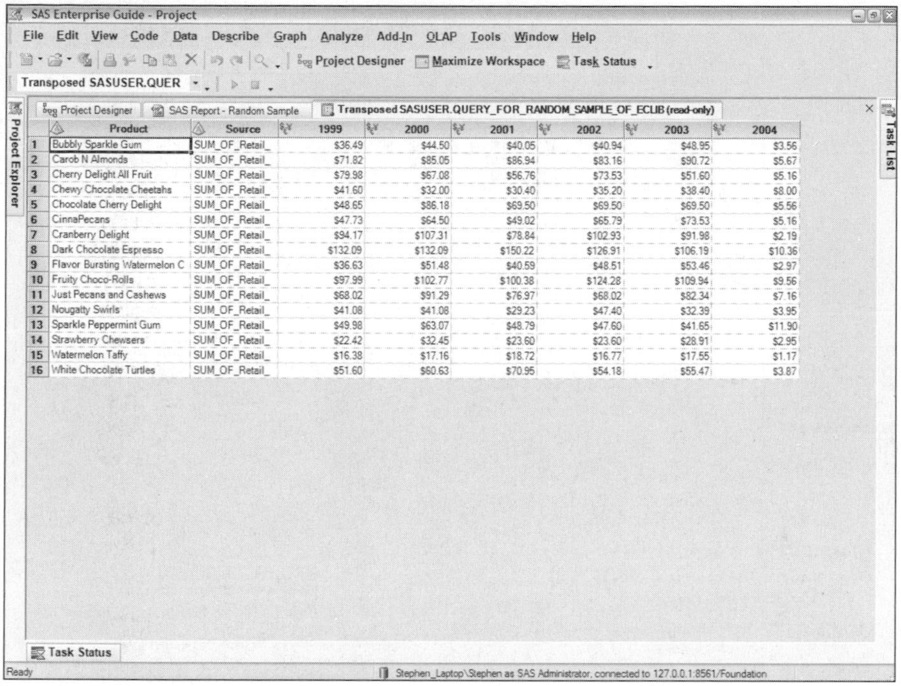

Figure 5-20:
Sales
summary
transposed
by year.

The Transpose task is useful for reporting in a columnar manner data that has many records over time. It is also used for certain statistical analyses that require data in a converted data form.

5. **Choose Data⇨Rank.**

   The Rank dialog box appears.

6. **Add columns named 1999 through 2004 to the Columns to Rank role.**

7. **Clear the Include Ranking Values check box.**

   You don't want the ranked values to appear in the original variable columns because they would use the current formatting for those columns. That would be a currency format rather than a standard numeric format.

8. **Click Run.**

   A data table similar to Figure 5-21 appears, with one column per year and one row per product.

The Rank task has many other ranking options: percentile ranks, deciles, quartiles, ntiles, percents, normal scores, and exponential distribution scores.

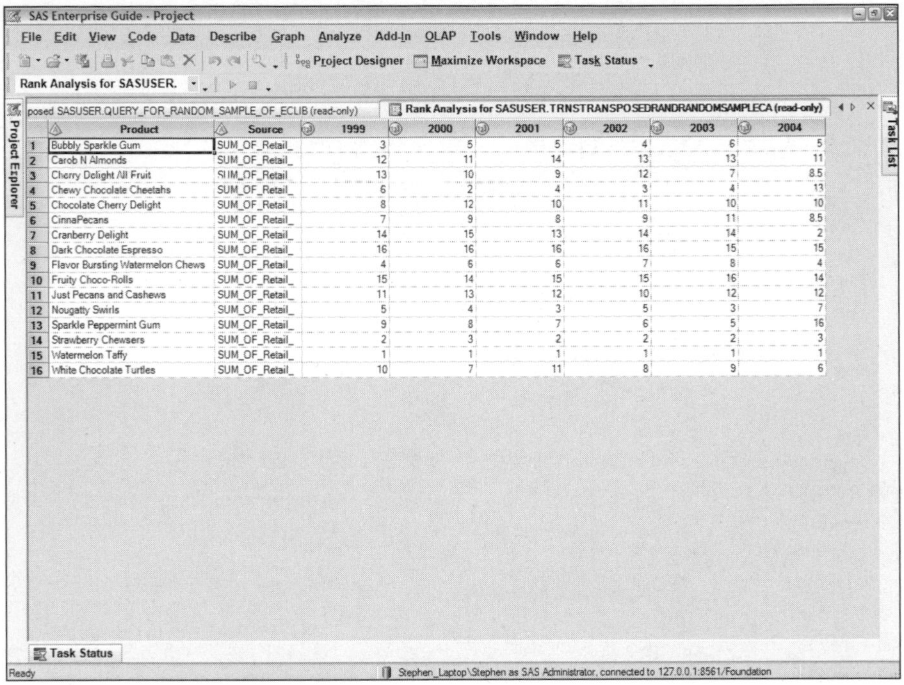

	Product	Source	1999	2000	2001	2002	2003	2004
1	Bubbly Sparkle Gum	SUM_OF_Retail_	3	5	5	4	6	5
2	Carob N Almonds	SUM_OF_Retail_	12	11	14	13	13	11
3	Cherry Delight All Fruit	SUM_OF_Retail	13	10	9	12	7	8.5
4	Chewy Chocolate Cheetahs	SUM_OF_Retail_	6	2	4	3	4	13
5	Chocolate Cherry Delight	SUM_OF_Retail_	8	12	10	11	10	10
6	CinnaPecans	SUM_OF_Retail_	7	9	8	9	11	8.5
7	Cranberry Delight	SUM_OF_Retail_	14	15	13	14	14	2
8	Dark Chocolate Espresso	SUM_OF_Retail_	16	16	16	16	15	15
9	Flavor Bursting Watermelon Chews	SUM_OF_Retail_	4	6	6	7	8	4
10	Fruity Choco-Rolls	SUM_OF_Retail_	15	14	15	15	16	14
11	Just Pecans and Cashews	SUM_OF_Retail_	11	13	12	10	12	12
12	Nougatty Swirls	SUM_OF_Retail_	5	4	3	5	3	7
13	Sparkle Peppermint Gum	SUM_OF_Retail_	9	8	7	6	5	16
14	Strawberry Chewsers	SUM_OF_Retail_	2	3	2	2	2	3
15	Watermelon Taffy	SUM_OF_Retail_	1	1	1	1	1	1
16	White Chocolate Turtles	SUM_OF_Retail_	10	7	11	8	9	6

Figure 5-21: Sales summary ranked by year across the products.

Creating a summary report

Finally, for the last part of this data management example, you create a report that summarizes the products ranked by sales in each year.

1. **Choose Describe⇨List Data.**

   The List Data dialog box appears.

2. **Add Product and columns 1999 through 2004 to the List Variables role.**
3. **Select the Options pane and clear the Print the Row Number check box and the Use Variable Labels as Column Headings check box.**
4. **Click Titles, click Report Titles, uncheck Use Default Text, and change the report title to Product Sales Ranking by Year.**
5. **Click Run.**

   A report similar to Figure 5-22 appears.

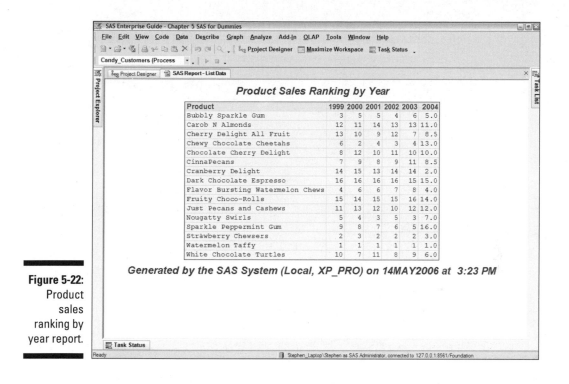

Figure 5-22:
Product
sales
ranking by
year report.

Chapter 6

Show Me a Report in Less Than a Minute

In This Chapter

▶ Using the various output types

▶ Creating simple listings and data summary reports

▶ Fine-tuning your formatting

*W*hen you mention *data reporting* to your colleagues, the phrase will likely invoke ideas ranging from simple listings of data tables to sophisticated combinations with graphs, data aggregations, complex data formatting, and even relevant statistical analysis in one report. SAS can cover a wide range of reports, from simple to complex.

That said, how you create a report with SAS is somewhat different from most other reporting applications. In SAS Enterprise Guide, reports can comprise a combination of output objects that you create in your project. For example, you can include a combination of a summary table of sales by quarter, a bar chart of new customers by quarter, and a line chart of sales by region over time on one page.

This chapter focuses on the tasks in SAS Enterprise Guide that allow you to generate data listings, data summaries, and summary tables (or cross-tabular reports). After you understand the building blocks of reports, you can combine the results of your labor into complex reports to meet most any need.

Discovering Your Reporting Options

Tasks that you run in SAS Enterprise Guide typically create a *report,* which is a type of textual or graphical output that you can view, print, or save as a file.

You can set the preferred output file type generated by tasks by choosing Tools⇨Options⇨Results General. The output file types available include

- ✔ **Plain text:** No formatting available — just text.
- ✔ **PDF:** The Adobe Acrobat Portable Document File format.
- ✔ **RTF (Rich Text Format):** An export format used by Microsoft Word and other popular word processing software.
- ✔ **HTML:** Formatting is possible, but printing often truncates important information.
- ✔ **SAS Report:** A SAS open standard report format. Formatting is possible, printing with proper formatting is possible, and your point-and-click format changes can be preserved if you rerun your project.

Although the preferred task output type is specified in Tools⇨Options⇨Results General, you can easily override this on a task-by-task basis. To force a task to generate different output than normal (say, if your colleague in Europe wants a PDF of the sales report), do the following:

1. **In the process flow or project explorer (tree view), right-click the task for which you want to specify a special type.**

2. **Choose Properties.**

3. **From the Properties dialog box that appears, do the following:**

    a. Click the Results tab.

    b. Select the Override the Preferences check box.

    c. Check the PDF file type (or whatever type you want).

   Figure 6-1 shows a task that has been modified in this way.

Note that you can select more than one output type; but be warned that for every output type you select, the task runs another time to generate it. For example, a task that takes one minute to create a long sales report in HTML takes about two minutes to generate the graph in both HTML and PDF formats. Obviously, it's to your advantage to request only the type of output you absolutely need.

Plain text reports

The least robust but simplest form of output that you can select is the plain text file. These files are much like the simple text files you can create in Windows Notepad: They bear the same limitations, including no character formatting, poor paragraph alignment control, and poor pagination when printed. Additionally, graphs in this format show up as low-resolution, character-based graphs — or not at all, depending on how the graph code is generated by SAS Enterprise Guide.

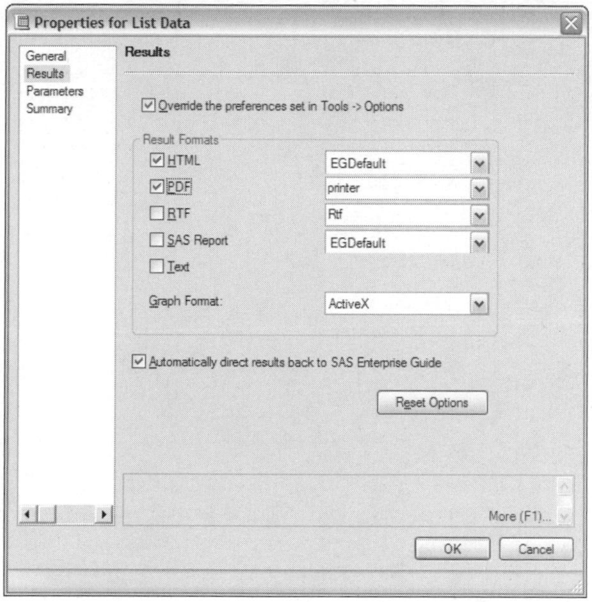

Figure 6-1:
Change the
file output
type for a
listing
report.

To view text files, you use a text viewer provided by SAS in SAS Enterprise Guide. You can also view these externally in Notepad or WordPad after exporting the output. There aren't many situations in which text files are useful unless you have a need to obtain reports in an unformatted manner or you want the smallest possible file size. Try to avoid this output type because of its many shortcomings. Figure 6-2 shows a sample text report generated by using the Characterize Data task with the Candy_Sales_Summary data set.

Adobe Acrobat (PDF) reports

SAS can also generate Adobe Acrobat files (PDFs). PDF is one of the most widely used file formats in the world because of parent Adobe's free Acrobat Reader program, which is preloaded in some form on most PCs. If you use this format for a report that is being sent to a wide audience of unknown people (say, you want to put the sales report on your company's Web site), you can be reasonably sure that everyone will be able view it.

Unlike plain text (which is also very portable), the PDF format has many formatting and layout advantages, including character formatting, paragraph alignment control, and pagination when printing. Additionally, graphs in PDF format show up in high resolution, and bookmarks are automatically created to quickly find your output in a large report.

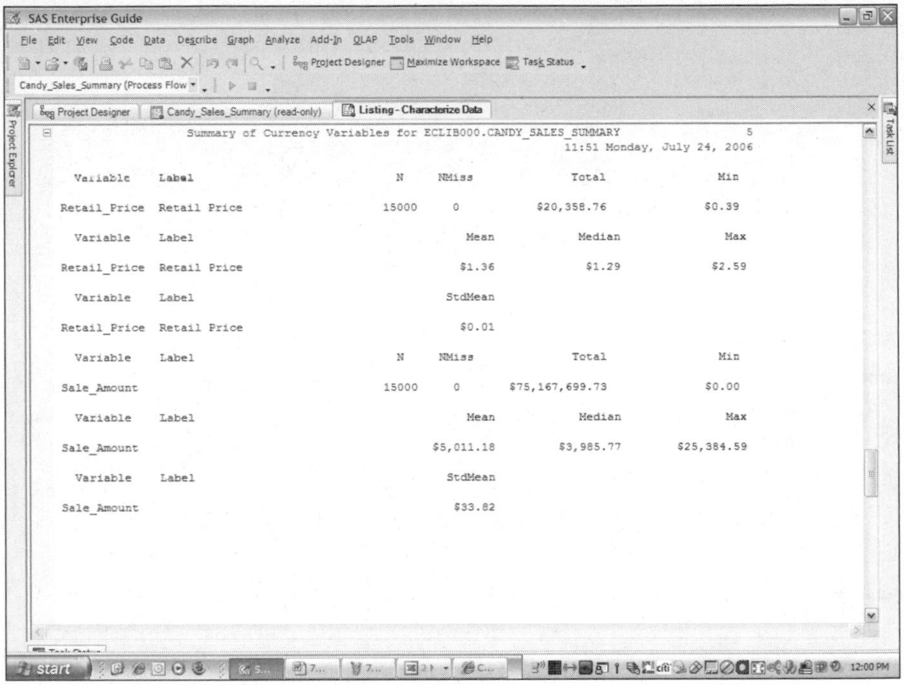

SAS Enterprise Guide

File Edit View Code Data Describe Graph Analyze Add-In OLAP Tools Window Help

Project Designer | Maximize Workspace | Task Status

Candy_Sales_Summary (Process Flow ▾)

Project Designer | Candy_Sales_Summary (read-only) | Listing - Characterize Data

```
                    Summary of Currency Variables for ECLIB000.CANDY_SALES_SUMMARY            5
                                                                11:51 Monday, July 24, 2006

   Variable    Label                       N       NMiss            Total              Min

   Retail_Price  Retail Price          15000           0       $20,358.76            $0.39

   Variable    Label                                 Mean          Median              Max

   Retail_Price  Retail Price                       $1.36           $1.29            $2.59

   Variable    Label                               StdMean

   Retail_Price  Retail Price                       $0.01

   Variable    Label                       N       NMiss            Total              Min

   Sale_Amount                          15000           0    $75,167,699.73            $0.00

   Variable    Label                                 Mean          Median              Max

   Sale_Amount                                   $5,011.18       $3,985.77        $25,384.59

   Variable    Label                               StdMean

   Sale_Amount                                      $33.82
```

start | ... | 12:00 PM

Figure 6-2:
Text output offers poor layout and no formatting.

A key limitation in using PDF reports is the inability to combine PDF output from more than one task. Several workarounds exist for this:

✔ **Use Adobe Acrobat:** The full featured editing and authoring product from Adobe lets you combine the exported output files.

✔ **Manually combine the SAS code for the various tasks into one SAS program that you can run:** However, this treads into the realm of SAS programming. See Chapter 17 for more information.

Adobe Acrobat Reader is used inside SAS Enterprise Guide to view PDF files. You can also view PDF output externally in Adobe Acrobat Reader after exporting the output (or right-clicking that output and choosing Open with Adobe Reader from the menu that appears). Figure 6-3 shows a sample PDF report generated by using the Characterize Data task with the Candy_Sales_Summary data set. In this example, the Statistical style is used instead of the default Printer style (intended for black-and-white printing) so that the graphs appear in color. (Chapter 10 contains more tips for how to control your output appearance.)

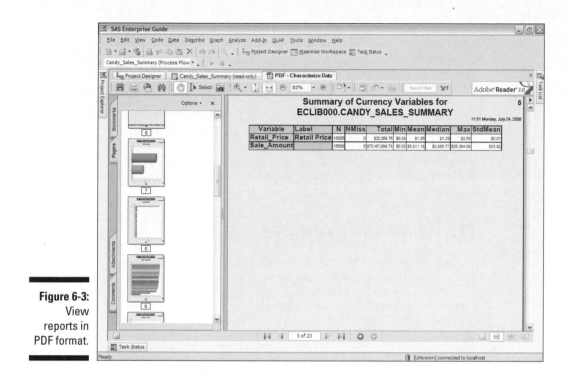

Figure 6-3:
View
reports in
PDF format.

Rich Text Format (RTF) reports

SAS is also capable of generating *Rich Text Format* (RTF) files as output, which is a standard import format for Microsoft Word. RTF is a flexible, but lesser-known, file format than PDF. When you use this format for a report that is being sent to a wide audience of unknown people (say, e-mailing a sales report to some of your investors), you can be reasonably sure that everyone will be able view it in Word or the less-functional (but free with Windows) WordPad.

WordPad is very limited. Sophisticated reports, especially those containing graphs, might not appear correctly in WordPad.

Like PDF output, using RTF has many formatting and layout advantages. Character formatting, paragraph alignment control, and pagination when printing are all available with RTF. Additionally, graphs in RTF format show up in high resolution and can be interactively modified with the ActiveX graph controls. (Just right-click the graph to see the available editing capabilities, such as the capability to change the color scheme.) Unlike in a PDF, however, bookmarks aren't automatically created to quickly find your output in a large report.

A key limitation of the RTF format is the inability to combine output from more than one task. Several workarounds exist for this: Use Microsoft Word or WordPad with the exported output files, or manually combine the SAS code for the various tasks into one SAS program to run. (Again, this ventures into the realm of SAS programming. See Chapter 17 for more information.)

To view RTF files, Word opens inside SAS Enterprise Guide. You can also view these files externally in Word or WordPad after exporting the output (or right-clicking the output and choosing Open with Microsoft Office Word from the menu that appears). A sample RTF report generated by using the Characterize Data task with the Candy_Sales_Summary data set is shown in Figure 6-4.

HTML format reports

SAS can generate HTML (HyperText Markup Language) files as output. HTML, the standard format for Web pages, is a moderately flexible format. If you use this format for a report that's being sent to a wide audience of unknown people (say, you want to place the sales report on your Web site), you can be reasonably sure that your viewers will be able see it in their standard Web browser.

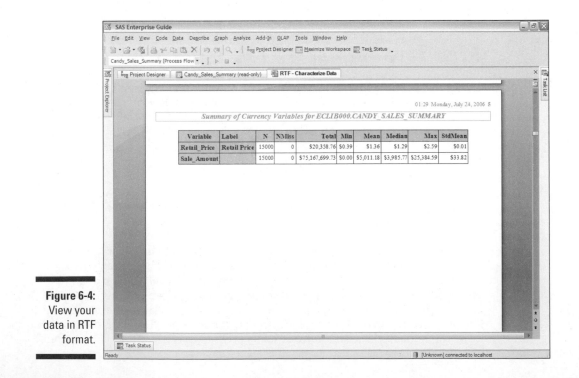

Figure 6-4:
View your data in RTF format.

Unfortunately, when you export HTML format, SAS usually creates multiple files (the HTML file and companion images). Therefore, e-mailing the output in this format can result in a confusing experience for the recipient.

HTML has some of the formatting and layout advantages of PDF and RTF, including character formatting and paragraph alignment control. Additionally, graphs in HTML format show up in high resolution and can be interactively modified by using the ActiveX graph controls. (Right-click the graph to see the available editing capabilities.) Unlike PDF, however, bookmarks aren't automatically created to quickly find your output in a large report. And unlike PDF and RTF, the pagination when printing is poor — for example, a big table may split in a very ugly manner across printed pages.

Unlike PDF and RTF, you can combine HTML output from more than one task. To access this capability, create at least one HTML output and then choose Tools⇨Create HTML Document. The HTML Document Builder lets you select entire HTML outputs or sections of output from HTML outputs in your project. It simply appends one HTML file to another, creating one long report.

To view HTML files, Microsoft Internet Explorer (IE) opens inside SAS Enterprise Guide. You can view these externally in IE or with other browsers, such as Mozilla Firefox. Figure 6-5 shows a sample HTML report generated by using the Characterize Data task with the Candy_Sales_Summary data set.

Figure 6-5:
View HTML output external to SAS Enterprise Guide in IE.

SAS Output - Windows Internet Explorer

C:\Documents and Settings\sasysm\Local Settings\Temp\SEG2412\e

File Edit View Favorites Tools Help

SAS Output

SAS Enterprise Guide®

The Power to Know.

Summary of Categorical Variables for
ECLIB000.CANDY_SALES_SUMMARY
Limited to the 30 Most Frequent Distinct Values per Variable

Variable	Label	Value	Frequency Count	Percent of Total Frequency
Category	Category	Candy	10318	68.7867
		Nuts	4682	31.2133
Discount	Discount	49%	334	2.2267
		27%	333	2.2200

Done   My Computer   100%

SAS Report (SRX) format reports

Starting with SAS 9, SAS can generate a new report standard format file as output. This output type is also referred to as *SAS Report Files* and is the standard format for SAS Business Intelligence (BI). This is a very flexible format combining many of the advantages of RTF, PDF, and HTML. If you use this format for a report that is being sent to users of SAS Business Intelligence (say, you want to place the sales report on your company's SAS BI Server for SAS Web Report Studio users), you can be certain that everyone will be able view, print, and modify it from their standard Web browser. At present, only SAS Enterprise Guide and SAS Web Report Studio can render SAS Report files.

Unfortunately, when you export SAS Report format, SAS usually creates multiple files (a file with an SRX extension, plus any companion graph images). Therefore, e-mailing it to someone can result in a confusing experience for the recipient.

SAS Report format has all the formatting and layout advantages of PDF and RTF, including character formatting and paragraph alignment control. Additionally, graphs in SAS Report format show up in high resolution and can be interactively modified by using the ActiveX graph controls. (Right-click the graph to see the available editing capabilities.) Further, if you interactively modify these graphs, the changes are remembered when you rerun the task. *Note:* This is an important capability because none of the other formats have this feature.

Bookmarks are automatically created so that you can quickly find your output in a large report, and pagination when printing is excellent. Finally, you can format the output with standard text formatting (bold, italics, different fonts, and so on), and the changes are retained if you rerun the analysis.

Like HTML, you can combine SAS Report output from more than one task. Going beyond HTML, though, the results of SAS Report can be laid out side-by-side as well as above or below each other, allowing you to create cool dashboard-like displays that can print on a single page (see the report shown in Figure 6-6).

To access this dashboard-type capability

1. **Create at least one SAS Report output.**

2. **Right-click one of the report outputs.**

3. **Choose Create Report.**

   The SAS Report Editor appears, allowing you to add entire SAS Report outputs or sections of output from SAS Report outputs in your project.

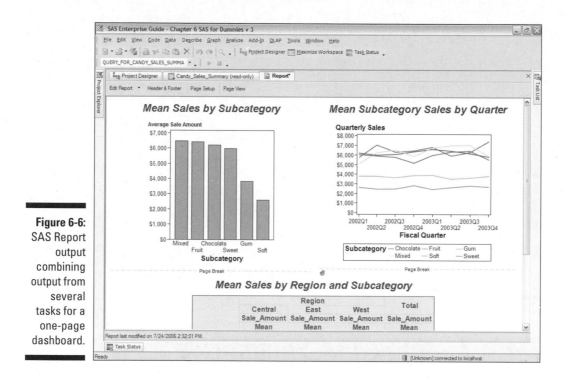

Figure 6-6:
SAS Report
output
combining
output from
several
tasks for a
one-page
dashboard.

The possibilities in the Report Editor are many and varied — from adding content with the Edit Report Contents dialog box (as shown in Figure 6-7) to selecting text and formatting it or interacting with the graphs in the report.

In this book, most examples use SAS Report format. It is the most flexible output type in terms of reporting layout and printing reliability.

See Chapter 11 to find out more about the various report formats and when to use them. Chapter 11 discusses how to select the appropriate report format for sharing results in different ways.

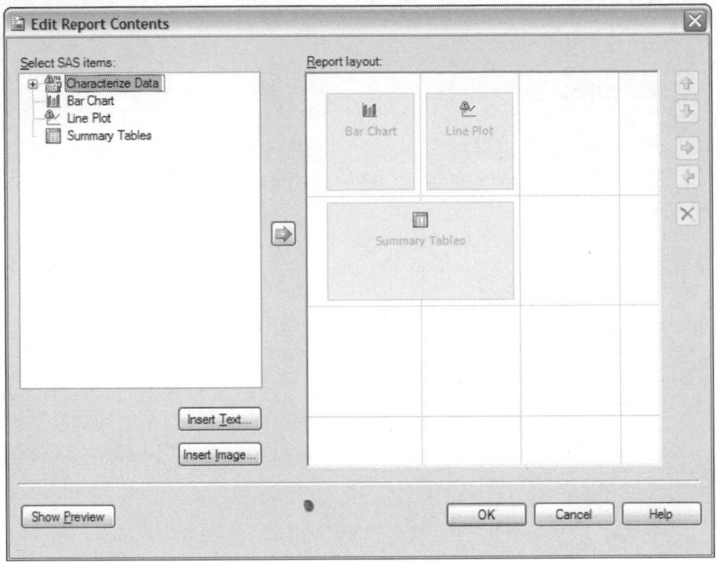

Figure 6-7:
The Edit
Report
Contents
dialog box in
the Report
Editor.

Data Listings and Summaries for the Listless

Most of the common data listing and summarization tasks for reporting are available in four tasks and wizards via the Describe menu in SAS Enterprise Guide. With these four tasks, you can easily create data listings, data summaries, or cross-tabular reports. A handy reference summary of these tasks is provided in Table 6-1, and the following sections describe each task in more detail.

Here are some common summary and listing tasks:

- ✔ **List Data:** Sales transaction detail report listing. Transactions are grouped by sales region with sales subtotals for each region.

- ✔ **Summary Statistics:** A quick and easy way to summarize sales by subcategory. Results are presented in tabular and graphical form in histograms as well as box and whisker plots. Histograms show frequency of sales by sales amount; box and whisker plots show average sales, the main range of sales amounts, and any extreme sales amounts.

- ✔ **Characterize Data:** Automatically summarizes every column in a data table. See Chapter 3 for an example of this task in action.

- ✔ **Summary Tables:** Also referred to as *cross-tabs*. A tabular summary of mean sales by region and subcategory in a compact cross-tabular layout.

The List Data task

The simplest form of a report is a detailed data listing. The List Data task makes data listings quick and easy. Some examples of common reports that you can create with this task are detailed reports such as warehouse inventory listings, detailed listings of cash register sales by item, or a detailed patient adverse event listing from a clinical drug trial. The key to this task is that it prints every record in your data source as a report. This task is available when you choose Describe➪List Data.

When you assign variables to List Variables using this task, the data columns are set to display in detail. If you want to sort the listing by certain variables, you add the variables to the Group Analysis by Variable role. Subtotals are linked to the group variables; adding a column to the Subtotal role enables subtotals at each change in the group variables. A grand total appears at the end of the entire data listing for each variable, designated as a Total role.

Figure 6-8 shows a sample sales report listing, and the following section walks you through creating one.

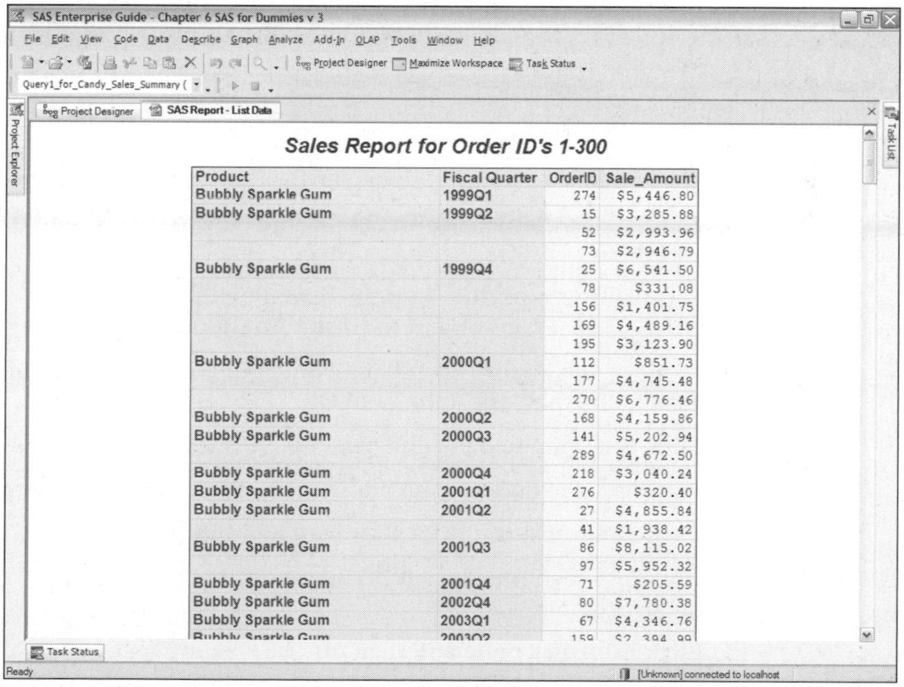

Product	Fiscal Quarter	OrderID	Sale_Amount
Bubbly Sparkle Gum	1999Q1	274	$5,446.80
Bubbly Sparkle Gum	1999Q2	15	$3,285.88
		52	$2,993.96
		73	$2,946.79
Bubbly Sparkle Gum	1999Q4	25	$6,541.50
		78	$331.08
		156	$1,401.75
		169	$4,489.16
		195	$3,123.90
Bubbly Sparkle Gum	2000Q1	112	$851.73
		177	$4,745.48
		270	$6,776.46
Bubbly Sparkle Gum	2000Q2	168	$4,159.86
Bubbly Sparkle Gum	2000Q3	141	$5,202.94
		289	$4,672.50
Bubbly Sparkle Gum	2000Q4	218	$3,040.24
Bubbly Sparkle Gum	2001Q1	276	$320.40
Bubbly Sparkle Gum	2001Q2	27	$4,855.84
		41	$1,938.42
Bubbly Sparkle Gum	2001Q3	86	$8,115.02
		97	$5,952.32
Bubbly Sparkle Gum	2001Q4	71	$205.59
Bubbly Sparkle Gum	2002Q4	80	$7,780.38
Bubbly Sparkle Gum	2003Q1	67	$4,346.76

Figure 6-8: A sales report created with the List Data task.

Creating a sales report

To help you better understand the List Data task, you can use it to create a sales report. As an example, say that the finance department in your company asks you to provide a listing of Bubbly Sparkle Gum orders from 2003 for a standard audit. You need to include the sale amount, the quarter when the product was sold, and how many customers placed orders. Because the auditor asked for the report to be organized by customer and quarter, you should sort it by these variables. To prepare the data first, you can use the Query Builder, a tool described in Chapter 2. Here are the overall steps:

1. **Open the sample table Candy_Sales_Summary.**

   Because you need to filter the data for just Bubbly Sparkle Gum and Fiscal Year sold for 2003, use the Query Builder first.

2. **Choose Data⇨Filter and Query and then select the Order_ID, Customer, Fiscal_Quarter, and Sale_Amount columns.**

3. **Filter on column Product for Bubbly Sparkle Gum and Fiscal_Year 2003.**

4. **Sort the data by this sequence: Customer, Fiscal_Quarter, and Order_ID; then run the query.**

   When subsetting your data, select only the variables needed for your next tasks; this reduces processing time and storage needed for your work. Sorting the data by the variables in sequence ensures that the records are grouped correctly for the following tasks.

5. **Choose Describe⇨List Data.**

   The List Data task appears, displaying the Task Roles pane.

6. **The detail variables are Order_ID and Sale_Amount; add them to List Variables.**

7. **Because you want to group the listing by Customer and Fiscal_Quarter, add them to Group Analysis By.**

8. **To make this report useful, total Sale_Amount at the end of each group, and then add it to Total Of.**

9. **Click the Options pane and select the Print Number of Rows option.**

   This displays the total number of rows in each group section.

10. **Clear (uncheck) the Print Row Number option.**

    You don't need this default because you are turning on the Print Number of Rows option.

11. **Click the Titles pane and turn off Use Default Text.**

12. **In the titles text area, type** Sales Report for Bubbly Sparkle Gum in 2003 **and click Run.**

The sales report appears, similar to Figure 6-9. As you can see, you can quickly find any customer, quarter, and the number and total amount of orders in each section.

Fine-tuning your sales report formatting

Look closely at Figure 6-9, and you might notice one problem: namely, the quarterly totals aren't formatting exactly as expected. The first value reads $28526.28 but *should* read $28,526.28 — the placeholder comma is missing. If you go to the last page, you will notice the grand total is even missing the $ sign. What's up with that?

If you look at the source table for this task, you can see that the format for Sales_Amount is DOLLAR9.2. This format dictates that one space is used by the dollar sign; one space is used for each comma separator for thousands, millions, and so on; three spaces are used for the decimal point and the cents; and the rest of the spaces are used for the dollar number characters. If the values of the dollar amount add up to something larger than $9,999.99, the DOLLAR9.2 format starts removing spaces for commas and other information you might like to see. This is a common problem when data is composed of small values but adds up to a large value when summed or averaged. (For example, you may not want cents shown, but that format is turned on in the default source variable.)

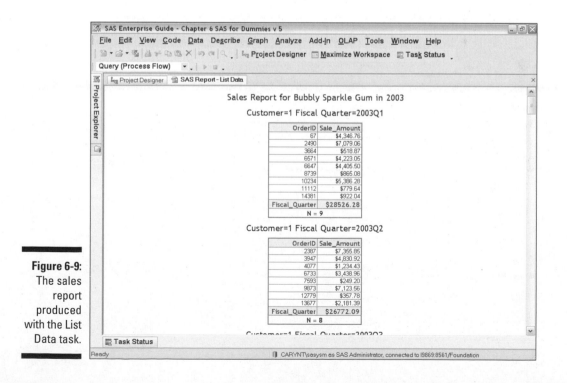

Figure 6-9: The sales report produced with the List Data task.

To fix this, change the format used by that variable in the query task or in the task where you are using it:

1. **Reopen the List Data task by double-clicking it.**

2. **Right-click Sale_Amount in the Total Of role and choose Properties.**

3. **In the Sale_Amount Properties dialog box that appears, click the Change button.**

   The format dialog box appears, displaying the current format DOLLARw.d, with Overall Width (w) set to 9 and Decimal places set to 2.

4. **Change the Overall Width to 15 and then click OK.**

5. **Click OK again to dismiss the Sale_Amount Properties dialog box and then click Run.**

   The updated sales report appears. Scroll to the bottom of the report, which looks like Figure 6-10. Much better!

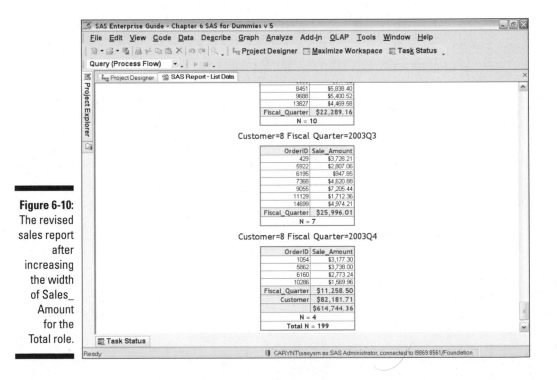

Figure 6-10:
The revised sales report after increasing the width of Sales_ Amount for the Total role.

The Characterize Data task: What did that guy in Accounting just give me?

If you receive some unfamiliar data to analyze and want a quick-and-dirty summary of every variable in a concise format, the quickest way to a simplified summary report is to use the Characterize Data task. Whereas you can use a combination of other tasks to summarize different variable types (character, numeric, date, and so on), this task uses a simplified approach to summarize the data. This task automatically groups the variables in your data source by type (for example, character, numeric, currency, and date) and provides compact listings of a simple summary of each variable.

This task is useful as a first glance at unfamiliar data to look for unusual, incorrect, or "dirty" data values (such as if variable gender has 50 males, 56 females, and 2 mails; or the minimum sales amount was –$9,012.46 and the maximum was $12,349.81 for a candy stand). You have very few options to think about in this wizard. On the first page of the wizard, you can select one or many data tables to analyze. On the second page, you can select whether you want a report, graphs, or output data sets of the summaries. All columns in each table are summarized by using frequency tables or summary statistics (n, n missing, total, min, mean, median, max, and standard mean). You can access this task by choosing Describe⇨Characterize Data. Refer to Figure 6-4 to see a sample Characterize Data report.

The Summary Statistics task: Get to the point!

Where are the statistics? This section shows how to get simple statistics for numeric variables. If you would like to analyze some sales data across product categories, you can start with the Summary Statistics task or Wizard. With this task, you can analyze numeric columns in your data for a variety of statistics.

The statistics available include mean, median, standard deviation, number of observations, min, max, 25th percentile, 75th percentile, confidence limits of the mean, t statistic, and 15 other univariate statistics.

You can optionally request data summaries graphically with histograms (shows distribution of a variable by frequency) or a box and whisker plot (shows median, 25th, and 75th percentiles, min, max, and outlier values shown as points). You can access this functionality by choosing Describe⇨ Summary Statistics or Describe⇨Wizards⇨Summary Statistics. The wizard has most of the functionality of the task; it just walks you through the steps in a controlled order and hides a few advanced options. If you need access to those advanced options, you can convert your use of a wizard to the full-on task. The method for doing that is discussed in "The Summary Tables (Cross-tabs) task: Easier than crosswords!" section later in this chapter.

To summarize by product category, add Sale Amount to the Analysis Variables role and Subcategory to the Classification Variables role. The histogram shows that Soft Candy sale amounts tended to be lower and more densely clustered around the mean amount than Sweet Candy sales. Figure 6-11 shows a sample sales report histogram by product category.

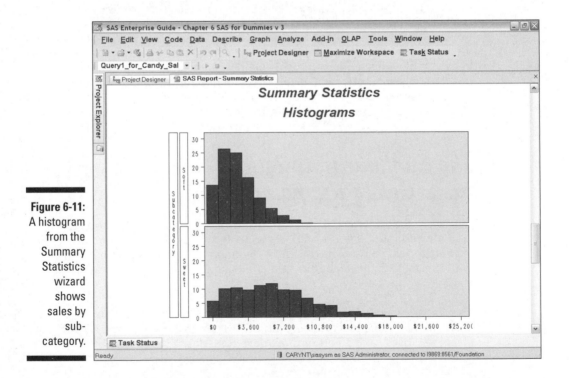

Figure 6-11:
A histogram from the Summary Statistics wizard shows sales by sub-category.

The Summary Tables (Cross-tabs) task: Easier than crosswords!

The Summary Statistics task is useful for analyzing numeric variables. However, if you want to add several category variables to analyze the data, these reports can become very long because there is one row per combination of category and analysis variables. If you want to analyze numeric data by several category variables, use the Summary Tables task and Wizard to use a minimum of space in a compact, cross-tabular format.

Summary tables are similar to pivot tables in Excel or crosstabulations that you have likely seen in various college courses or corporate financial statements. Suppose you want to analyze median and mean sales by region, product category, and subcategory. The Summary Tables task makes it possible to present this in a very concise form, as shown in Figure 6-12. Note that you can easily compare across regions or products as well as compare overall regional and product performance via the Total columns. Likewise, you can compare median and mean sales for each product and region. Comparing median and mean can quickly clue you whether sales are skewed to the left or right of the mean, which is a key indicator of a few large sales skewing the mean up or down. (And all this from a compact table!)

Figure 6-12: A Summary Table analyzing sales by region, category, and subcategory.

Median and Mean Sales by Region and Subcategory

Category	Subcategory	Product	Central Median	Central Mean	East Median	East Mean	West Median	West Mean	Total Median	Total Mean
Candy	Chocolate	Chewy Chocolate Cheetahs	$2,815	$2,884	$3,116	$3,065	$2,419	$2,790	$2,895	$2,940
		Chocolate Cherry Delight	$4,729	$5,119	$5,114	$5,141	$5,254	$5,314	$4,891	$5,150
		Dark Chocolate Espresso	$8,547	$9,172	$9,104	$9,398	$10,352	$10,760	$9,074	$9,427
		Fruity Choco-Rolls	$8,727	$8,876	$8,413	$8,752	$7,194	$9,089	$8,537	$8,857
		White Chocolate Turtles	$4,296	$4,561	$4,807	$4,844	$4,396	$4,436	$4,464	$4,655
	Gum	Bubbly Sparkle Gum	$3,054	$3,231	$3,309	$3,411	$2,773	$3,078	$3,071	$3,279
		Sparkle Peppermint Gum	$4,226	$4,311	$3,943	$4,234	$4,612	$4,824	$4,140	$4,346
	Soft	Flavor Bursting Watermelon Chews	$3,568	$3,670	$3,444	$3,690	$3,428	$3,717	$3,503	$3,684
		Nougatty Swirls	$2,780	$2,885	$2,927	$2,999	$2,602	$2,876	$2,814	$2,926
		Strawberry Chewsers	$2,207	$2,218	$2,018	$2,190	$1,907	$2,030	$2,106	$2,186
		Watermelon Taffy	$1,479	$1,569	$1,384	$1,414	$1,655	$1,569	$1,473	$1,510
Nuts	Fruit	Cherry Delight All Fruit	$4,897	$4,961	$4,785	$4,858	$3,847	$4,601	$4,702	$4,874
		Cranberry Delight	$7,450	$8,066	$7,145	$7,835	$8,585	$8,623	$7,490	$8,056
	Mixed	Just Pecans and Cashews	$5,907	$6,360	$6,841	$6,934	$4,863	$5,602	$6,086	$6,480
	Sweet	Carob N Almonds	$6,561	$6,908	$7,323	$7,384	$6,205	$6,626	$6,868	$7,035
		CinnaPecans	$4,825	$5,035	$5,211	$5,014	$3,839	$4,086	$4,853	$4,900
Total			$4,011	$4,968	$4,021	$5,066	$3,771	$5,020	$3,986	$5,011

Statistics available in the task include sum, mean, median, standard deviation, number of observations, min, max, 25th percentile, 75th percentile, confidence limits of the mean, t statistic, row or column sums, row or column percents, weighted sums, and ten other univariate statistics. The wizard offers a subset of the statistics and limited data formatting relative to the task, but it is easier to master than the task. You can access this wizard by choosing Describe⇨Summary Tables or Describe⇨Wizards⇨Summary Tables.

Creating a summary table

The easiest way to understand summary tables is to create one. As a sample scenario, say that the sales director of your company asks you for a summary of sales data by region, category, subcategory, and product. In the summary, she wants to see whether some regions are getting more of their sales revenue from large orders, so she has also asked that the summary show median and mean sales amount. If the mean is much higher than the median, the data can be said to be *skewed* by a small proportion of larger sales.

1. **Open the sample table Candy_Sales_Summary and choose Data⇨ Wizards⇨Summary Tables.**

   The Summary Table wizard appears. The Verify Data screen of the wizard shows the data being used. This screen shows the server being accessed and the data in use.

2. **Click Next.**

   The Select Analysis Variables and Statistics screen appears.

3. **Because you want to analyze median and mean sales, add the variable Sale_Amount to the Analysis Variables dialog box by clicking Add and selecting Sale_Amount.**

4. **Change the default statistic (Sum, in the drop-down box next to Sale_Amount) to Median.**

5. **Add Sale_Amount a second time to the Analysis Variables dialog box.**

6. **Change the second instance of Sale_Amount to Average.**

7. **Change the value of the Analysis Variables Label from In Columns to Hidden.**

   Hiding these labels saves space because they provide excessive detail for a summary table anyway. The screen should look similar to Figure 6-13.

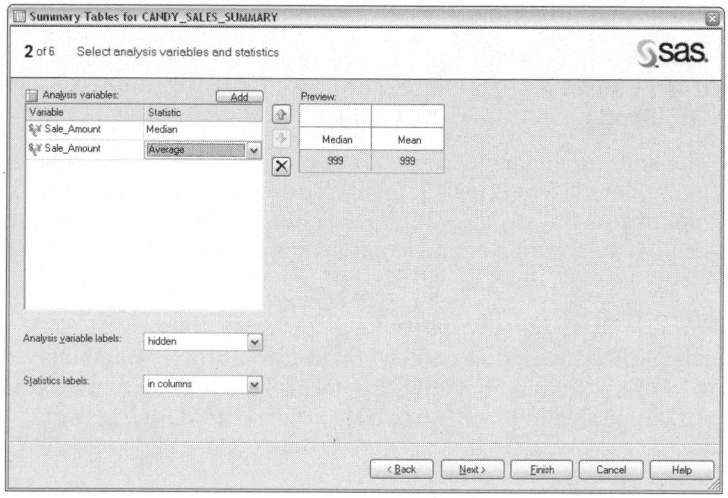

Figure 6-13: The Select Analysis Variables and Statistics screen.

8. **Click Next.**

   The Select Classification Variables screen appears.

9. **Add Region to the Columns dialog box and Category, Subcategory, and Product to the Rows dialog box.**

   A simplified preview with mock data is shown on the right side of the pane, as shown in Figure 6-14.

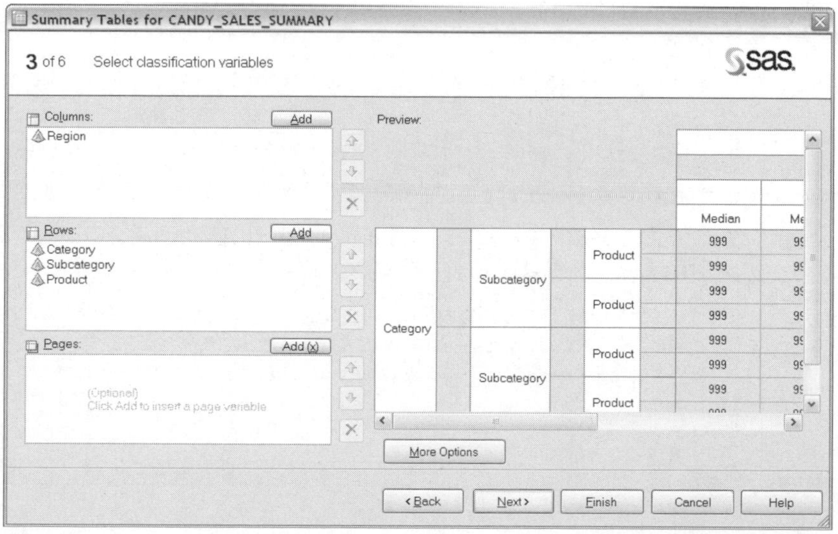

Figure 6-14: The Select Classification Variables screen of the Summary Tables Wizard.

10. **Click Next three times.**

11. **In the Provide a Title and Footnote screen that appears, change the title to Mean and Median Sales Summary by Category, Subcategory, and Product and then click Finish.**

    The sales summary appears, as shown in Figure 6-15. You can glean many details from this summary. The West region seems to have the most skew toward larger sales, pushing up the mean above the median. Fruity Choco-Rolls in particular seems to be the extreme case.

Enabling formatting in wizards

Wizards, unlike tasks, don't allow you to format the results. One way around this is to open the wizard in the task form. This feature allows you to transfer the work specified in the wizard to the full-featured task version.

To do this, follow these steps:

1. **Right-click the wizard node in the project and choose Open in Advanced View.**

Figure 6-15: The Summary Tables results.

Category	Subcategory	Product	Central Median	Central Mean	East Median	East Mean	West Median	West Mean	Total Median	Total Mean
Candy	Chocolate	Chewy Chocolate Cheetahs	2815.20	2884.28	3116.00	3065.30	2419.20	2790.36	2895.20	2939.89
		Chocolate Cherry Delight	4728.78	5119.07	5113.81	5140.98	5254.20	5313.80	4891.41	5150.17
		Dark Chocolate Espresso	8547.00	9171.90	9103.85	9397.68	10352.23	10760.10	8974.35	9426.97
		Fruity Choco-Rolls	8727.09	8875.59	8412.80	8752.22	7193.90	9089.28	8537.08	8856.81
		White Chocolate Turtles	4295.70	4561.27	4806.54	4843.68	4396.32	4436.04	4464.05	4655.19
	Gum	Bubbly Sparkle Gum	3054.48	3230.92	3309.02	3410.88	2773.24	3078.02	3070.50	3278.97
		Sparkle Peppermint Gum	4225.69	4310.68	3943.07	4234.05	4612.44	4823.67	4140.01	4345.81
	Soft	Flavor Bursting Watermelon Chews	3567.96	3669.87	3444.21	3689.94	3428.37	3717.11	3502.62	3683.66
		Nougatty Swirls	2780.01	2884.88	2926.95	2999.37	2602.26	2876.41	2813.98	2925.84
		Strawberry Chewsers	2206.60	2218.39	2017.80	2189.57	1907.47	2029.82	2106.30	2185.57
		Watermelon Taffy	1478.88	1569.13	1384.11	1414.04	1655.16	1569.50	1472.84	1510.08
Nuts	Fruit	Cherry Delight All Fruit	4896.84	4960.89	4785.26	4858.15	3847.43	4601.19	4702.05	4874.30
		Cranberry Delight	7450.38	8065.73	7144.88	7834.57	8584.80	8623.37	7489.80	8056.14
	Mixed	Just Pecans and Cashews	5907.00	6360.03	6841.38	6934.41	4863.43	5601.57	6086.00	6479.79
	Sweet	Carob N Almonds	6561.14	6907.70	7322.81	7383.86	6204.87	6626.06	6868.26	7034.95
		CinnaPecans	4824.60	5035.03	5210.96	5014.33	3839.04	4085.77	4852.98	4900.43
Total			4011.02	4968.44	4020.84	5066.27	3770.69	5020.05	3985.77	5011.18

Generated by the SAS System (Local, XP_PRO) on 28JUL2006 at 3:19 PM

The Summary Tables task appears, from which you can update the formats for the sales median and means.

2. **Select the Summary Tables pane, right-click Median and Mean in the column headers, and then choose Data Value Properties.**

   The Data Value Properties window appears.

3. **Select the Format tab, and select an appropriate number format for the results (for example, DOLLARw.d in the Currency category).**

4. **Click OK to apply the format selection.**

   After you open a wizard in advanced mode and save it, you can open it only in task form. Tasks cannot be converted to wizard form because some features are inaccessible in the simplified wizard view.

Chapter 7

You Want Fries with That Graph?

*U*sing pictures of your data — *graphs* — to tell a story is the most widely used method in business, science, and education to convey complex information quickly and with a minimum of additional explanation. Like mastery of spatial depth or the human form for a great artist, learning to create graphs that are useful, concise, and tell the story behind the data can be one of the most useful skills you can acquire for your career. The great news is that SAS has virtually the full palette of "colors and hues" in the graph world available to you!

Creating graphs with SAS can be an amazing journey. You can harness large volumes of data and explore their nuances and relationships via the most logical method. Applications like Microsoft Excel or PowerPoint have their advantages, but if you want to explore larger data volumes or use powerful and highly customized graphs, SAS trumps them hands down. After you have a set of graphs that convey the story you want to tell, SAS offers a rich array of options to customize and tweak the graphs for exactly the look and feel you need.

Graphing Basics

The following list includes the basics that you need to consider when you are envisioning a graph:

✔ **Decide the question you want to answer or the information you want to convey before deciding on the graph to use.** Graphs often do a poor job of conveying a clear and compelling message — because there isn't one! When in doubt, think long and hard about what you need to say with your graphs before proceeding.

✔ **Figure out what data will be the basis for your graph's story.** Sometimes, the data might need to be filtered, updated with new or calculated columns, or even transposed or rearranged to arrive at a data structure needed for your desired graphs.

✔ **Be sure that a graph is the best way to convey the message.** Graphs are good for providing your audience with the overall shape of the data or allowing quick comparisons of the relationship between many data points at once. For example, you might want to compare sales by region in a line graph to show that most regions have the same seasonal sales patterns. Perhaps you select a bar chart of the relative amount of sales for each region.

Summary tables might be more useful than graphs if any of the following are your primary purpose:

✔ You are providing details for values lookup rather than overall comparisons.

✔ Precise values of the data are key to the purpose.

✔ You want to concisely present information on the same topic that uses the same unit of measurement.

Here are some examples of when to use summary tables instead of graphs:

✔ Sales summaries for accountants who require precise reconciliation for each region

✔ Presenting sales by quarter for the year in dollars, yen, units sold, and as a percent of the prior year sales amount

Turn off the 3-D effects that are the default for most of these graphs because they add little value (people thought they were cool at one time) and can actually make it harder for people to correctly compare values in most charts.

Graphs for Every Occasion

If you decide that a graph is the best way to present your information, you then need to decide which graph type will most clearly tell your story. The following sections describe the graph types available to you in SAS Enterprise Guide, their typical applications, and additional points to consider.

Bar charts

Bar charts are useful when you want to compare the relative differences among distinct groups. A good example would be a bar chart of sales by region for the current year, as shown in Figure 7-1.

Make sure that the vertical (y) axis starts at zero; otherwise, you can end up with charts that are very deceiving to people at first glance because the relative height of the bars is what people tend to see, with little attention paid to the scale.

You can choose between horizontally or vertically oriented bar charts. Most of the time, vertical bar charts are fine. However, if you have many bars or long descriptions for each group, horizontal bar charts are the better choice.

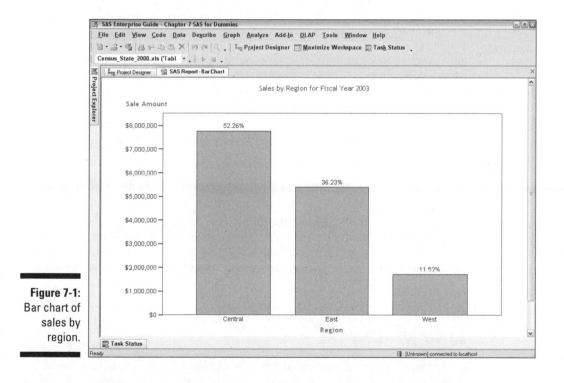

Figure 7-1: Bar chart of sales by region.

You can further expand the value of bar charts by using subgroups of bars or by stacking various subgroups in a bar. A subgroup example could be a graph of Quarter 1–4 sales by region, subgrouped on each quarter, allowing a quick comparison of regions per quarter. Likewise, you could create the same chart for each quarter instead of creating multiple subgroups on the same chart. This is particularly useful if you have many categories or many groups you want to examine, which could quickly make a single bar chart unreadable. A major downside of stacked bar charts is that most people have difficulty comparing the same stack piece across the various bars, but if only a few groups are in each stack, this can still be useful.

Pie charts

Pie charts are one of the most popular types of charts among business users. Unfortunately, many graph experts are strongly opposed to pie charts because of difficulties understanding the information, leading to an inability for people to make effective decisions from them. A bar chart is usually superior at conveying the same information as a pie chart, from a comparison of individual values to a comparison of multiple values. That said, if you still want to use pie charts because everyone at your company or your audience just loves them, here are a few points to consider:

- ✔ Avoid creating pie charts with more than six to eight values.
- ✔ Ensure that there are fairly large differences between the values.
- ✔ Use colors with high contrast to make viewing easier.

Pie charts are available in standard, stacked, and grouped form. Standard pie charts are much like bar charts in function, charting sales by region, as shown in Figure 7-2. Stacked pie charts are difficult for most people to understand but are similar in function to stacked bar charts because you can chart sales by region stacked by sales channel. Grouped pie charts are similar in function to grouped bar charts because you could chart sales by region in each pie and group the pies on product line.

Line plots

Line plots are useful for examining trends over time. A chart showing sales over the past three years conveys the overall long-term sales trend as well as the seasonal shape of sales throughout a given year, as shown in Figure 7-3.

With SAS, you can create a variety of specialized line charts that go beyond the standard line chart. Among these are specialized forms of line charts, including splines, needles, step, regression, smoothed, standard deviations, Lagrange interpolations, and overlay plots. You can also produce line plots with multiple groups displayed on a single graph or with one graph per group.

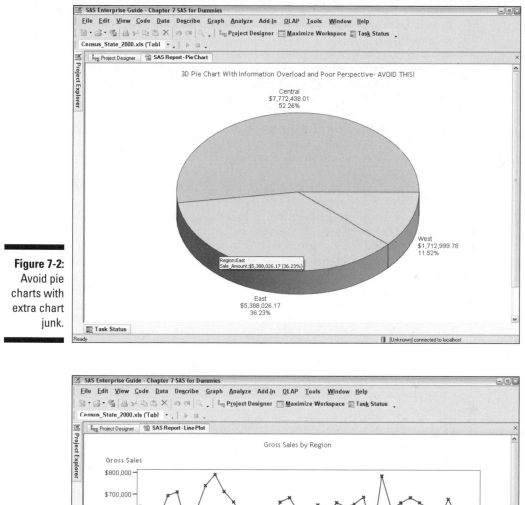

Figure 7-2:
Avoid pie
charts with
extra chart
junk.

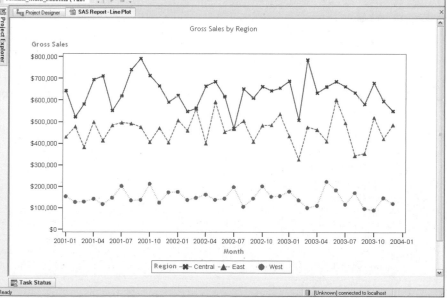

Figure 7-3:
Line plots
showing
monthly
sales by
region over
several
years.

Deciding whether to add symbols for each data point on your line plot should largely be a function of whether you want to emphasize the overall trend only (lines only) or the trend and the individual points (lines and points). Finally, you can choose to display two different vertical (y) axis variables in a line plot — one on the left side and one on the right side. These can be of different scale (say, number of units sold on left and dollars revenue on right), and each can have a separate line per measure displayed.

Beware the scaling effect! No, don't reach for that fungus treatment; the scaling effect afflicts only your bar and line charts. When two variables with values of a different magnitude are shown on the same chart (for example, net sales is in the millions, and net returns are in the thousands), the change in the variable with the large scale is perceived as much larger than the smaller scale variable. If returns double from the start to the end while sales increase 10 percent, the sales increase still appears larger at first glance. This is especially important when you compare growth rates of competing groups that start at very different values. One solution to solve this problem is to convert the data to the logarithmic scale, which is an option readily available in the line plot task, as shown in Figure 7-4. Note that the variations from month to month for the West region appear much larger in the log graph than the standard graph in Figure 7-3. Likewise, the variation from month to month for the other two regions appears much smaller because we have removed the scaling effect.

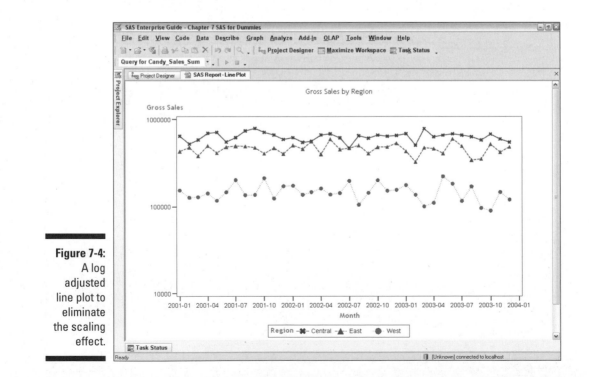

Figure 7-4:
A log adjusted line plot to eliminate the scaling effect.

Scatter plots

Scatter plots are great at showing the relationship between two variables of interest, which is a concept often referred to as examining the correlation of the two variables. A chart showing the relationship of total amount of each sale with the percent discount given in each sale is a great example of examining correlations.

A good rule is to place the variable that you believe influences the second variable (typically called the *independent variable* or the *cause*) on the x axis. Place the second variable, also known as the *dependent variable* or the *effect*, on the y axis.

Scatter plots can be further enhanced by the addition of a fitted regression line. Without getting overly technical, the *regression line* is the closest fit among the weighting of the data points. The line can be used for an approximation of the overall trend and "center" of the data displayed. Figure 7-5 is an example of a scatter plot with a regression line fitted to the data. An interesting observation from this plot is that larger discounts appear to yield overall smaller orders. Salespeople often argue that larger discounts lead to larger sales, but this graph contradicts that argument. More investigation might be warranted based on this simple analysis.

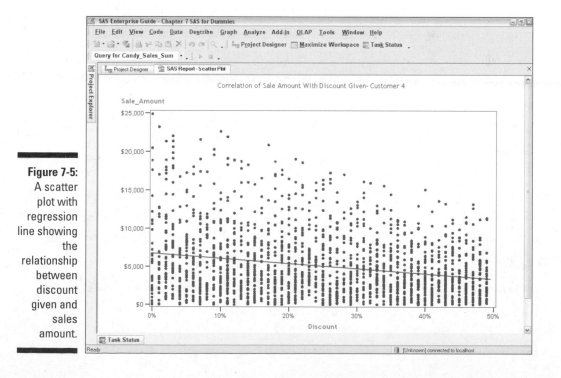

Figure 7-5:
A scatter plot with regression line showing the relationship between discount given and sales amount.

Area plots

Area plots are a form of the line plot with the area below the line colored to emphasize it. In general, these add little value over line plots. In the case of trying to display multiple groups on one plot, area plots can be very difficult to read and interpret. Figure 7-6 shows the same information as Figure 7-1. Notice how difficult it is to read the area plot, especially with overlapping areas.

Bubble plots

Bubble plots are a specialized form of a scatter plot, using bubbles of various size rather than points for each data point. The bubble sizes are scaled according to a third variable displayed in the plot. Figure 7-7 is a classic example of using bubble plots to display two attributes of group data in a simple-to-read plot.

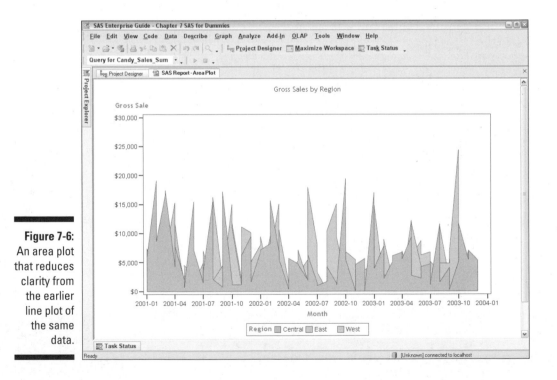

Figure 7-6: An area plot that reduces clarity from the earlier line plot of the same data.

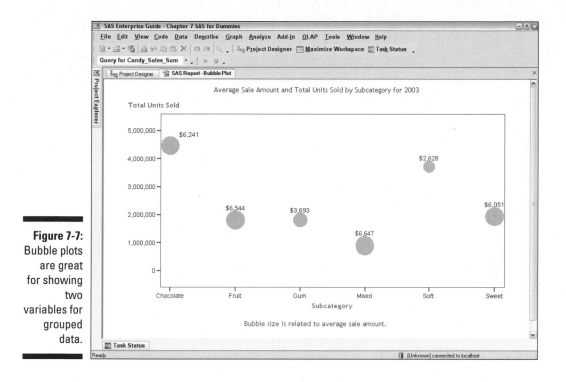

Figure 7-7:
Bubble plots
are great
for showing
two
variables for
grouped
data.

Box plots

Box plots are great for comparing the distribution of a variable for two or more categories or over time. A box plot displays the median and the four quartiles of the data for each category of data on the x axis:

- ✔ **Bottom line (or "whisker"):** The 0–25th percentile (lower quartile)
- ✔ **Bottom part of the box:** The 25th–50th percentile (second quartile)
- ✔ **Horizontal line in the box:** The median
- ✔ **Top half of the box:** The 50th–75th percentile (third quartile)
- ✔ **Top line (or "whisker"):** The 75th–100th (fourth quartile)

A great use of a box plot is to compare the distribution of sales by product category, as shown in Figure 7-8.

Variations on the standard box plot include hi-lo plots, hi-lo-close plots, and box plots that use interquartile range instead of quartiles. A hi-lo plot or a hi-lo-close plot can show the high, low, and closing price of a stock over time.

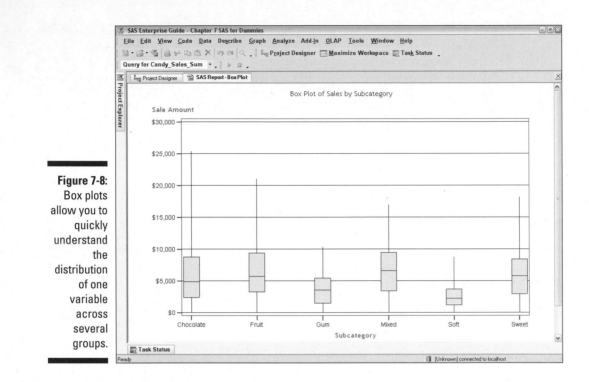

Figure 7-8:
Box plots
allow you to
quickly
understand
the
distribution
of one
variable
across
several
groups.

Donut charts

Donut charts are similar to pie charts except that a hole appears in the middle of a donut chart. Because they are an even more confusing form of pie charts, we don't recommend that you use them. According to multiple studies by graphing experts, accurately interpreting a donut chart is very difficult for most people.

Contour plots

Contour plots allow you to show the relationships between three numeric variables in a two-dimensional plot. Much like a map that shows elevation of land contours, a contour plot allows you to show the relationship between two variables like a scatter plot but with coloring or gradient lines highlighting the third value in your plot.

A good example of a contour plot is to display the relationship of time of day, store number, and sales amount at a chain of retail stores. The time of day would be on the x axis, the store number would be on the y axis, and sales amount would appear as various shades of different colors showing sales amount, as shown in Figure 7-9. This figure shows quickly how different stores have varying times of day that might be ideal for deliveries, inventory, and restocking.

Contour plots can be useful for finding trends such as the time of day with highest sales, day of week with most returns by store, or day of month by clinical trial investigator with the most patient visits.

Radar charts

A *radar chart* allows you to present graphically the frequency or intensity in value of four to ten variables at different points in time or by using different conditions or various test subjects. Classic users of radar charts include quality control folks and marketing research types. On a radar chart, the values for each variable are displayed along spokes that radiate from the center of the chart and are often stacked on top of one another, thus giving them the look of a radar screen. Marketing researchers might want to show several attributes of a product and several consumer opinions of a product by each attribute, as illustrated in Figure 7-10. With one glance, you can see that only one test consumer rated the product high on all attributes and also that most disliked the product on more than half the attributes deemed important to product success. Back to the drawing board!

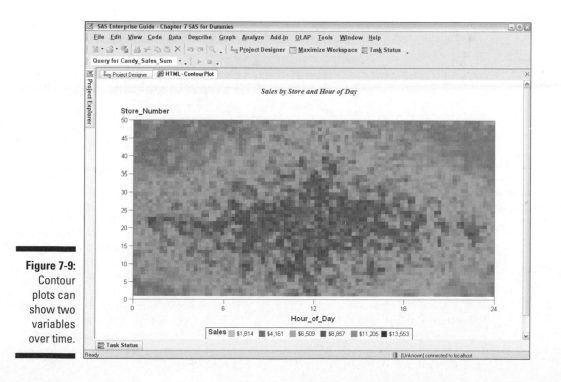

Figure 7-9:
Contour plots can show two variables over time.

Map graphs

Map graphs in SAS enable you to overlay data values for a location, city, county, state, country, or continent on a map of your choice. A two-dimensional U.S. map can be used to show the states by population, as shown in Figure 7-11. In this map, population is bucketed into five groups based on population ranking. You can quickly find the most and least populous states and their proximity to one another. Variations on this include three-dimensional maps with the state rising above others based on population and two-dimensional maps with bars rising from each state, indicating population.

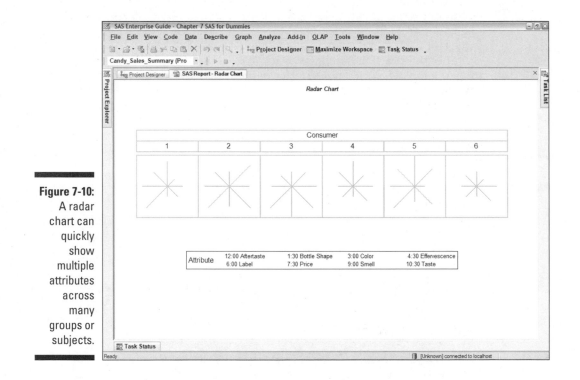

Figure 7-10:
A radar chart can quickly show multiple attributes across many groups or subjects.

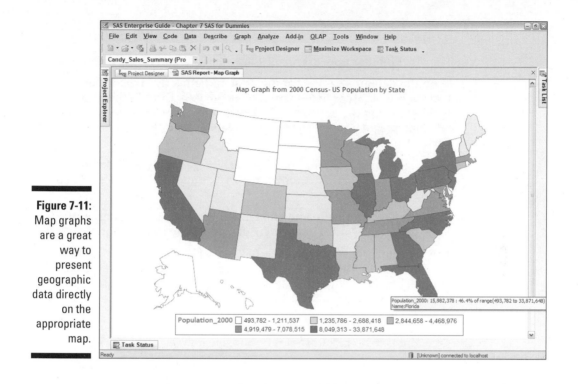

Figure 7-11:
Map graphs
are a great
way to
present
geographic
data directly
on the
appropriate
map.

Creating Graphs with SAS

It's time to put some of these graphing principles to practice. This section provides examples of creating useful plots with SAS — plots that contain relevant information about your data and convey a meaningful message.

A box plot example: Finding the extreme products

The shipping department folks have asked you to see if there is a way to avoid shipping so many large orders. Large orders frequently cause them to keep people late, resulting in overtime, expedited shipping requests, and employees who are more likely to quit because of stressful deadlines. They want you to analyze sales by category so that they can talk with the appropriate sales manager about reducing the number of large orders placed and receiving more frequently placed, manageable, and smaller orders. Follow these steps to perform this analysis:

1. **Open the sample table Candy_Sales_Summary and choose Graph⇨ Box Plot.**

   The Box Plot task appears, displaying the Box Plot type selection pane.

2. **Keep the default selection of Box Plot and click the Task Roles pane. You want to analyze orders by subcategory (because managers are divided among the subcategories) and analyze overall sale amount, so add Subcategory to the Horizontal role and Sale_Amount to the Vertical role.**

   As we mentioned earlier in the chapter, you generally want to place the causative variable on the horizontal (x) axis and the result variable on the vertical (y) axis.

3. **Click the Box Plot pane and change the Whisker Length Percentile selection from +– 1.5 Times Interquartile Range to High/low Extremes.**

   This change forces the whiskers that extend beyond the 25% and 75% quartiles to include all data points in the horizontal group, including potential outliers. If you don't care about seeing the individual extreme values, this is a good setting to keep your graph clean and easy to view.

4. **Click the Titles pane and turn off Use Default Text.**

5. **Type the title** Box Plot of Sales by Subcategory.

6. **Change the selected section to Footnote and turn off Use Default Text.**

7. **Clear the default footnote text and leave blank.**

8. **Click Run.**

   The box plot appears, similar to Figure 7-12. An interesting note is that Mixed has the highest median amount of order while Chocolate has the highest range of order value, with Fruit a close second. This could indicate more infrequent ordering of chocolate and perhaps an opportunity to work with the Chocolate sales manager and focus more on receiving smaller, more frequent orders for this product category.

A line plot example: Tracking the regions

The finance department has asked you to provide a chart showing the monthly pattern of sales by region for 2003. Understanding the relationship of varying sales cycles among the regions is key for this chart.

Prepping your data

To prep your data for a line plot graph, follow these steps:

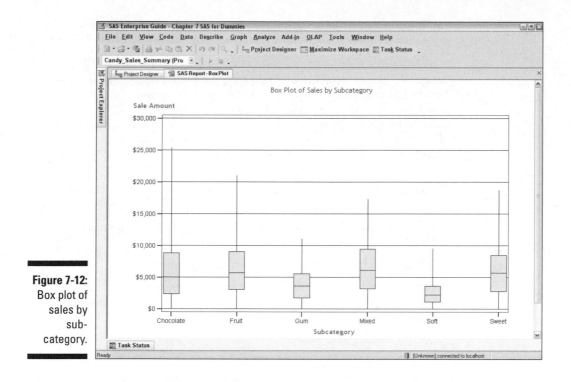

Figure 7-12:
Box plot of
sales by
sub-
category.

1. **Open the sample table Candy_Sales_Summary.**

2. **Open the Filter and Query task by choosing Data⇨Filter and Query.**

3. **Add the Sale_Amount and Region columns to the Select Data pane.**

4. **Select the Filter Data pane and add a filter for Date between '01JAN2003'd and '31DEC2003'd (use the entire value, including the apostrophes).**

SAS dates are always stored as numbers, so unless you know the internal number used by SAS to represent these dates, you need to use a special quoted version of the date as shown here. The day, three-letter month, and four-digit year enclosed in single quotes and appended by a lowercase *d* tells SAS that you want this text string converted to a SAS date value.

6. **Click the Computed Columns button and then choose New⇨Build Expression.**

7. **In the expression text, add the following function and then click OK:**

```
INPUT( PUT( YEAR(Candy_Sales_Summary.Date )*10000 +
       MONTH(Candy_Sales_Summary.Date ) *100 +
       1,8.0),YYMMDD8.)
```

8. **Click the newly computed column — Calculation1 — and select Rename, rename the column to Month, and then click OK.**

    This formula uses the YEAR and MONTH function to extract the year and month values as numbers and add them to form a number representation of the year and month with the day always equal to *01* (for example, 20030301.) The number is then converted to text so that it can be read in as a date value, with the day from every record converted to the 1st. Note that you could have used the Recode feature instead of the Expression Builder to accomplish the date range remapping to the first of each month.

9. **Return to the Select Data pane and double-click Month to change the format for this newly created column.**

10. **Click the Change button and select Category Date and format YYMMDw.d.**

11. **Click OK and then click Run to execute your query.**

    A data table similar to the one in Figure 7-13 should be created. You now have the data needed to create a great line plot of monthly sales by region!

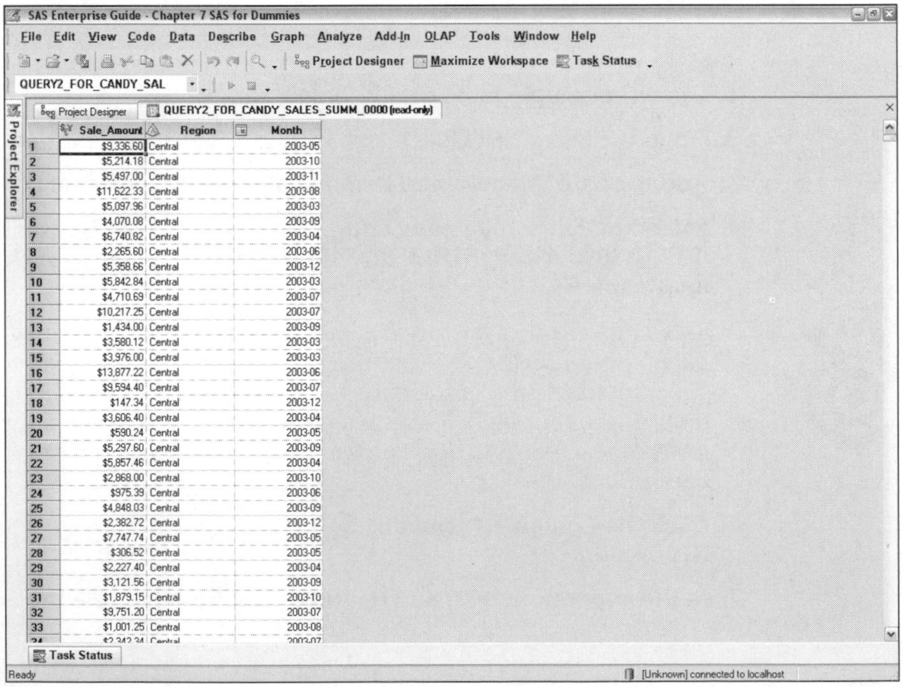

Figure 7-13: Data prepped for your analysis of sales in 2003.

Creating your line plot graph

From prefiltered data, you can create a line plot graph by following these steps:

1. **Open the sample table Candy_Sales_Summary and choose Graph⇨ Line Plot.**

   The Line Plot task appears, displaying the Line Plot type selection pane.

2. **Select the last choice: Multiple Line Plots by group Column.**

   This allows the graphing of multiple lines on one graph based on the grouping column specified in the next step.

3. **Click the Task Roles pane.**

4. **You want to analyze sales by month, grouped by region, so add Month to Horizontal, Sale_Amount to Vertical, and Region to Group.**

5. **Click Sale_Amount and select Sum from the Summarize for Each Distinct Horizontal Value drop-down list.**

6. **Click the Titles pane and turn off Use Default Text.**

7. **Type the title** 2003 Gross Sales by Region. **Change the selected section to Footnote and turn off Use Default Text.**

8. **Clear the default footnote text and leave blank.**

9. **Click Run.**

   The line plot should appear, similar to Figure 7-14. An interesting note is that the regions have different sales patterns, with the Central region having their biggest months early in the year and the East and West having bigger months in the middle of the year. Also, East and Central appear to have similar patterns in the last part of the year.

For some interesting variations, you can change the Sum value set in Step 5 to Average. Remember to update your title when you do this. Click Run. The mean sales line plot should appear, similar to Figure 7-15. You will notice very different patterns than in the gross sales plot. The West region has the most variable average order amount, whereas the Central and East regions average order amounts correlate more smoothly with their total sales for each month.

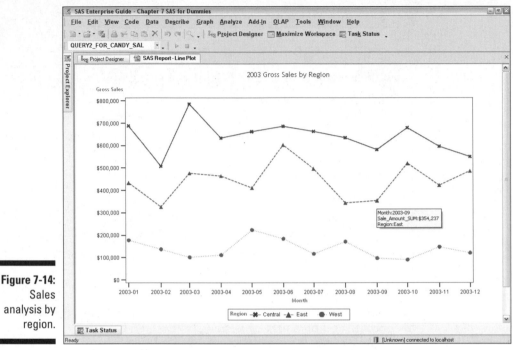

Figure 7-14:
Sales
analysis by
region.

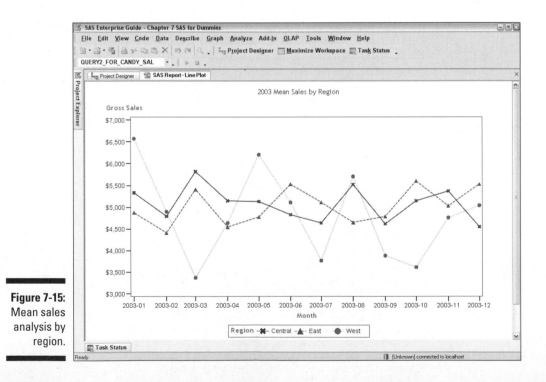

Figure 7-15:
Mean sales
analysis by
region.

Part III

Impressing Your Boss with Your SAS Business Intelligence

The 5th Wave   By Rich Tennant

"Right here. Analysis shows the well-run small criminal organization should have no more than nine goons, six henchmen, and four stooges. Right now, I think we're goon heavy."

In this part . . .

People spend lifetimes studying statistical methods and applied analytics, collecting Ph.D. after Ph.D. In this part, we distill the entire field down to just a couple of chapters. Obviously, our treatment of this area cannot be considered comprehensive — and there is no diploma at the back of this book.

However, we hope that it's enough to raise your interest in the topic and inspire you to discover more. In the meantime, you can pick up enough lingo and concepts to recognize how SAS brings the power of analytics to almost any problem you can imagine.

Chapter 8

A Painless Introduction to Analytics

*L*everaging the power of analytics that SAS has to offer is a reason why many customers buy and continue to use SAS. The ability to leverage past data to better understand what happened, to make better decisions about what to do today, and to forecast future behavior and outcomes is what statistics and analytics are about. This chapter and Chapter 9 provide an overview of what each analytic area is about, why you would want to leverage it, and the value you can obtain with it. Note that an in-depth understanding of general principles in each analytic area is beyond the scope of this book, but is crucial to getting the most from these techniques.

Analytic Concepts Useful for Everyone

Unfortunately, this book can't make you an expert in statistics. But we do provide a basic overview of the analytic capabilities of SAS.

We don't cover many of the specialized capabilities here. We recommend that you do some additional reading on the methods you're most interested in so that you can more fully understand the assumptions, use, and interpretation of the results from these powerful tools.

It's variable

The fundamental principle behind almost every form of statistical analysis is the concept of *variability*, which is the most important concept for understanding most results of various analyses. The simplest way to illustrate variability is with a coin toss. If you toss a fair coin repeatedly — *fair*, meaning that the coin has an equal chance of landing heads up or tails up — say ten times, you would expect the same number of heads and tails to be counted (five heads and five tails). However, multiple iterations of this ten-toss scenario show that many times, the number of heads counted in ten tosses isn't five, but rather six or seven or four or three. In fact, if you bet $1 on five heads per ten tosses in order to win $2 per ten tosses, you would become poor very quickly. In Table 8-1, you can see that you would win $2 only 24.6 percent of the time, meaning an average return of just $0.492 ($2 won multiplied by 24.6 percent of the time) on each $1 bet. This example summarizes variability quite nicely.

Many early statistical methods were developed to examine gambling outcomes like the one used in this example!

Table 8-1	Chance of Various Outcomes from Tossing a Coin Ten Times	
Number of Heads	*Number of Tails*	*Chance of Seeing This Outcome*
0	10	0.1 percent
1	9	1.0 percent
2	8	4.4 percent
3	7	11.7 percent
4	6	20.5 percent
5	5	24.6 percent
6	4	20.5 percent
7	3	11.7 percent
8	2	4.4 percent
9	1	1.0 percent
10	0	0.1 percent

p-values

If you understand the idea of variability, you have the beginning of understanding the annoying p-values frequently cited by various studies, journals, and newspapers. A *p-value* is often used to explain how rare the outcome is, given certain assumptions from the analysis used. Suppose that you want to ask whether a coin in question was indeed fair. (See the preceding section for a definition of *fair*.) If a coin is indeed fair, you expect a 50 percent chance of a head or tail if you conduct enough tosses.

Say you come across a questionable coin and doubt that it is fair, believing it to be rigged to land on tails more than 50 percent of the time, which would obviously provide an advantage to someone in a game. If you flip that coin ten times and see zero heads turn up, you would likely believe that the coin was fixed. You could assign a p-value of 0.001 (0.1 percent) to this outcome because a fair coin would exhibit this behavior in just one of a 1,000 ten-toss tries! Sure, it *could* be a fair coin, but most people would likely insist on using a new coin because 1 head in 1,000 tosses seems like a pretty good indication that the coin is fixed.

In many fields of study, a p-value less than 0.05 is usually considered *statistically significant.* Be sure not to confuse this type of statistical significance (for example, drug A is more effective than drug B based on one measure of success) with practical or real-world significance (for example, drug A is 5 percent faster than drug B at relieving bunion pain but costs 10 times more — not something of practical value to most people).

How confident are you?

The third foundation concept to help with analytics is that of *confidence intervals,* which are ranges of values that attempt to contain within them the true value being estimated. For example, suppose you create a sales forecast for the next month based on the last three years of sales. Offering a single number to your boss — say, $10,000,000 — seems simplistic and even dangerous! It is an estimate of the next month that doesn't seem to take into account the variability of prior months, unless they were always $10,000,000. The greater the prior months' variability, the wider the confidence interval needs to be. If the variability of prior sales were low, you would expect a smaller confidence interval range. You might offer your boss a 95 percent confidence interval of $7,200,000 to $15,000,000, with an expected value of $10,000,000, as a more informative sales estimate.

What is variance?

Suppose your manager asks for a report summarizing the average sale by region for your new product, Super Chocolate Toffee Bears. Suppose the West has a mean sales price of $1.25, and the East has a mean sales price of $1.28. These don't seem all that different — but are they?

Suppose we told you that 95 percent of all sales in the West were between $1.20 and $1.30 and that 95 percent of all sales in the East were between $1.01 and $1.61. Now do they seem similar? What does this additional information

tell us? Perhaps you could focus your marketing dollars to first penetrate the markets where the candy is selling at higher prices — and hopefully higher margins!

The missing piece added by these confidence intervals is in the concept of *variance*. Variance is the measure of spread of values for a given measure — in this example, sales price. Variance is central to all statistical analysis and is the key to calculating confidence intervals in this example.

Most people new to statistics think that a 95 percent confidence interval means there is a 95 percent chance that the interval contains the true value of the statistic. But that's not how it works! A 95 percent confidence interval actually means that if the overall data for the subject at hand were collected 100 times, 95 of the 100 confidence intervals would contain the true value. Approximately five of those times, it would not contain the true value.

What did your mother say about making assumptions?

Every statistical method and technique has a variety of assumptions that must be met for the results to be useful and meaningful. You need to check these assumptions prior to using statistical techniques by using the diagnostic checks frequently available with the analysis output. If your data doesn't meet the standard assumptions for a given statistical technique, perhaps another technique has broader or different assumptions that would make analyzing your data possible. Likewise, you may be able to transform your data to make it meet the assumptions required of your selected statistical technique. Suppose, for example, that you use an analysis that assumes your data is normally distributed. If the data isn't normally distributed, the assumptions haven't been met, and the results and interpretations will lead you to incorrect conclusions. This is why it is so important to check the assumptions required by your analysis technique to ensure that you use the right test and make correct conclusions!

Distribution Analysis — Describing Your Data

A common question asked about data is the type of distribution that it mimics or originates from. Most people who are familiar with statistics have heard of *normal distribution,* which is the assumed distribution for analyses, like simple correlation, analysis of variance (ANOVA), and linear regression. Knowing the distribution that your data mimics is important in selecting the proper transformation and appropriate analytic technique.

The Distribution Analysis task (available by choosing Describe⇨Distribution Analysis) enables you to examine your data for conformance to a variety of distributions, including the normal, lognormal, exponential, Weibull, beta, gamma, and kernel distributions. Tabular summaries, fit statistics, and a variety of graphical presentation including histograms, probability plots, quantile plots (you may have heard of them as percentile, decile, or quartile plots), and box plots are also readily available.

Figure 8-1 shows a sample histogram from the Candy_Sales_Summary data provided with SAS Enterprise Guide. In this plot, the lognormal distribution is overlaid on the frequency counts of the Sale_Amount data. Visually, this appears to be a very good fit to the lognormal distribution. You can also examine the actual goodness-of-fit statistics to see whether the data actually conforms to the lognormal distribution. Other output from this task can help statistically test the value of the mean and the standard deviation. Also handy from the standard summary tables are the confidence intervals for the mean, standard deviation, and variance of the data.

Analyzing Counts and Frequencies

In customer demographic and health care research, collecting responses for one or more categorical variables is common. Examples of categorical variables include a favorite day of the week, a favorite car type, ethnic background, gender, disease progression status, a grade received in a course, marital status, home ownership status, citizenship status, and employment status. Some categorical variables have inherent order, and others are just categories with no implicit order to the categories. Gender is a good example of a *nominal variable,* a variable with no explicit order to the values: male and female. Disease progression status is a good example of an *ordinal variable* because Stage I of a disease occurs prior to Stage II, and so on. Ordinal variables simply have an order of the categories, but they have no exact ratio of difference among the categories: That is, Stage I is not necessarily half as advanced as Stage II.

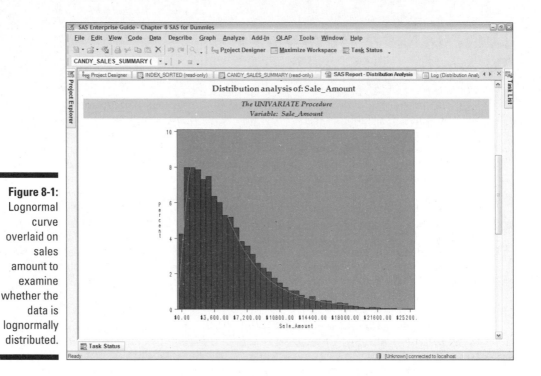

Figure 8-1:
Lognormal
curve
overlaid on
sales
amount to
examine
whether the
data is
lognormally
distributed.

An example of a *two-way contingency table* is shown in Figure 8-2. This is a table of chocolate preference by gender generated with the Table Analysis task (available by choosing Describe⇨Table Analysis). This type of table is also referred to as a *contingency table* or *cross-tabular summary.* The Table Analysis task can produce contingency tables based on many variables, but practical experience shows that no more than three or four variables can be examined easily. The Table Analysis task adds more value than the Summary Tables task (covered in Chapter 6) because of the availability of many statistical methods to determine whether the differences among the various categories are statistically significant.

Examining Figure 8-2, you might wonder whether the taste profile of males and females would be the same in the general population as in this 200-person sample. Various statistical tests, such as the Chi-square test or the Mantel-Haenszel Chi-square test, can be applied with the Table Analysis task to determine whether a true taste preference difference exists among a potential customer base or whether chance resulted only from the differences between men and women in this sample.

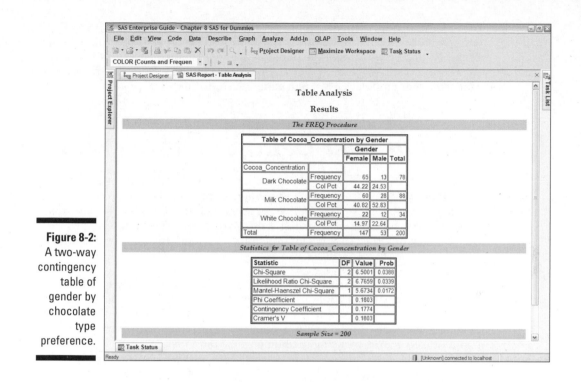

Figure 8-2:
A two-way contingency table of gender by chocolate type preference.

After examining the statistics in Figure 8-2, a significant difference apparently likely exists between males and females in the general population in their taste preferences for chocolate. This is very valuable information when designing marketing campaigns, packaging, and so on.

A very wide array of statistics is available from the Table Analysis task, as outlined in Figure 8-2. The table breaks down the tests and measures into the following categories:

- ✔ **Association:** The most commonly used area, examining whether two or more variables are related *(correlated)*

   Being correlated does *not* mean that causality exists.

- ✔ **Agreement:** Used with *dichotomous* variables only (yes/no or positive/ negative)

- ✔ **Differences:** Tests for differences among classes for an ordinal variable

- ✔ **Trend:** Examines the outcome of a two-level variable against an ordinal variable

Other ways of addressing categorical data analysis are available, some of which are covered in the following sections. Additional methods that can be useful for analyzing categorical data include regression, analysis of variance (ANOVA), logistic regression (very heavily used in marketing research), generalized linear models (GLM), and generalized estimating equation.

Transforming Your Data for Further Use

Before or after analyzing your data, you might realize that certain assumptions about your data aren't met. For example, perhaps your data isn't normally distributed, but your analysis requires the data to be normally distributed. You can either select another analytic method with different or broader assumptions, or you can transform your data to meet the assumptions of your selected analysis.

The Standardize Data task in SAS Enterprise Guide (available by choosing Describe⇨Table Analysis) allows you to transform data from a variety of distributions (uniform, lognormal, and so on) to a standard normal distribution. You can easily convert data with percentiles (uniformly distributed) into standardized scores by using the Standardize Data task.

You can also use tasks covered in previous chapters for transforming your data. You can use the Rank Data task to convert data to percentiles, ranks, normalized scores, or exponential scores. Various functions with calculated columns from the Query task can also be useful in transforming your data (for example, LOG, EXP, and LOG10).

Basic Data Analysis via Correlation Techniques

Correlation analysis is useful to examine whether two or more variables share a relationship. In a simpler form, you're examining whether one variable increases, decreases, or stays the same while the other variable increases. Note that this does not imply causality: That is, correlated variables are not necessarily causing the other to vary. A simple example of correlated variables that aren't causal is measuring the body temperature of a dog and a person who have been in a steam bath for more than 15 minutes. Both temperatures would rise over the 15-minute period (positive correlation: as one rises, so does the other), but the actual cause is the steam bath temperature and exposure time to the steam bath, not each other's temperatures.

With any statistical analysis, presuming causality is very dangerous simply because there is a significant p-value or a described relationship! Unless you design a controlled study in which all other variables can be controlled or adjusted for, do not assume causality in any case!

That said, correlation or positive p-values *could* be indicative of causality, especially when combined with practical experience with the process at hand. Still, scientists should reject the notion of finding causality unless they verify the results with a controlled experiment. A *controlled experiment* implies that you can keep all other conditions constant or that you have a known way of adjusting for the conditions you can't control. This way, you can focus on just the causal variables change and the resulting change in the outcome of interest.

The Correlation task (available by choosing Analyze⊃Multivariate⊃ Correlations) enables you to examine the relationship between one or more variables with each other. The default technique for this task, Pearson correlation, assumes your data in both variables are from normal distributions. Other techniques available with this task — Hoeffding, Kendall, and Spearman — have fewer assumptions about the data distribution being used to obtain the strength of correlation.

Most laypeople refer to Pearson correlation when they talk about correlation. This task generates p-values that measure the probability that the correlation seen with your selected data could happen by chance or whether they were not correlated at all. In addition, this task provides you with the correlation coefficient, which is either positive or negative, depending on whether the two variables increase together (positive) or whether one decreases as the other increases (negative). Scatter plots showing the relationship of each variable with the other can also be displayed with your analysis.

An example of a Pearson correlation table and scatter plot is shown in Table 8-2 and Figure 8-3. The data used in this example is in the data set Corn, which is available in the sample data provided with the SAS Enterprise Guide. This data set is a historic record of corn yield over 33 years and various environmental variables that could influence the corn yield. Note that only three of the eight selected variables exhibit a p-value less than 0.05: July_Rain, July_Temp, and August_Temp. Rainfall appears to be positively correlated (more rain likely results in better yield, adding subjective assessment to the result), and higher temperature generally results in lower yield — a negative correlation. To definitively state causality, a controlled experiment would be needed. Note that in this case, it is highly unlikely that corn yield is influencing the weather!

Table 8-2	Pearson Correlation Table Examining Corn Yield Data
Variable Correlated to Corn Yield	**Pearson Correlation Coefficient**
Pre_seasonPrecip	0.15116
	0.4011
May_Temp	-0.11893
	0.5098
June_Rain	-0.13907
	0.4402
June_Temp	-0.14536
	0.4196
July_Rain	0.57407
	0.0005
July_Temp	-0.57884
	0.0004
Aug_Rain	0.20946
	0.242
Aug_Temp	-0.34749
	0.0475

One final observation based on experience is that the temperatures in July and August are likely correlated and that the rainfall in July is likely correlated with the temperature in July. This is often referred to as *interaction,* where one predictive variable influences not just the outcome of interest but the other predictive variables. Therefore, to find the true strength of various variables on the outcome, controlled experiments where only one of these variables is allowed to vary would be useful. More sophisticated statistical techniques are also available that can help you separate this interaction, or covariance, of predictors.

Canonical correlation is often used in marketing analysis to compare multiple variables grouped together against another variable (available by choosing Analyze➪Multivariate➪Canonical Correlation). It is similar to the Correlation task in concept except that you can group several related variables, such as July and August temperatures, and correlate them with one or more outcome variables, such as corn yield.

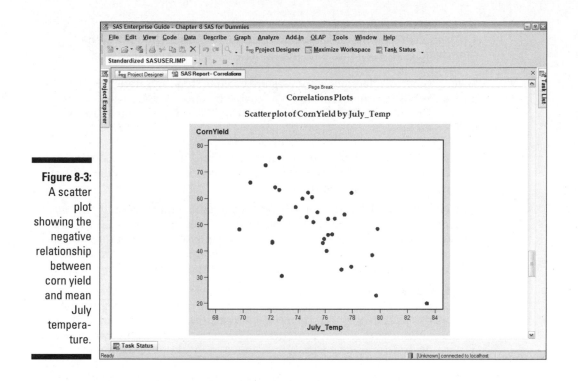

Figure 8-3:
A scatter plot showing the negative relationship between corn yield and mean July temperature.

ANOVA and Regression: No PhD Required!

Analysis of variance (ANOVA) and *regression analysis* are two forms of statistical analysis frequently used in a wide range of applications to describe the relationship between two or more variables. These two forms of analysis are fairly related and can even be combined into one analysis type. Analysis of variance lets you examine the strength of the relationship between a discrete predictor variable (for example, a car type) and a continuous, predicted variable (for example, a car price.) The primary purpose of ANOVA is to allow you to determine whether a categorical variable has differing averages across the various groups.

Regression is similar to correlation analysis in that both the predictor and the predicted variable must be continuous (for example, horsepower and car price). Regression provides you with an equation for the line (the y-axis intercept and the slope of the regression line) that best describes the relationship between the predictor and predicted variable. Regression analysis also provides you with the statistical strength of the regression line for predicting other values you can obtain in the future.

Several types of analytic techniques are grouped together under the ANOVA submenu in SAS Enterprise Guide (available by choosing Analyze⇨ANOVA): t Tests, One Way ANOVA, Nonparametric One Way ANOVA, Linear Models, and Mixed Models:

- **t Tests:** Used to examine the effect of a treatment with two categories (for example, aspirin versus a placebo) on one continuous measure (for example, blood pressure).

- **One Way and Nonparametric ANOVA:** Enable you to examine the effect of a categorical variable with many levels (for example, aspirin versus placebo versus acetaminophen versus naproxen) on a continuous measure (for example, blood pressure). The nonparametric form has no underlying distribution assumption about the continuous measure.

- **Linear Models and Mixed Models:** These are the most generalized forms of ANOVA and combine concepts from ANOVA and regression analysis. They are also the most complex form of this type of analysis to use and interpret. Linear Models lets you relate one or many continuous or discrete predictor variables to one or many continuous predicted variables. Mixed Models further generalize on Linear Models in that the various predictors can be correlated and can exhibit nonconstant variability across the range of predicted values.

An example of a one-way ANOVA is shown in Figure 8-4 using the SAS Enterprise Guide sample data set CARS_1993. This example explores the relationship between car type and car price. The box plot shows the mean and range of the price across the categories in the box plot. Note a few possible surprises here: for example, midsize cars have some of the highest prices and compact cars can rival large car prices. The table above the box plot shows the R-Square and the p-value for this model. *R-Square* is a measure of how much of the variance in mean price is explained by the model; in this case, about 42 percent of the variance is explained in the model. The p-value, less than 0.0001, indicates that there is less than a one in 10,000 chance that the mean is equal among the car groups. You can conclude that car type is a good predictor of car price, explaining about 42 percent of the variability in car price.

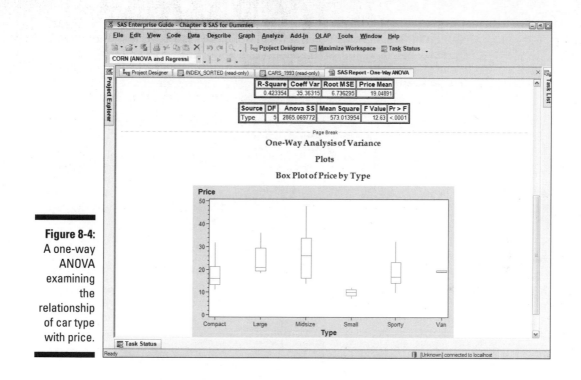

Figure 8-4:
A one-way
ANOVA
examining
the
relationship
of car type
with price.

Several types of analytic techniques are grouped under the Regression submenu in SAS Enterprise Guide (available by choosing Analyze⇨Regression): Linear Regression, Nonlinear Regression, Logistic Regression, and Generalized Linear Models:

- ✓ **Linear Regression:** Attempts to fit a line to your data; an example is a model car price based on horsepower.

- ✓ **Nonlinear Regression:** Extends the concept of linear regression where you must specify the general form of the model to fit your data: for example, a cubic relationship between horsepower and price.

- ✓ **Logistic Regression:** Widely used in marketing research and one of many data mining techniques. Logistic regression allows you to add binary (yes, no) and categorical variables (low, medium, and high income) to the linear regression model, as both predictors and predicted values.

- ✓ **Generalized Linear Models:** An extension of linear regression that enables you to add data not normally distributed, such as counts or proportion measurements.

Figure 8-5 shows an example of linear regression. This example shows the predicted linear relationship and prediction limits between horsepower and car price. The graph shows the positive relationship between horsepower and car price, along with prediction bands, between which 95 percent of all data points should lie.

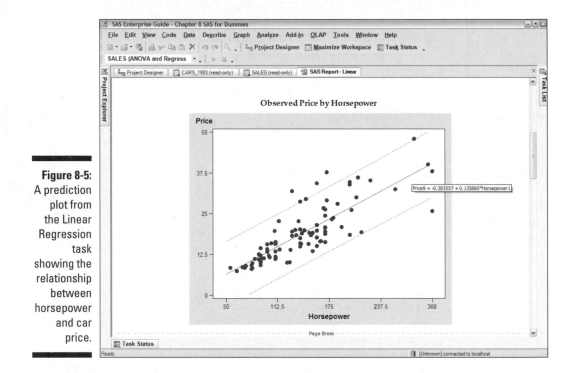

Figure 8-5:
A prediction plot from the Linear Regression task showing the relationship between horsepower and car price.

Chapter 9

More Analytics to Enlighten and Entertain

As you might expect, one chapter isn't enough to cover the analytics available with SAS. In addition to Chapter 8, you can delve even deeper into analytic capabilities in this chapter. We review some of the more modern and advanced analytic techniques available with SAS, including the following:

✔ **Survival analysis:** Enables you to compare the lifespan of similar products, for example, or to determine whether one treatment increases time to illness or death versus another treatment.

✔ **Quality control methods:** Provide a broad range of tools to understand and optimize your manufacturing or customer service process.

✔ **Forecasting:** Enables you to make simple or sophisticated models that can help project business outcomes for the coming week, month, quarter, or year.

✔ **Multivariate analysis:** Lets you examine and link vast numbers of predictor and predicted variables related to your business; this effectively reduces complex data in your business.

✔ **Data mining:** Helps you determine the most lucrative customers so that you can provide them with exemplary service; also identifies customers who may be a drain on your resources.

Staying Alive with Survival Analysis

Survival analysis might sound morbid, but death doesn't have to overshadow this area of statistical analysis. Although survival analysis can indeed be used to model time until death for people or products (light bulbs are a classic example of the latter), other outcomes (besides death and failure) can be substituted in this technique. Think of *yes* or *no* types of outcomes, for example: Yes, he defaulted after 678 days on his loan; No, she didn't default as of 893 days as a loan customer.

When comparing two drugs that prevent the onset of a new stage of a disease, the arrival of symptoms is sometimes used as the endpoint outcome for survival analysis. The amount of time until a customer cancels or closes his account is another example of an event of interest to model.

The principle behind survival analysis revolves around determining the failure rate of various groups (called *strata*) relative to an outcome of interest (death, product failure, or a customer cancelling his account). Examples of strata include patient lifestyle, patient treatment, light bulb filament type, or promotional program offered to new customers at time of recruitment.

Figure 9-1 shows a classic example of time to relapse or death for cancer patients. The control group (the bottom line in the graph) received no preventive therapy after their cancer was in remission. The maintenance therapy group received a drug being tested for the prevention of cancer recurrence. When relapse occurred, the patient was counted as a failure. (Patients unable to be contacted for follow-up are considered *censored* at their last visit and are treated a specific way by the analysis.)

As you can see, the maintenance therapy group appears to have better survival rates. (That is, at 40 months, about 38 percent in the maintenance group are still in remission versus about 18 percent in the control group.)

Two types of survival analysis techniques — Life Tables and Proportional Hazards — are grouped together under the Survival Analysis submenu in SAS Enterprise Guide (available by choosing Analyze⇨Survival Analysis):

✔ **Life Tables:** The Life Tables task estimates the survival distribution of each group. Usually, you want to compare survival curves to determine whether two groups differ significantly from one another. The Life Tables task computes rank tests and a likelihood ratio test to test for differences across the groups.

✔ **Proportional Hazards:** The Proportional Hazards task uses regression analysis principles for survival data. *Proportional hazards* are widely used in the analysis of survival data to explain the effects of explanatory variables on survival times. An example would be to expand the previously mentioned cancer survival study and add the number of cigarettes smoked per day by each patient during the trial. This could have a significant impact on cancer recurrence rates that was incorrectly attributed to the treatments. The Proportional Hazards task enables you to separate out the extraneous factors that could influence survival rates.

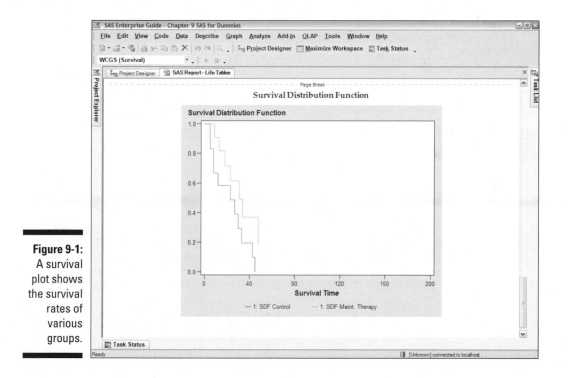

Figure 9-1:
A survival plot shows the survival rates of various groups.

Quality Control: You Want Something That Works?

Most organizations want to provide quality products and services. SAS can help you monitor and improve the quality of your products and services based on quality standards set by you and your organization. Just as important, increasing quality often results in considerable time and cost savings — from efficiency to customer satisfaction to fewer returns and cancellations.

A wide variety of quality control techniques are available — from control chart methods to specialized tools that can help improve products, maintain high quality, and increase levels of customer satisfaction. These techniques can help you

✔ Identify key issues that contribute to low quality

✔ Examine historic product quality to help set future standards

✔ Determine the quality of products or services as they are produced or delivered to minimize waste

The following sections introduce you to the wide range of quality control tasks available in SAS Enterprise Guide.

Histograms

One of the simpler quality-control techniques you can use is a histogram. *Histograms* show the counts or percent of observed values across a range of values for a selected variable. You use a histogram to compare the results of a user-selected process with the user-defined specification limits. With a quality histogram, you can graphically see the distribution of measured values, how many items are out of specification, and how widely dispersed the outlying values are from the desired specification.

The following example uses the sample TubeAngle data set included with SAS Enterprise Guide. This data is from a bicycle manufacturing operation that creates frames for off-road bicycles. It is critical to the performance of these bikes that the tube angle is within the specification limits of 73.7 to 74.3 degrees.

You use the Histogram task by choosing Analyze⇨Capability Analysis⇨ Histograms. The histogram in Figure 9-2 shows the counts of parts produced by angle. As you can see in the histogram, the specifications appear as dashed lines at each end of the chart, and out-of-range bars appear in a different color beyond the dashed lines. Overlaid on the histogram is the normal distribution for the given data based on the mean and standard deviation of the given data. You can see that the mean is slightly above the ideal 74.0-degree angle; you could probably improve this process by slightly recalibrating the equipment used to achieve a smaller angle.

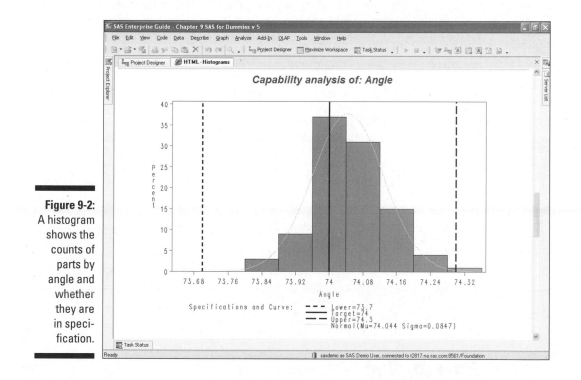

Figure 9-2:
A histogram shows the counts of parts by angle and whether they are in specification.

Q-Q plots and probability plots

Q-Q plots and *probability plots* are useful for examining the data from your process and checking whether the data is distributed according to an expected statistical distribution (such as normal, exponential, or lognormal). Q-Q plots are more useful for deriving the actual distribution parameters and capability indices, and probability plots are more useful for examining actual versus expected percentiles. These tasks are available by choosing Analyze⇨Capability Analysis.

Control charts

Control charts (or *Shewhart charts*) allow you to visualize product quality variation due to common or regular causes versus variation due to special or sporadic causes. Control charts can help you identify new problems that arise from factors such as undertrained personnel, new equipment that might not be properly calibrated, or out-of-specification products from suppliers.

Mean and Range, Mean and Standard Deviation, Mean Individual Measurement, Box, p, np, q, and c charts are useful for continuous monitoring of your process to determine whether it is in specification or possibly moving out of specification. This is very helpful in monitoring any type of manufacturing process or customer service scenarios to decide whether to stop the production line or add more sales representatives at a given point in time. Determining the chart type to use depends on the type of data being collected and the type of process you're monitoring.

The Mean Individual Measurement chart in Figure 9-3 shows two possible times that the production of bike frames should have been examined and adjusted to minimize future defects. On 3/17, a frame was made out of specification, and the moving range of the values was high enough to warrant examination. On 3/26, just the moving range was large enough to possibly indicate a problem in production, but perhaps it was just an adjustment made to the equipment. You can access these tasks by choosing Analyze⇨Control Charts.

Pareto charts

Pareto charts are similar to bar charts, but they are specifically designed to identify top causes of failure so that priorities can be set for eliminating product failure from your process. The Pareto chart in Figure 9-4, available by choosing Analyze⇨Pareto Chart, shows that the majority of defects in the bike frame example are linked to just two causes: stray file marks and burrs. Eliminating or greatly reducing these two errors could cut down on defects by more than 50 percent!

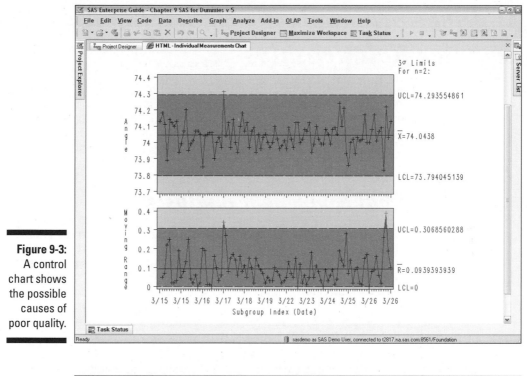

Figure 9-3:
A control
chart shows
the possible
causes of
poor quality.

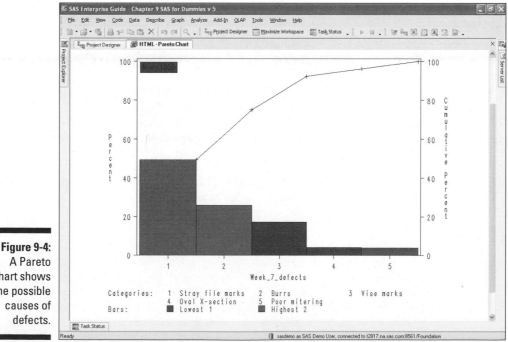

Figure 9-4:
A Pareto
chart shows
the possible
causes of
defects.

Multivariate Analysis: Understanding Complex Relationships

Multivariate analysis is a set of techniques for examining relationships among multiple variables in one analysis. You can use principal component analysis when you're interested in collapsing many variables and discovering new relationships among the variables of interest. You can use cluster and discriminant analysis to find logical groupings or clusters of your data.

Principal component analysis

The Principal Components task can allow you to simplify data across multiple variables by collapsing the variables to fewer composite variables. These composite variables are reductions based on the analytic results from the Principal Components task, which identifies the relative correlation of each variable with the outcome of interest.

Suppose that you have the crime rates for 7 categories and 12 predictive variables for each of the 50 U.S. states. With so many variables, visually examining all the variables is very difficult. You can use principal component analysis to summarize the data down to two or three dimensions and to help you visualize the relationships.

Cluster analysis and discriminant analysis

The *Cluster Analysis* and *Discriminant Analysis tasks* (available when you choose Analyze⇨Multivariate⇨Cluster Analysis/Discriminant Analysis) create *clusters,* or logical groupings of data. You specify how many clusters you want from your data and the task clusters different records together based on the attributes you provide. The task can also chart the results of hierarchical clustering to produce a tree diagram (a *dendrogram*). A cluster example is shown in Figure 9-5. Various ZIP codes have been clustered, based on an income scale and a crime index scale.

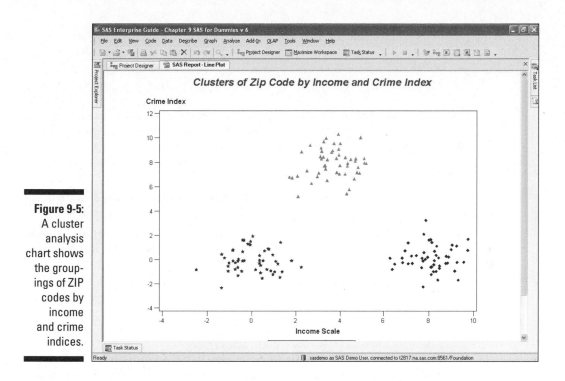

Figure 9-5:
A cluster analysis chart shows the groupings of ZIP codes by income and crime indices.

Forecasting: Using the Crystal Ball

When you think of forecasting, you likely think of the weather and the forecasts you read in the paper or see on television. You can use the forecasting function in SAS Enterprise Guide for this, but it is more frequently used for forecasting in a wide range of business and economic areas. Some examples of forecasting include predicting

- The number of patients admitted to a hospital in the next day, week, month, quarter, or year
- The number of music players that will be sold next month
- Whether we can increase the number of music players we sell next year by increasing the sales staff by 30 percent and tripling the marketing budget; by doing these things, how many more music players might we sell

✔ The number of homicides in a city next year

✔ The number of people who will die of various causes in the next ten years

✔ How many flights will be delayed tomorrow versus the same day last year

Forecasting is concerned with how to collect historical data and use it to effectively project future results. Various factors play into the effective analysis of data to produce forecasts, including

✔ **How much historical data can be gathered**

✔ **Whether the forecasts are seasonally affected:** For example, more beer is sold in May in Miami, which is a low sales point time in Sydney.

✔ **Whether to break down the data being forecasted into various groups:** For example, newer beer brands might have different sales patterns than existing brands.

✔ **Examining variables that help predict the outcome:** Temperature, the number of marketing programs, the number of stores that carry the brand, and so on.

The example shown in Figure 9-6 contrasts a forecast of beer sales based only on historic sales amounts with a forecast also incorporating predictive variables (the number of TV ads and the effect of a specific weather forecast for the year 2006). The power of incorporating future predictive variables is likely apparent very quickly. This example demonstrates the importance of understanding your data and using predictive variables when creating forecasts.

Figure 9-6: Contrast a simple forecast with a more refined forecast using predictive variables.

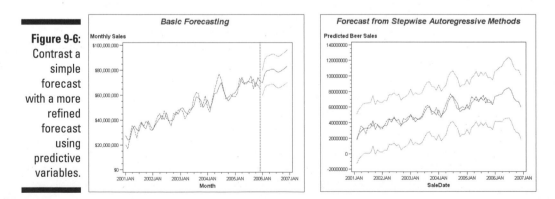

SAS Enterprise Guide provides you with two tasks to prepare your data for forecasting. Forecasting is performed on a standard time interval of your choice, such as days, weeks, or months. These tasks enable you to prepare your historical data to conform to these time period intervals.

Say that you have daily sales data, but you only want to produce monthly sales analysis. With the Prepare Time Series Data tasks (available by choosing Analyze⇨Time Series⇨Prepare Time Series Data), you can collapse the 28 to 31 records per month into one monthly record.

The Create Time Series Data task is similar to the Prepare task but is intended for large volumes of data or to perform more complex transformations of your existing data. This task is available by choosing Analyze⇨Time Series⇨ Create Time Series Data.

Four tasks are available to create forecasts of your data, from a simple forecast based only on prior sales amounts to more sophisticated modeling techniques that allow you to add predictive variables and change the underlying assumptions about your data.

- ✔ **Basic Forecasting, ARIMA Modeling and Forecasting:** Basic Forecasting (Analyze⇨Time Series⇨Basic Forecasting) and the ARIMA Modeling and Forecasting tasks (Analyze⇨Time Series⇨ARIMA Modeling and Forecasting) both provide a simple approach to producing forecasts based solely on the trends in your historical values.

- ✔ **Regression Analysis with Autoregressive Errors:** This task, available from Analyze⇨Time Series⇨Regression Analysis with Autoregressive Errors, allows you to add predictor variables to your forecast model.

- ✔ **Regression Analysis of Panel Data:** This task (Analyze⇨Time Series⇨ Regression Analysis of Panel Data), enables you to specify advanced details about the model errors and to add cross-sectional data analysis to your time series analysis.

- ✔ **Cross-sectional analysis:** Enables you to examine the correlation between various groupings of your data over time. An example would be to forecast beer sales and potato chip sales over time and to examine the correlation between these two time series: Do chip sales go up as beer sales go down?

Data Mining: Precious Jewels in Your Data

Loosely speaking, *data mining* is leveraging your data via key variable selection, data exploration, and data modeling to make informed decisions. Data mining is famous for the wide array of applications in customer insight and customer management. Banks use data mining to predict whether a customer is a good loan risk, whether a customer will likely accept a new marketing offer, and even to assign a predicted lifetime profit value to each customer. Retailers such as Amazon.com use data mining to personalize your shopping experience and proactively make recommendations for your next item to add to your shopping cart.

Data mining with SAS is primarily performed with an application specifically made for data mining, SAS Enterprise Miner. Although SAS Enterprise Miner is not covered in depth in this book, we do cover using work created by this application. SAS Enterprise Miner is an expert desktop client interface that allows extensive data mining capabilities for your mining experts. SAS Enterprise Guide can use work performed by your data mining team via the Model Scoring task.

The Model Scoring Task, available from Analyze⇨Model Scoring, allows you to obtain the essence of the work published by your data mining team and leverage it from SAS Enterprise Guide. After your data mining team has explored and modeled data for a particular subject — take customer loan risk, as an example — a data mining model is available to business users to score their data.

Scoring data comprises taking some new data (say, recent loan applicants) and then scoring their attributes — such as income, education, recent credit history, debt load, location, and loan purpose — to obtain a score. Scores are typically a numeric value such as 0–100%, with applicants receiving scores higher than 70% considered an acceptable credit risk to grant a loan. You might even base the interest rate on the value of their score.

Figure 9-7 shows an example of some data that was scored using the Model Scoring Task and then summarized with a box plot chart. This chart shows that for these groups of potential customers, office workers appear to be the lowest risk of loan default group, and sales and "other" groups of applicants appear to be of much higher risk. If you were to reject any applicant with a greater than 5 percent chance of loan default, you would accept about half the managers, about 75 percent of office workers, and only about 25 percent of "other" workers.

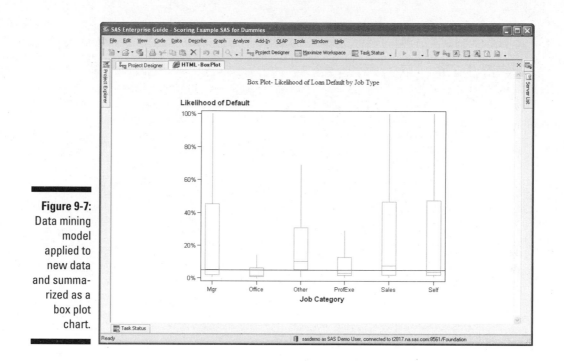

Figure 9-7:
Data mining model applied to new data and summarized as a box plot chart.

Chapter 10

Making It Pretty: Controlling Your Output

In This Chapter

▶ Adding some style to your report

▶ Painting your own custom styles

▶ More than just a pretty face: Making your styles mean something

▶ The demise of plain text? Not even close!

*I*f you've ever read a badly formatted report — the ones that use single spacing between lines, with too-small 7 point (pt) text, quarter-inch margins, and 15 different fonts — you know that the aesthetics and appearance of a report can be almost as important as the content. If the formatting is bad enough, people might not want to read it. In fact, some organizations divide the job of report creation among different people: a report writer and report formatter, for example. With the techniques presented in this chapter, you can master both jobs (after which you should lobby to receive both salaries).

Perhaps your report needs to comply with a corporate standard for size, colors, and typefaces. Or you might be a finicky author who wants to ensure that the report is as pleasing to the eye as it is accurate and informative. Using effective formatting is more than just good looks, though. You can also use formatting to call attention to important parts of your report, such as summary total lines or results that you might consider exceptional. In this chapter, we show you how to use the style capabilities of SAS to control many aspects of your report's appearance to ensure that the presentation of the information in your report is the best that it can be.

Output Delivery with No Extra Postage Required

Styles, the templates that control the appearance of reports, are a relatively recent phenomenon for SAS users. In the old days (up until about 1999), SAS output was exclusively plain, unformatted text. If you've ever tried to make plain text stand out and look pretty, you probably realize what a futile exercise that is. You can spend hours getting columns to align and pages to break just so, but that's about the extent of it. Even with that limited control, some professionals make careers out of controlling the appearance of SAS reports.

Getting cozy with ODS

Thankfully, modern SAS applications can take advantage of an Output Delivery System (ODS). Its name makes it sound like a commercial shipping service, and that metaphor is actually appropriate. The tried-and-true SAS procedures control the content of your output as they always have, but ODS controls how it gets to you and in what format.

An output format type in ODS is a *destination*. Although SAS supports many destination types, only a few big ones relate to report format and appearance:

- **HTML (HyperText Markup Language):** The most popular format for Web-based output. Use this format when you want to share your results on a Web page. It's great for viewing, but not so hot for printing.

- **PDF (Portable Document File):** The ubiquitous printer-friendly format supported by Adobe Acrobat. Use this format when "printability" is paramount.

- **RTF (Rich Text Format):** A format usable within most word processing applications, most notably Microsoft Word. If you intend to include your results in a larger report that you want to edit, this is a good choice.

- **SAS Report:** A proprietary format used and sharable by a selection of SAS products and applications. It views like HTML, prints like PDF, and provides flexible layout options; however, it's usable only within SAS applications such as SAS Enterprise Guide and SAS Web Report Studio.

Creating a report with style

SAS Enterprise Guide understands ODS and "baked-in" styles, making the creation of SAS reports with a specific format and style quite simple. When you create an HTML report with SAS Enterprise Guide, the default style used is EGDefault, which is a simple, inoffensive style featuring neutral colors and a banner image with the SAS logo.

Figure 10-1 shows two versions of the same report displayed side by side within SAS Enterprise Guide. They are identical except for one setting: The report on the left uses the default style for HTML in SAS Enterprise Guide, and the report on the right uses the built-in Analysis style.

SAS Enterprise Guide makes it easy to select which types of output to create as well as which styles to use for each of those output types. To see what types of output will be created, view the settings by choosing Tools⇨Options⇨ Results General. Each active output type is marked with a check box. The Options window contains a subsection for each of the possible output types: HTML, RTF, PDF, and SAS Report. In each of these sections, you can choose from the available styles. See Figure 10-2 for a view of the HTML section of the Options window, which shows a subset of the available styles.

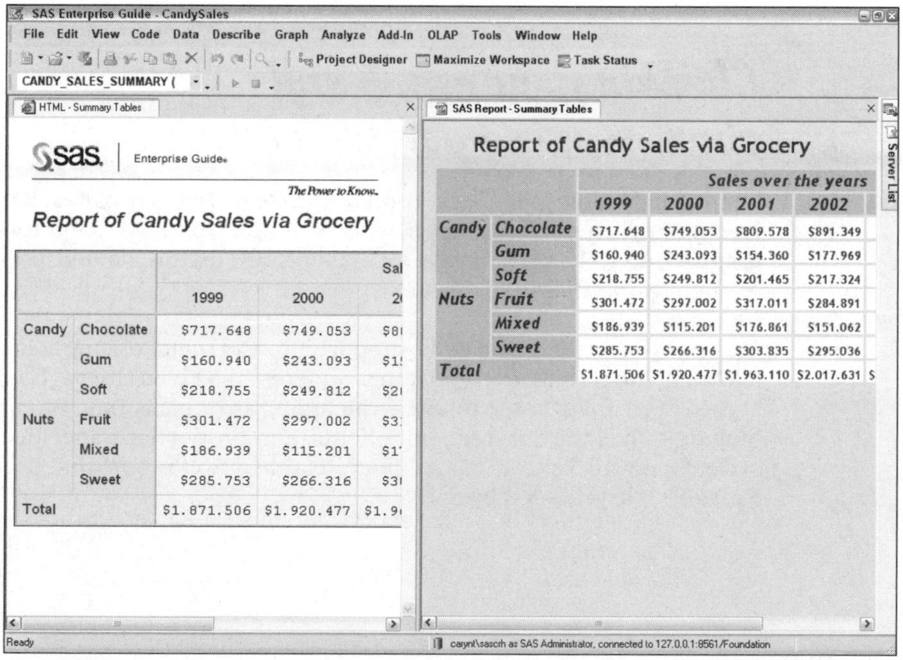

Figure 10-1:
The same report with two different styles applied.

Some of the styles that SAS provides are designed for use with a specific output type. For example, the *sasweb* style is meant for HTML output, whereas the *printer* style is optimized for PDF. Note the RTF style — can you guess which output type you might use with that one?

Checking out graph styles: A chart-topping performance

Immediately after the introduction of ODS and style templates, SAS users enjoyed stylish control over all aspects of their reports except for one: graphs. SAS 9 changed that by including a new feature named, appropriately enough, *graph styles*.

Graph styles extend ODS style support into the realm of charts and plots, allowing you to create a report that adheres to a given theme. Using graph styles, everything in the report — including any charts that you happen to include — has the color schemes, fonts, and proportions specified in that style. Figure 10-3 shows a combination table-graph report that uses the *Seaside* style provided by SAS.

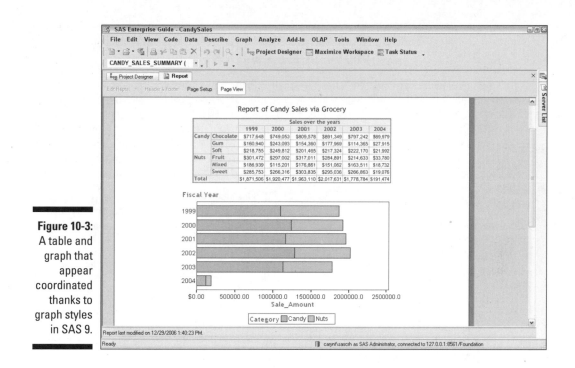

Figure 10-3:
A table and graph that appear coordinated thanks to graph styles in SAS 9.

Graph styles seem like a simple concept, but the technology represents a big step in style support. Prior to using graph styles, you could change the style of a tabular report with a simple style option, but changing the appearance of a graph required much more work. It was kind of like dressing your report in a coordinated suit that a fashion consultant put together for you but then leaving you to weave your own necktie to complete the ensemble.

At the time of this writing, the current version of SAS software supports graph styles only in two graph image formats: ActiveX and Java.

SAS supports a wide variety of standard image formats, including JPEG, GIF, BMP, and many others. However, those image types (often referred to as *static image types* because after SAS generates them, users cannot alter them) do not support the modern graph styles. ActiveX and Java graph formats are traditionally interactive types, rendered in a Web browser, using Windows and Java technology, respectively, which allows you to play with them — change colors, rotate them, and so on. If you don't want that interactivity (or if you're using an output type that doesn't support interactivity, such as PDF), you can use a static image flavor of either graph format: ActiveX Image or Java Image.

How styles work

A *style template* is the component of ODS that controls the appearance of your output. When SAS creates output with ODS, it tags the various parts of your output according to its function. For example, a report title is tagged as a System Title element, a data value within a table is tagged as a Data element, and a column heading is tagged as a Header element. Each style template can define dozens of stylistic elements.

With every piece of output tagged according to its function, the style template defines how to treat each output element with respect to its appearance. For example, a style's definition might state that a System Title should be left-aligned, use the Verdana typeface in 18-point bold, and have a white foreground with a navy blue background. The same style element in a different style template might use completely different formatting; SAS looks to the loaded template to determine how to format a given element.

ODS translates these style instructions as appropriate for each output destination that you specify. For HTML output, the style is usually controlled with Cascading Style Sheet (CSS) notation. For RTF and PDF, the documents contain formatting instructions using rich text codes and PostScript instructions, respectively.

SAS 9 includes about 40 built-in style templates, offering a variety of appearances and layouts that provide a good base for those users just getting started.

Savvy SAS users can create their own style templates, either from scratch or as variations of what SAS provides, using the SAS TEMPLATE procedure. For documentation on the TEMPLATE procedure and examples of its use, see the SAS Online Documentation at http://support.sas.com.

Power of the Palette: Creating Your Own Styles

If you use SAS Enterprise Guide, you aren't confined to the 40 or so built-in styles that ship with SAS. SAS Enterprise Guide provides a style editor tool that lets you create and modify your own styles for use with HTML and SAS Report results.

The geography of styles

SAS Enterprise Guide categorizes style definitions according to where those definitions reside. The three categories are

✔ **Built-in styles:** These are the styles provided with SAS and that are installed with SAS Enterprise Guide. Most of them correspond to ODS style templates that are built into SAS: hence, the descriptor *built in.*

✔ **External styles:** These can take the form of remote CSS files (referenced on a Web site, for example), or they might simply be names of customized ODS style templates defined for your SAS session. In either case, these are usually centrally located styles that someone else has defined for your use.

✔ **My Styles:** These are the styles that you create or modify within the Style Editor in SAS Enterprise Guide. They reside as CSS files in your personal profile area on your computer.

Sweetening your output with a custom style

To see how easy it is to transform the appearance of your output with a few simple style tweaks, follow these steps:

1. **Choose Tools⇨Style Manager.**

   The Style Manager screen appears, as shown in Figure 10-4, showing you a list of all the styles that you have available. From this window, you can manage all your style definitions, adding and deleting custom and external styles.

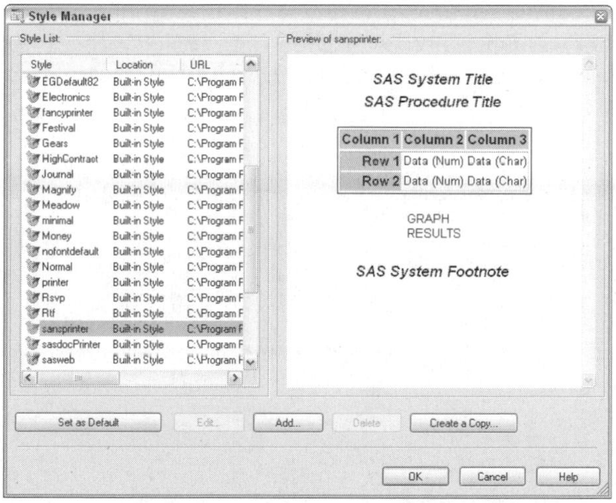

Figure 10-4:
Wow! That's a lot of styles to manage!

2. **Click Add.**

   The Add New Style dialog box appears, as shown in Figure 10-5.

   The Style Manager doesn't force you to start from scratch when creating a new style. Instead, you can select the existing style that most closely meets your needs and then use it as a template for a new style. The *sansprinter* style is a simple clean style that works well as a starting point for this example.

Figure 10-5:
The Add
New Style
screen.

3. **Select the Add New Based on Existing Style option, name the style (we named ours CandyBar), select sansprinter from the Based On field, and then click OK.**

   The list of styles in the Style Manager screen now contains one more: your style (the CandyBar style, in this case). Currently, it's an exact copy of the *sansprinter* style, but after a few more steps, it will be a true original.

4. **With your new style selected, click the Edit button.**

   The Style Editor screen appears, as shown in Figure 10-6. The left side of the screen contains a preview area to give you an idea of what your style will look like. However, this preview area is for more than just looking: You can click items within the preview area to activate a style element to edit, and then you can edit its attributes with the controls on the right side of the screen.

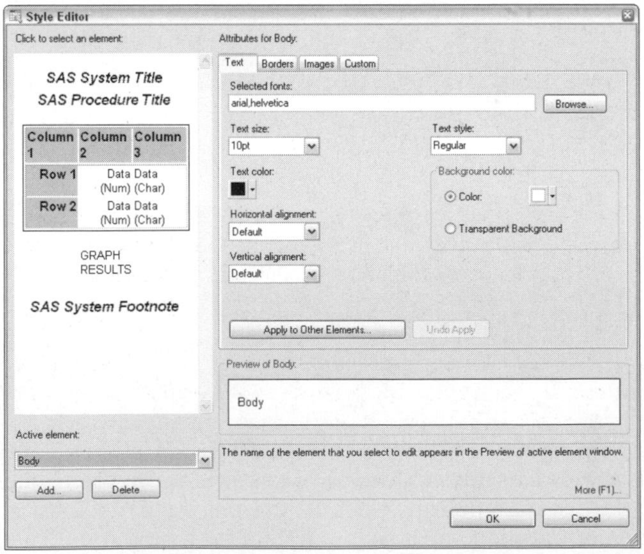

Figure 10-6:
The Style
Editor
screen with
the start of
your custom
style.

5. **For this example, click the words SAS System Title in the preview area.**

   Notice how the right side of the Style Editor window changes. The top label now reads `Attributes for System Title`, and all the text settings reflected in the controls within are those that apply to the System Title element. Because almost all reports contain a title, make your mark on this style by changing the title appearance.

6. **In the area next to the Selected Fonts field, click Browse.**

   The Browse Available Fonts dialog box appears. It contains two areas: a list of available fonts to choose from, and a list of the currently selected fonts.

7. **Scroll the Available Fonts list and select one (we chose Comic Sans MS), click the right arrow to add it to the Selected Fonts list, click the up arrow on the right to move Comic Sans MS to the top of the list to register that font as your "first choice" (as shown in Figure 10-7), and then click OK.**

   In the Style Editor window, the preview area on the left shows the font change in the SAS System Title, and the Selected Fonts field on the right shows the new font selection.

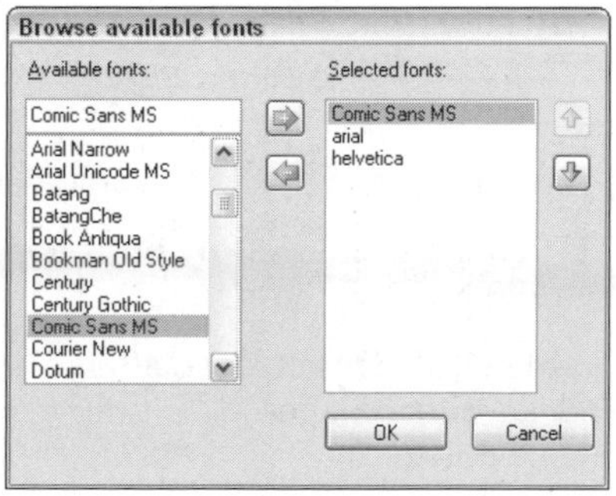

Figure 10-7:
The Browse
Available
Fonts
screen with
a new font
selection in
place.

8. **Click the down arrow next to the color block underneath the Text Color field. Then, in the palette of colors that appears, click a color block (such as the red block to select Red as the color).**

   The preview area shows the title in the color you choose.

You can repeat these steps for every element that you want to change, but that would get tedious after a few repetitions. Fortunately, the Style Editor contains a shortcut button that lets you apply the text settings for the current element to as many other elements as you want. In the following steps, see how to change a few other title-like elements to look just like the System Title.

9. **With System Title still as the active element, click the Apply to Other Elements button.**

The Apply to Other Elements dialog box appears, as shown in Figure 10-8. Here, all the available elements are listed on the left, and a preview area shows on the right.

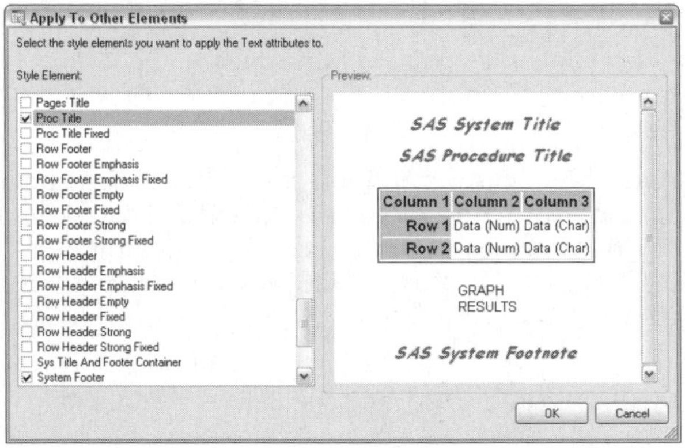

Figure 10-8:
The Apply to Other Elements screen helps you change many elements at once.

Apply To Other Elements

Select the style elements you want to apply the Text attributes to.

Style Element:

- [ ] Pages Title
- [✓] Proc Title
- [ ] Proc Title Fixed
- [ ] Row Footer
- [ ] Row Footer Emphasis
- [ ] Row Footer Emphasis Fixed
- [ ] Row Footer Empty
- [ ] Row Footer Fixed
- [ ] Row Footer Strong
- [ ] Row Footer Strong Fixed
- [ ] Row Header
- [ ] Row Header Emphasis
- [ ] Row Header Emphasis Fixed
- [ ] Row Header Empty
- [ ] Row Header Fixed
- [ ] Row Header Strong
- [ ] Row Header Strong Fixed
- [ ] Sys Title And Footer Container
- [✓] System Footer

Preview:

SAS System Title

SAS Procedure Title

Column 1	Column 2	Column 3
Row 1 Data (Num)	Data (Char)	
Row 2 Data (Num)	Data (Char)	

GRAPH
RESULTS

SAS System Footnote

OK   Cancel

10. **Scroll through the element list, find Proc Title, and then select the check box next to it. Repeat this step for System Footer and then click OK.**

The preview area of the Style Editor screen reflects the changes you made.

SAS Enterprise Guide provides a handy Undo Apply button in case you mistakenly apply changes to too many elements.

You could change so much more within this style to affect the text formatting, borders, and even background images — but move on to see how to use this style within your output.

11. **In the Style Editor window, click OK.**

12. **In the Style Manager window, with your style as the selected style, click the Set as Default button and then click OK to close the Style Manager window.**

Your style is set as the default style for HTML and SAS Report output that you create in SAS Enterprise Guide.

TIP

Two (or more) fonts are better than one

When creating a style for use with HTML reports that might be viewed from a Web browser, we recommend specifying a list of fonts (instead of just one font) to guarantee the best appearance everywhere. Why? Not every computer has all of the same fonts installed. You can list your preferred font first and then follow that with acceptable alternatives. Include a generic font type at the end of that list: serif, sans-serif, or monospace. That way, if none of your named fonts are available, at least the report will show a font from the same basic family of typefaces.

Mixing Style and Substance: Conveying Meaning with Style

SAS Enterprise Guide provides a few tasks that allow you extra control over the formats of your results. One example is the Summary Tables task, which uses the TABULATE procedure to enable you to enhance your output by applying special formatting to the table, headings, and data values.

In the following example, we show you how to create a simple tabular report to summarize candy sales across product categories. The bottom line is important, so you want to emphasize the totals. And because the numbers in the report represent dollars, you need to make sure that the proper currency format is applied. Here are the steps:

1. **Open the Candy_Sales_Summary sample table from the SAS Enterprise Guide sample data folder and choose Describe➪Summary Tables to open the task window.**

2. **On the Task Roles page, add the Sale_Amount column to the Analysis Variables role, add the Category column to the Classification role (as shown in Figure 10-9), and then click the Summary Tables item on the left pane to move to the next page.**

Figure 10-9:
Assigning
the columns
to use in a
report.

3. **On the Summary Tables page, click and drag the Category variable to the empty box on the left side of the Preview area and then release the mouse button, dropping the variable in place.**

   The table region should look like Figure 10-10.

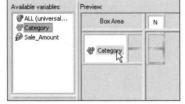

Figure 10-10:
The first
classifica-
tion variable
in place —
Category.

The table preview shows that the current report would produce a count of records (*N* is SAS shorthand for *number of observations*) that fall into each category. But you don't want to analyze the count; you want to analyze the sales in dollars.

4. **Repeat this motion for the Sale_Amount variable, dropping it on the rectangle at the top (just to the left side of the N).**

   The result should look like Figure 10-11.

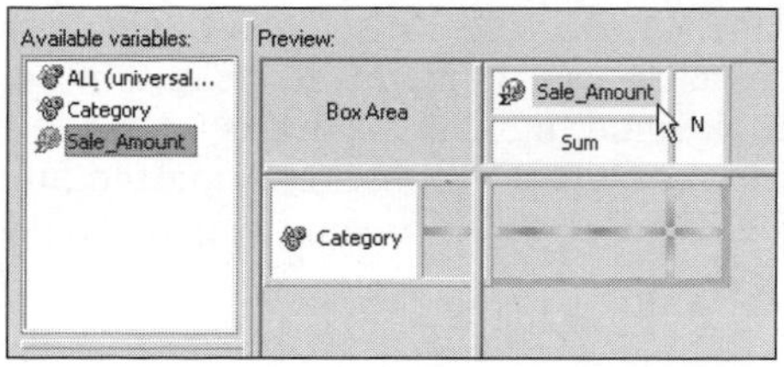

Figure 10-11:
Adding the
variable to
analyze.

Now the table preview shows the default analysis statistic, Sum, that
will be used in the report. Note that N is still off to the side as the last
column; you want to remove that.

 5. **Right-click the N column header and choose Remove Cells from the
    contextual menu.**

    The extra N column is dropped, resulting in the table shown in
    Figure 10-12.

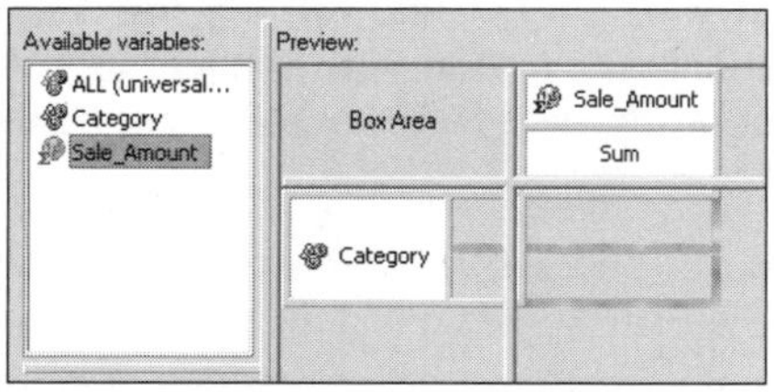

Figure 10-12:
The report
minus N is
a little bit
cleaner.

The table preview shows that the report contains sum of sales across
each category, but it still doesn't contain a row for the grand totals for
the categories combined.

 6. **Select the ALL variable; drag and drop it in the area just below
    Category in the left portion of the table.**

    The table now looks like Figure 10-13.

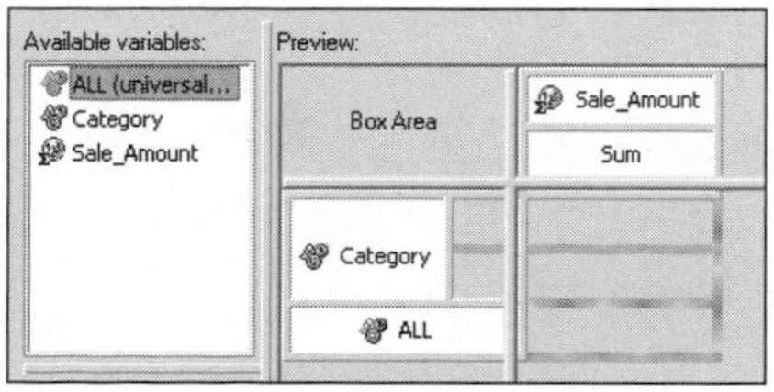

Figure 10-13:
ALL is now
in place at
the bottom.

All the content is in place: categories, statistic, and a totals line. However, if you run the task now, you might be disappointed with the results, which would look something like Figure 10-14. Sure, it has all the information, but it looks clunky with big unformatted numbers and some extra column labels. With a few more steps, you can give it a more professional appearance.

Figure 10-14:
First draft: Not bad, but nothing to brag about.

	Sale_Amount
	Sum
Category	
Candy	45855883.51
Nuts	29311816.22
All	75167699.73

7. **(Optional. If you didn't run the task yet, you can skip this step.) If you ran the task to see what it would look like, reopen the task by double-clicking the Summary Tables task within your project and then clicking the Summary Tables item on the left pane to get to the Summary Tables page.**

8. **Fix the appearance of the summary numbers by right-clicking the Sum box and choosing Heading Properties.**

   The Heading Properties dialog box appears, as shown in Figure 10-15.

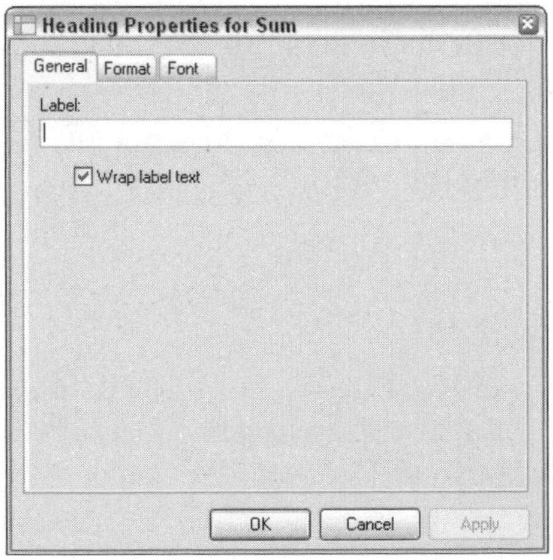

Figure 10-15:
Striking out the Sum heading.

Heading Properties for Sum

General | Format | Font

Label:

☑ Wrap label text

OK | Cancel | Apply

9. **Delete the Sum text from the Label field and then click OK to close this window.**

Why delete the text? When you blank out the label text, SAS omits that Sum title cell from your report table, making your report appear more concise.

10. **To apply a currency format to the data values, right-click the Sum box and choose Data Properties.**

The Data Value Properties window appears.

11. **Click the Format tab, choose the Currency category from the Categories list (as shown in Figure 10-16), and then choose DOLLARw.d from the Formats list.**

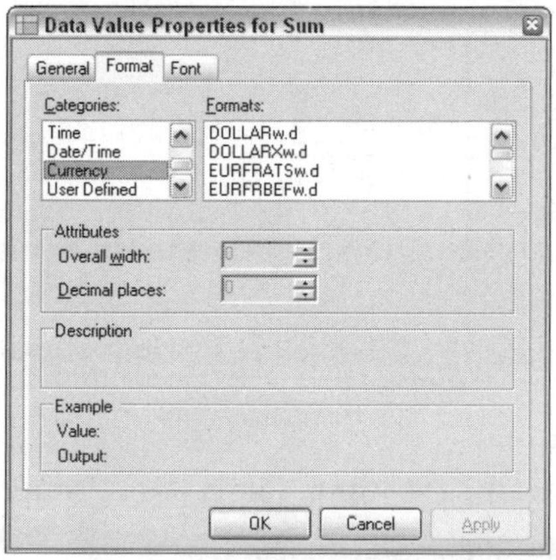

Figure 10-16: Making room for the big DOLLAR numbers: That's good, right?

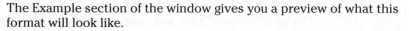

The totals are large (in the millions), so you need to increase the format width from its default size of six characters to give enough space for all the digits, comma separators, the decimal separator (a period), and the dollar sign.

For this report, don't worry about the cents column. Keep reading to see how to adjust the precision of the format.

12. **Change the Overall Width value to 15 to leave enough space for the big numbers, commas, and dollar sign. However, leave the Decimal Places value at 0. Click OK to close this window.**

The Example section of the window gives you a preview of what this format will look like.

Work on the bottom line of the report. Similar to the previous steps for the Sum values, you adjust the label and appearance of the ALL row.

13. **Right-click the ALL box and choose Heading Properties.**

    The Heading Properties dialog box appears.

14. **On the General tab, change the label value from ALL to Total Sales.**

15. **With the Heading Properties window still open, select the Font tab, select a Font Style of Bold and a Size of 4, and change the Foreground color to Dark Blue. Click OK to close this window.**

    The window should look something like Figure 10-17.

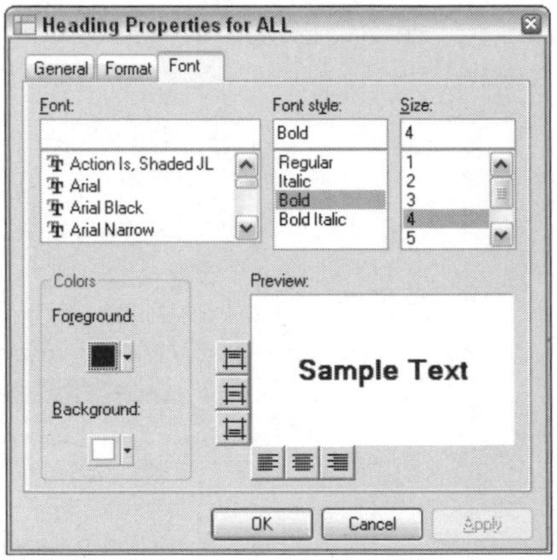

Figure 10-17:
Changing
the fonts
on the
bottom line.

16. **Right-click the ALL box again. This time, select Data Properties.**

    The Data Values Properties dialog box appears.

17. **Select the Font tab, change the Font Style to Bold Italic and the Size to 4, change the Foreground color to Dark Blue, and then click OK to close this window.**

    Just a few more steps, and this report will be all ready to go!

18. **To eliminate the Category heading, right-click Category and choose Heading Properties.**

    The Heading Properties dialog box appears.

19. **On the General tab, blank out the label field just like you did for the Sum heading, and then click OK to close this window.**

20. **To adjust the text of the Sales_Amount heading, right-click Sales_Amount in the table preview area and choose Heading Properties.**

    The Heading Properties dialog box appears once again.

21. **On the General tab, change the label to read simply Sales and then click OK to close this window.**

    After all your hard work, you're finally ready to view the final product!

22. **Click Run on the Summary Tables task window.**

    The resulting report should look something like Figure 10-18.

Figure 10-18:
The final
report, crisp
and clean.

	Sales
Candy	$45,855,884
Nuts	$29,311,816
Total Sales	*$75,167,700*

In addition to the TABULATE procedure, the other SAS procedures that offer similar formatting control include the PRINT procedure and the REPORT procedure. If you want to get fancy and invest some more time, you can even apply formatting to table values based on *exception rules.* For example, you can define SAS formats that change appearance when a value exceeds a certain threshold. SAS Enterprise Guide does not provide a point-and-click method for doing this, but the tools to make it happen are all baked into the FORMAT procedure (and you can read all about that in SAS online documentation).

Plain Text Is Not Dead Yet

As boring as plain text might seem — especially after reading about the exciting things you can do with styles — plain text reports remain in use in many places. Plain text (also known as *listing reports*) offers several advantages over some of the other output types:

- ✓ Output files are usually much smaller (in terms of disk space) than their fancier counterparts.

- ✓ Plain text makes it easy for other computer applications to process and parse the report results.

And who knows? Perhaps some companies have a huge investment in 132-column, green bar, fan-folding report paper and aren't quite ready to abandon it.

Figure 10-19 shows an example of a listing report in SAS Enterprise Guide.

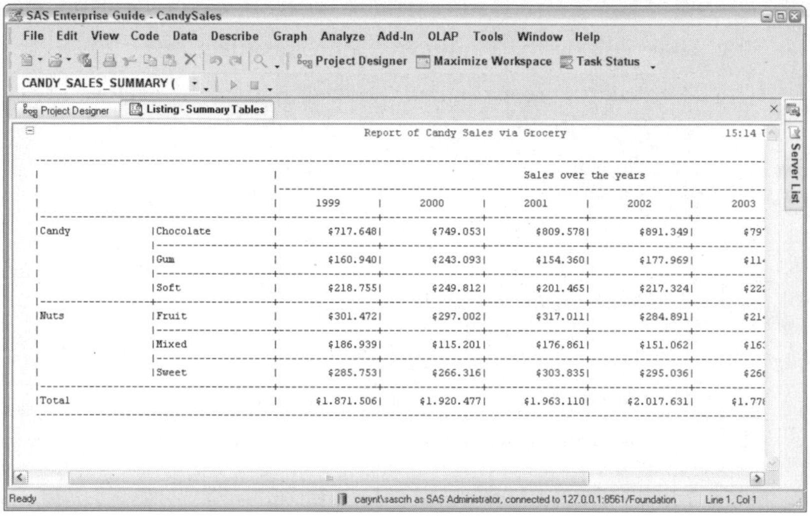

Figure 10-19:
A plain text
listing
report, as
reliable now
as it was 30
years ago.

Part IV
Enhancing and Sharing Your SAS Masterpieces

The 5th Wave   By Rich Tennant

"The top line represents our revenue, the middle line is our inventory, and the bottom line shows the rate of my hair loss over the same period."

In this part . . .

This part is where the rubber meets the road. Here, you can see how you can apply analytics and create reports in the place where you live. Do you spend all your time in Microsoft Excel? You can create SAS reports from the SAS Add-In for Microsoft Office. Are you equipped only with a Web browser? SAS Web Report Studio lets you create reports with only a few clicks. Do you need to process data and create reports to give to others? See how to use SAS Enterprise Guide on your desktop to analyze, report, and distribute your results — SAS programming is optional.

Chapter 11

Leveraging Work from SAS to Those Less Fortunate

In This Chapter

▶ Saving results

▶ Exporting data

▶ Having it your way with customized reports

▶ Portals: Your path to the rest of the world

▶ Stored processes: Dynamic content for everyone else

*I*t used to be that getting results from SAS meant getting results from SAS programmers. That is, your SAS results were only as accessible as the programmers/analysts in your organization. Bribes of cookies, candy, and caffeine were commonplace.

Fortunately, SAS tools now exist that allow you to not only perform your own analyses and create your own results but also help you share those results with the world (or at least the part of the world that you care about). In this chapter, you see how to use SAS Enterprise Guide to transform your SAS reports and data into something your audience can use. You can also read about the various ways you can deliver this information to your audience.

Pulling Out Results without Pulling Teeth

Using SAS Enterprise Guide to run SAS programs ensures that your results are captured within your SAS Enterprise Guide project. As you work, you might see dozens of output items within your project, including HTML, RTF, PDF, and SAS data sets. When you save your project on your computer, however, only one file is created. This file is a SAS Enterprise Guide *project file,* which carries an .egp file extension, and it contains the collection of everything you've done.

What makes "temporary" data temporary?

"Nothing is permanent," to quote Buddha. Still, some things are less permanent than others. In SAS, *temporary data* is data that is stored in a temporary location. SAS *libraries* — the folder-like structures where SAS stores data — can be defined in such a way that they exist only for the duration of your SAS session. Every SAS session has at least one temporary library named WORK. The contents of WORK are discarded when you exit the SAS application (or when you close SAS Enterprise Guide, as in our examples).

When you reopen the project file, all your work is still visible in the project. You can open many of your results, such as HTML output. However, some of your output data might be inaccessible even though a placeholder item still exists in the project for it.

The reason: Working with SAS tasks and programs sometimes results in *temporary data:* that is, data that doesn't persist across SAS Enterprise Guide sessions. Figure 11-1 shows a project flow that contains a reference to temporary data (joined_cust_products). In this example, the temporary data is a means to an end; it doesn't represent the final result but instead serves as a sort of scratch pad to help on the way.

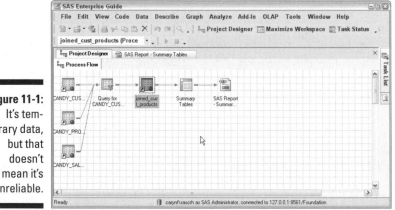

Figure 11-1:
It's temporary data, but that doesn't mean it's unreliable.

Most of the time, it's okay that you have some temporary data referenced in your project. After all, a project is like a recipe for how to cook up interesting results, and that recipe is the valuable part of your hard work. With that intact, you can rerun your project — and once again, like magic, your temporary data rematerializes and is available for your use.

Exporting results, duty-free

When viewing your results in SAS Enterprise Guide, capturing a snapshot of the results is as simple as choosing File⇨Export. This works for HTML, PDF, RTF, and even output data sets.

When you export HTML results, the result is an HTML file that you can view or send or place on a Web site. Similarly, when you export PDF and RTF results, you end up with files of each respective type. However, when you export data, you have many more options:

✔ **Export SAS data as SAS data sets (of course).**

✔ **Transform data as part of the export process.** SAS Enterprise Guide can export data in a variety of formats, including Microsoft Excel; text-based formats, such as comma-separated or tab-delimited values; and even older file formats, such as dBase or Lotus 1-2-3.

When sharing SAS data with people who don't have access to SAS applications, Microsoft Excel is by far the most popular file format. Use SAS Enterprise Guide to show a simple example of transforming SAS data into the spreadsheet vernacular.

1. **Open the Candy_Sales_Summary table from the SAS Enterprise Guide sample folder.**

   The table is added to the current project and opens in the data view.

2. **Choose File⇨Export⇨Export Candy_Sales_Summary.**

   The Export *filename* To window appears, as shown in Figure 11-2.

Figure 11-2:
The first
question
when
exporting
data: local
or long
distance?

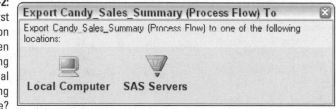

This window offers a choice between

- *Local Computer:* Anywhere on your computer or on your local network

- *SAS Servers:* Any remote SAS server that you have access to

The choice you make here determines whether you see the familiar file window that you see in other applications when you save files, or instead see a window specific to SAS that lets you navigate to a remote SAS server. Because the objective of this example is to create a spreadsheet file that you can work with on your computer, act locally (but keep thinking globally!).

3. **Select Local Computer by clicking the icon.**

   The Export window appears.

4. **From the Save as Type drop-down list, choose Microsoft Excel Files (*.xls).**

   The list offers over a dozen different types of files.

5. **Use the Export window to navigate to the location where you want to store the file (for example, somewhere in My Documents).**

6. **(Optional) Change the name of the file in the File Name field.**

   You do not have to specify the .xls extension; SAS Enterprise Guide adds that for you.

7. **Click Save.**

   The window closes, and SAS Enterprise Guide saves the file as a Microsoft Excel spreadsheet file. It might take a minute or two for the export operation to complete.

The EXPORT tax in SAS

For years, SAS has offered an EXPORT procedure so that programmers can include the export step as part of their SAS programs. This can make exporting SAS data to a text file convenient — for example, in comma-separated values (CSV) form — while running SAS programs in a batch environment. However, in order to use PROC EXPORT to transform SAS data to a Microsoft Excel file, you must have an additional SAS product module installed on your SAS server: namely, SAS/ACCESS to PC File Formats. This product module is not part of the basic SAS package; you must license it separately.

One of the most common questions posed by SAS programmers who begin using SAS Enterprise Guide is whether they need SAS/ACCESS to PC File Formats in order to export SAS data to Microsoft Excel. The answer is no. Instead of using PROC EXPORT, SAS Enterprise Guide uses built-in data access components to transform the data to third-party data files.

These steps result in a spreadsheet file that you can share with anyone who has Microsoft Excel. It isn't difficult to accomplish, but this can get tedious if it's something you need to do often. The next section looks at ways to automate the process.

Export as a step: Baking it into the recipe

Imagine that you design a tremendous project in SAS Enterprise Guide. It's a project that has something for everybody: for example, a summary report for Stan in Sales, a series of charts for Mel in Marketing, and output data table for Alice in Accounting. Just rerun the project each week to refresh the results with the latest data.

Oh, and you need also to get the information out and delivered to the people who need it. Perhaps Stan prefers PDF files delivered to his mailbox whereas Mel needs HTML for his Web site. And Alice, of course, needs a spreadsheet file for the data to be of any use to her.

SAS Enterprise Guide has a feature that lets you "bake in" the process for saving files outside of your project file and then replay those processes each time that you run your project. Figure 11-3 shows an example project with these types of steps included.

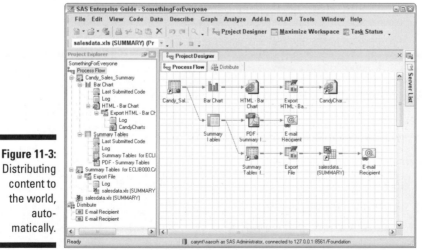

Figure 11-3:
Distributing content to the world, automatically.

Here's how to break down the work in this project:

1. First, the Bar Chart task creates an HTML result.

2. Next is an Export step, which saves the HTML file (and any images that it contains) to a file location on the network, hopefully to a location where Mel can access it.

3. Next is a Summary Tables task that produces two items: a PDF report and an output data set.

4. The PDF report feeds into the E-mail Recipient step so that it can be sent to Stan.

5. The output data set feeds into an Export step, transforming the file from a SAS data set to a Microsoft Excel spreadsheet file.

6. The spreadsheet file then leads into the E-mail Recipient step, sending the file to Alice in Accounting.

Each time you run this project, all the steps run with it. SAS Enterprise Guide uses SAS to create the reports and then automatically distributes the output using Export and E-mail steps.

Before you can use SAS Enterprise Guide to send e-mail on your behalf, you need to configure some options to teach SAS Enterprise Guide about your e-mail system. The options are set in Tools⟹Options, within the E-mail Settings page (last page of the Options window). You might need help from a system administrator to determine the correct values for your e-mail server settings.

The following example shows you how to create a step to automatically e-mail a PDF report. The steps in this example assume that you already have a project with a PDF result. In fact, these steps will work for any type of result, including RTF or HTML.

1. **Click the item in your project that represents the PDF result.**

   For example, in the project shown in Figure 11-3, the PDF result is the one labeled PDF - Summary Tables.

2. **Choose File⟹Send To⟹E-Mail Recipient as a Step in Project.**

   The Send window appears, as shown in Figure 11-4.

   Initially, the Send window contains a list of just the one item that you intend to send.

   You can use the Add button to select additional files to attach to the e-mail message. These additional files can come from within your project, or they might be files located on your computer or on a remote SAS server.

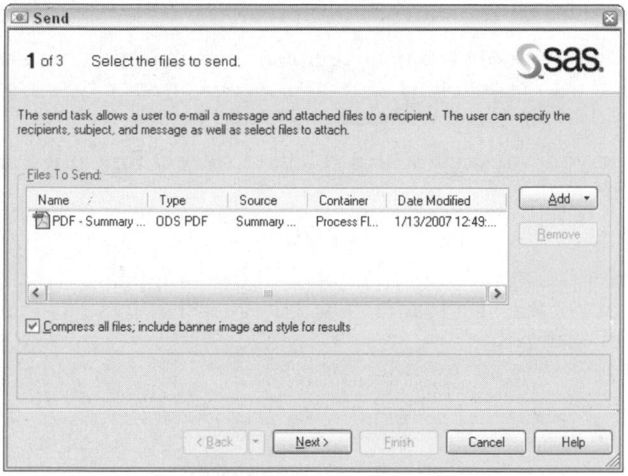

Figure 11-4:
All the
results
that are fit
to mail.

Notice the Compress All Files check box at the bottom. With this option enabled, SAS Enterprise Guide compresses all the attached files into a Zip archive file. Your intended recipients, especially those with limited network bandwidth, will thank you for delivering big results in a smaller package.

3. Click Next.

The second page of the Send window appears, as shown in Figure 11-5. This is the page where you complete all the e-mail related information.

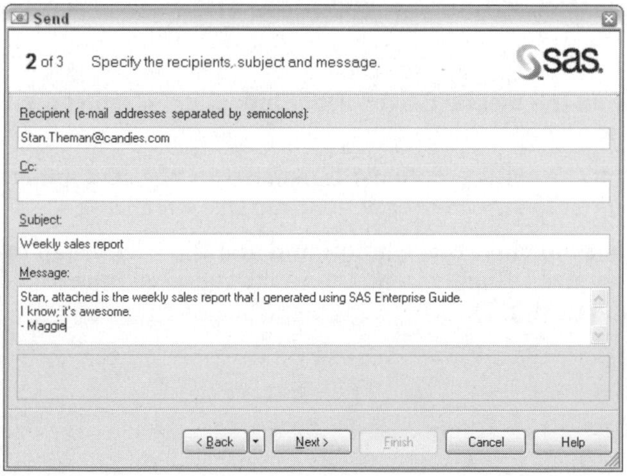

Figure 11-5:
Fill out the
address and
write the
note. Don't
forget to lick
the stamp!

4. **Add an e-mail address for the Recipient.**

   You can specify more than one recipient by separating the e-mail addresses with semicolons. Optionally, you can specify one or more e-mail addresses in the Cc field in the same way.

5. **Complete your message with a relevant subject line and a short message body.**

6. **Click Next.**

   The third page — the confirmation window — appears. This page shows a summary of the files to attach and the message to send. Figure 11-6 shows an example.

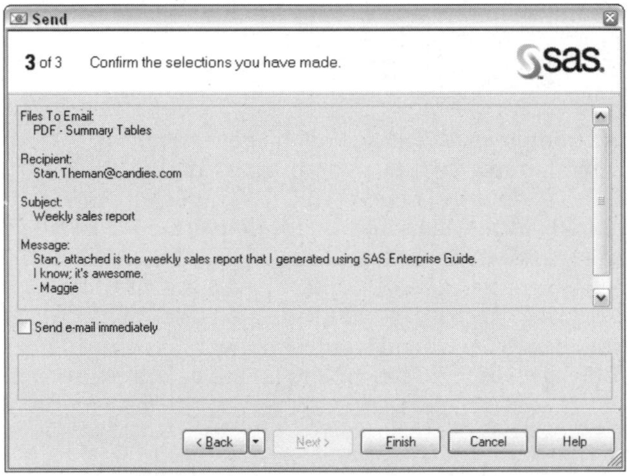

Send

3 of 3   Confirm the selections you have made.   §sas.

Files To Email:
    PDF - Summary Tables

Recipient:
    Stan.Theman@candies.com

Subject:
    Weekly sales report

Message:
    Stan, attached is the weekly sales report that I generated using SAS Enterprise Guide.
    I know; it's awesome.
    - Maggie

☐ Send e-mail immediately

    ‹ Back [▾]   Next ›   Finish   Cancel   Help

Figure 11-6:
Double-check before you send it.

---

7. **If you want the message to be sent immediately, select the Send E-mail Immediately check box.**

   If you don't select this option, the e-mail won't be sent until the next time you run the project (or at least run this e-mail step).

8. **Click Finish to close this window and add the e-mail step to your project (and, optionally, send the e-mail message immediately, as described in Step 7).**

Getting content to the channel surfers

SAS can distribute information through channels. Think of a *channel* as simply a location to store information, where people in your organization can subscribe to the content that interests them (and that they are permitted to see). Channel content is similar to an e-mail distribution list except that it's not limited to e-mail. Channel content can also appear within intranet portals. SAS offers one such portal: the SAS Information Delivery Portal.

If your organization has a portal infrastructure with configured channels, you can use SAS Enterprise Guide to push your content out to the channel-surfing audience.

The process is similar to the export and e-mail steps described earlier:

1. **Select the content you want to share.**

2. **Click the item in your project that you want to publish and then choose File⇨Publish to Channels.**

   The Publish window appears, as shown in Figure 11-7.

Figure 11-7:
The Publish
window.

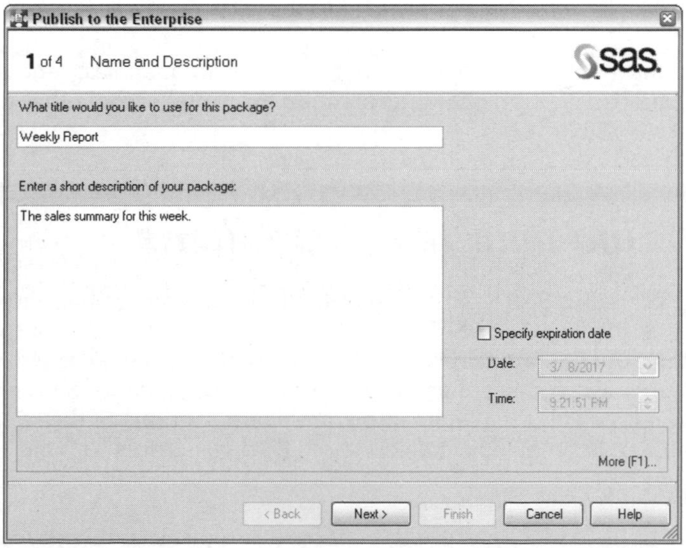

Publish to the Enterprise

1 of 4   Name and Description   §sas.

What title would you like to use for this package?

Weekly Report

Enter a short description of your package:

The sales summary for this week.

☐ Specify expiration date

Date: 3/ 8/2017

Time: 9:21:51 PM

More (F1)...

‹ Back   Next ›   Finish   Cancel   Help

3. **Configure options in the Publish window to describe the "package" you want to publish.**

4. **Select a channel and add additional content to include.**

   The Publish step is added to your project; your updated content is republished each time you run your project.

Using Only the Good Bits: Assembling Reports in a Snap

People of a certain age will remember spending too much time making "mix tapes" to collect all their favorite songs in one place. You could spend hours pulling the best songs from your favorite albums in order to make an audio cassette that contained just the songs you wanted, played in the order that you wanted to hear them.

What if you could make a "mix report" in the same way, using SAS output? You could take the most interesting tables and charts from various tasks within your SAS Enterprise Guide project and then assemble them into a single, concise report that you want to share with the world.

It turns out that HTML and SAS Report formats are malleable enough to make this possible, and SAS Enterprise Guide contains tools that can help you.

Selecting your mix ingredients

When SAS creates SAS Report or HTML output, it divides that output into sections according to the SAS procedures that created it. The output from a single task can contain tables, charts, or a combination of the two. As you view the results, you see them as a single document, but SAS Enterprise Guide can break up the results into component sections in the same way that a child can break up a collection of LEGO structures to build a new masterpiece.

With the tools in SAS Enterprise Guide, you can disassemble those sections and reassemble them in a form that makes sense to your audience.

For example, you can take portions of results from different tasks — a table here, a plot there, a chart from over there — and recombine them into a single coherent document.

After you complete this work once, your project then contains a *recipe* that points to its component ingredients. When you rerun the tasks that make up the document, the document is automatically refreshed with the latest results. You can then export or e-mail the completed document by using the techniques discussed earlier in this chapter.

Before you get started on this adventure, you have a decision to make: Will you use HTML or SAS Report format?

Use HTML when

- ✔ The report must be shared on the Web (in a Web browser).
- ✔ You don't need much control over the exact layout of the report.

Use SAS Report when

- ✔ You intend to print this report, and you want control over the page layout, sizes, and printing options.
- ✔ You need extra control over the report layout, including flexibility to arrange tables and charts horizontally as well as vertically.
- ✔ You need to resize charts to make them fit better.
- ✔ You intend to share this report with others using SAS Web Report Studio.
- ✔ You do *not* need an HTML version of the report for users who do not have SAS to view.

HTML Document Builder: Stacking it up for the Web

To get started with the HTML Document Builder, create or open a SAS Enterprise Guide project with at least one task or program that creates an HTML result. Then choose Tools➪Create HTML Document to launch the Document Builder window. Figure 11-8 shows an example of the Document Builder window with some content already selected.

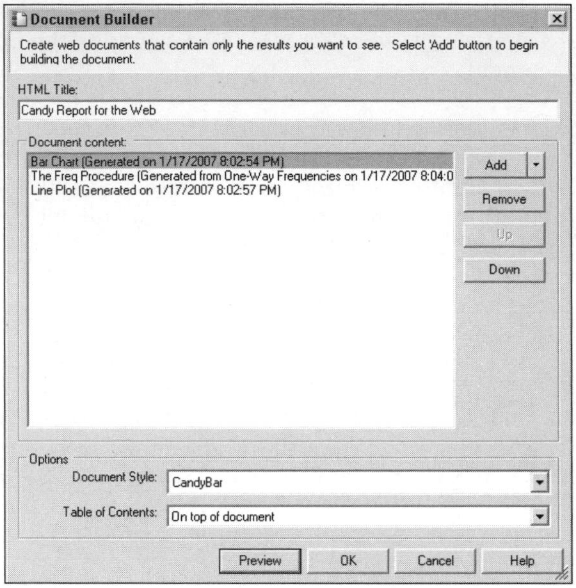

Figure 11-8:
Document
building; no
cellophane
tape is
necessary.

To select additional content for the document, click Add. You can add sections of HTML output that you have in your project. You can also add notes and links to external documents. Figure 11-9 shows the Add Results window with a list of all of the available HTML results in your project.

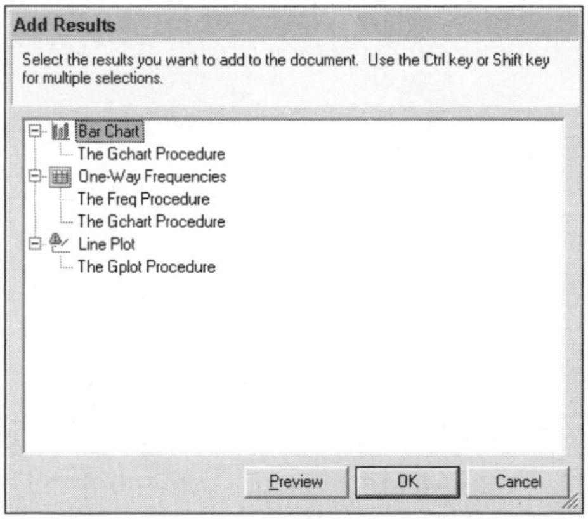

Figure 11-9:
All the HTML
results that
are fit to
print.

Creating reports suitable for framing

SAS Enterprise Guide has always had the ability to arrange HTML; it's a capability that is both utilitarian and effective.

In contrast, arranging SAS Report output within SAS Enterprise Guide can be downright fun. Why? Because you can

- ✔ Interact with your report by dragging pieces into place.
- ✔ Add and resize elements, such as charts and images.
- ✔ Add and apply formatting to titles and other text.

To build a new report with SAS Report results, create or open a SAS Enterprise Guide project with at least one task or program that creates SAS Report output. Then choose File⇨New⇨Report. A window similar to the one shown in Figure 11-10 appears.

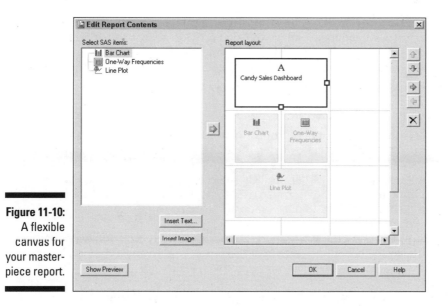

Figure 11-10:
A flexible canvas for your masterpiece report.

Practicing feng shui in report design

As you can see in Figure 11-10, all your eligible SAS Report items appear on the left part of the window in the Select SAS Items section. The right side of the window shows the report layout in a grid canvas.

To add SAS Report items to your report, simply click an item on the left and drag it over to the right, dropping it on a grid cell. (As an alternative to drag and drop, you can also use the arrow buttons to move an item over and then arrange it within the grid.)

After items are in the grid, you can arrange them by clicking them and dragging them around. You can stack them vertically, and you can arrange them side by side (horizontally). Although it might not seem like a big deal to those new to SAS, many SAS programmers regard side-by-side output, such as placing a chart next to a table, as sort of the "cold fusion" of SAS reporting. That is, everyone suspects that it's theoretically possible but only a select few can reliably achieve it. This report builder window sets out to change that perception.

You can also annotate the report with additional items such as text and images. The Insert Text and Insert Image buttons provide access to windows that allow you to specify and format text, or select an image file, and place those in the report grid. After these items are added, you can arrange them in the same way you arrange the other items on the grid.

Harmony is just a few clicks away

To affect the placement and proportion of the items within the report layout, you can "stretch" an item by using the mouse to grab its handles and resize it. For example, the Candy Sales Dashboard text item in Figure 11-10 has been resized to span the Bar Chart and One-Way Frequencies items, ensuring that it will appear centered over those two items. Likewise, the Line Plot item spans the bottom portion of the report.

Figure 11-11 shows the final report, appearing exactly as it will when you print it. Notice how the elements of the report are arranged just the same as they appear in the New Report window in Figure 11-10.

When you re-run your project, the report refreshes with the most current content while also retaining the layout you worked so hard to achieve.

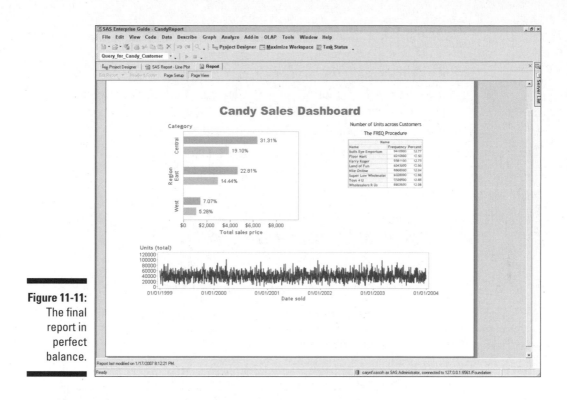

Figure 11-11:
The final
report in
perfect
balance.

Canning Your Work for Others to Use in Stored Processes

If you've read this chapter to this point, you've seen how to use SAS Enterprise Guide to push the fruits of your labor out to the world. But what if you work with people who want to pick their own fruit?

As a person who provides SAS content for others, your goal is to equip your audience with access to relevant and correct information, without necessarily burdening them with all the details of how it came to be.

This sounds like a job for . . . stored processes!

A *stored process* is fundamentally a SAS program, but it's a special SAS program because

- ✔ It's stored in a central location.
- ✔ It contains information about parameters and prompts, so the results can be tailored each time you run it.
- ✔ It's secured, so you can control who can access/run it.
- ✔ It runs from a variety of environments, including within your Web browser, SAS Web Report Studio, Microsoft Office, and SAS Enterprise Guide.

Almost like cloning yourself

A *stored process* is a SAS program that you can publish for others to run in the environment that makes sense for them. Your audience doesn't need to know anything about SAS programming or building SAS Enterprise Guide projects in order to benefit from your stored processes. All your viewers need to know is how to answer the prompts that you can build into the stored process to customize their results.

It's like packaging up a little bit of your smarts so that others can access it anytime, from anywhere, to get answers to the specific questions that you design into the process. And after you publish it, it can all happen without further intervention from you.

Distilling the complex down to the simple

Stored processes are a great way to take a process with many parts and boil it down to a single step. For example, consider the project flow shown in Figure 11-12.

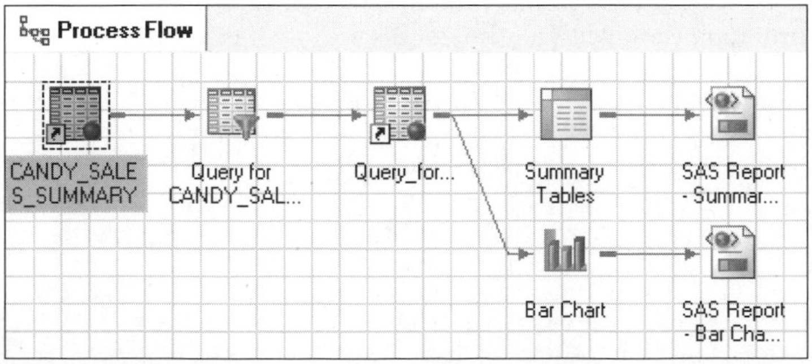

Figure 11-12: A project with a few too many steps for some people.

You can see that it starts out with some data (Candy_Sales_Summary) and then passes it through a query step. The output of the query is then used for a summary tables report and a bar chart. The part you don't see is that the query contains a filter that references two parameters, which allows you to specify the sales region and product category when you run the project. All in all, it's a nice little project that offers some flexibility at run time, which is great as long as you're willing to always run it with SAS Enterprise Guide.

To share this work with others who don't use SAS Enterprise Guide or even use SAS at all, you can create a stored process. To get started

1. **Right-click an empty spot on the process flow canvas and choose Create Stored Process.**

   The Create New SAS Stored Process Wizard appears, similar to Figure 11-13.

   Notice that the title indicates that this screen is the first of eight steps! Don't worry; it won't take very long to step through them all. The first page of this wizard is for general information.

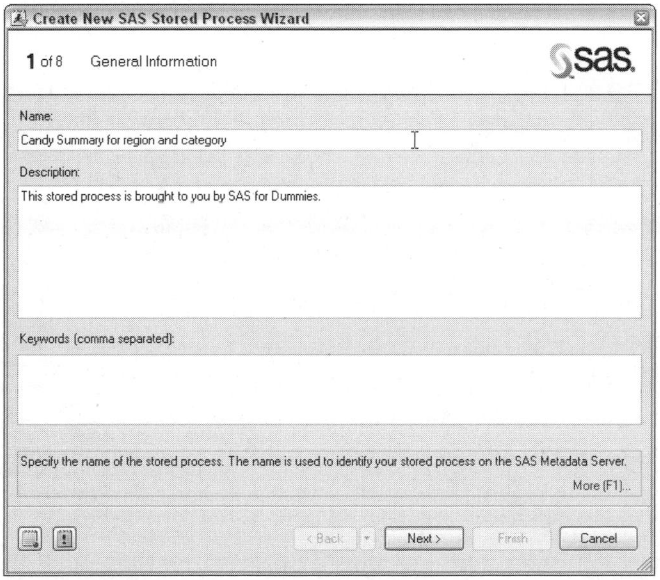

Figure 11-13: The start of the Create Stored Process Wizard.

2. **Name your stored process and provide a description.**

   The optional Keywords field is useful only in environments that allow you to search for content (such as the SAS Information Delivery Portal).

3. **After you name your stored process, click Next.**

   The second page of the wizard (as shown in Figure 11-14) displays the SAS code that is going to be the core of the stored process. In this case, SAS Enterprise Guide generated the code within the flow, so nothing further is needed here.

Figure 11-14:
The "process" part of your stored process: the SAS program.

```
Create New SAS Stored Process Wizard                              ⊠

 2 of 8    SAS Code                                          §sas.

  -------------------------------------------------------- */
  ⊟ PROC TABULATE
     DATA=WORK.QUERY_FOR_CANDY_SALES_SUMMARY
                                                          I
       ;
       VAR Sale_Amount;
       CLASS Fiscal_Year / ORDER=UNFORMATTED MISSING;
       TABLE /* Row Dimension */
  Fiscal_Year
  ALL={LABEL='Total' STYLE={FONT_SIZE=3 FONT_WEIGHT=MEDIUM FONT_STYLE=ITALIC}
  /* Column Dimension */
  Sale_Amount*
     Sum={LABEL=''}*F=DOLLAR15.0      ;
       ;

  ◄                        ||                           ►

  [ Replace with code  ▼ ] [ Include code for  ▼ ] [ Clear code ] [ Reset code ]

                                                      More (F1)..

  [□] [□]                      [ < Back ] [▼] [ Next > ] [ Finish ] [ Cancel ]
```

---

4. **Optionally, experienced SAS programmers can use this screen to change the code to alter the stored process behavior.**

5. **When your eyes glaze over from staring at the SAS code, click Next.**

   The third page of the wizard (as shown in Figure 11-15) lets you select the desired location of the stored process. You can select a location from the folder structure defined in your SAS environment.

6. **Specify a location for your stored process and then click Next.**

   Page 4 of the wizard is where you can specify what stored process server to use and where to store the SAS program. Figure 11-16 shows an example of this screen with all the fields completed. Your options here depend heavily on how the SAS environment is configured in your organization. The good news is that after you make these selections for one stored process, SAS Enterprise Guide remembers these preferences for your next visit to this window.

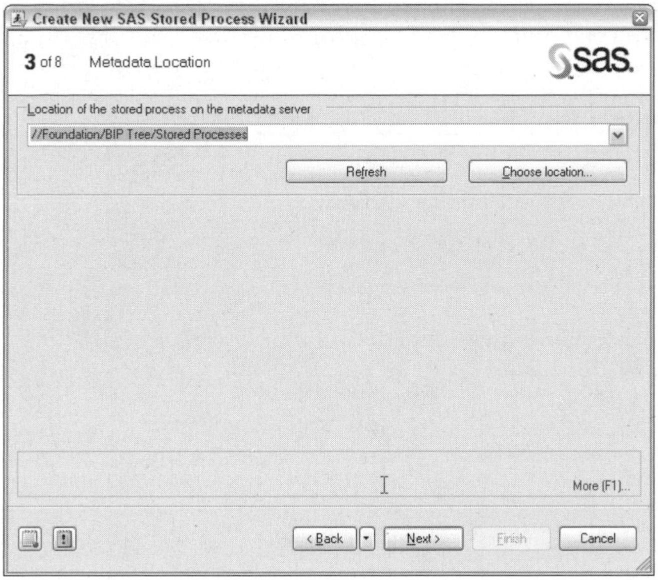

Figure 11-15:
Location, location, location: putting the "stored" in "stored process."

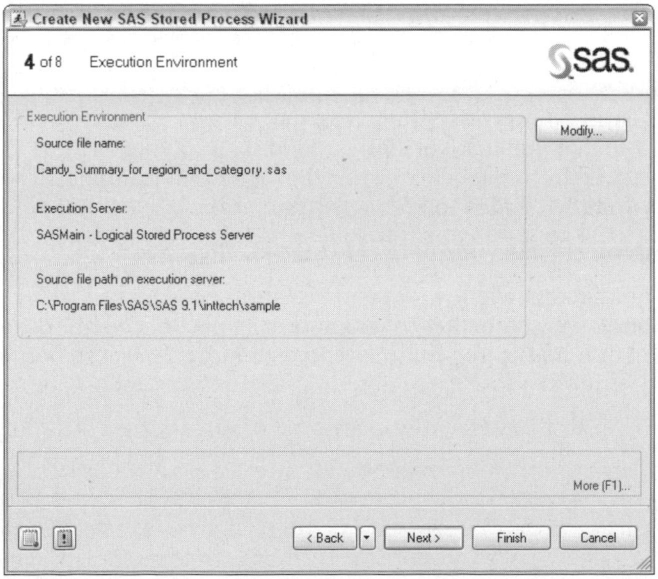

Figure 11-16:
The Execution Environment window. You can survive it.

7. **Select the options for your stored process and then click Next.**

The Librefs window appears, as shown in Figure 11-17. This window is actually one of the smartest parts of this wizard. This screen shows you the data references that you use in your project flow, and it gives you the chance to adjust those references if necessary to run in the stored process environment.

Create New SAS Stored Process Wizard

5 of 8   Librefs

§sas.

Library	LIBNAME statement
☑ Sample Data	Libname SAMPLE V9 'c:\program files\sas\enterprise guide 4\sample\data'
☐ WORK	<SAS built-in library, no LIBNAME statement required>

☑ Include LIBNAME statement in SAS code

Library Name: Sample Data

Type: INPUT

Host name: 19692.na.sas.com

☐ Use custom LIBNAME statement

Libname SAMPLE V9 'c:\program files\sas\enterprise guide 4\sample\data'

More (F1)...

< Back   Next >   Finish   Cancel

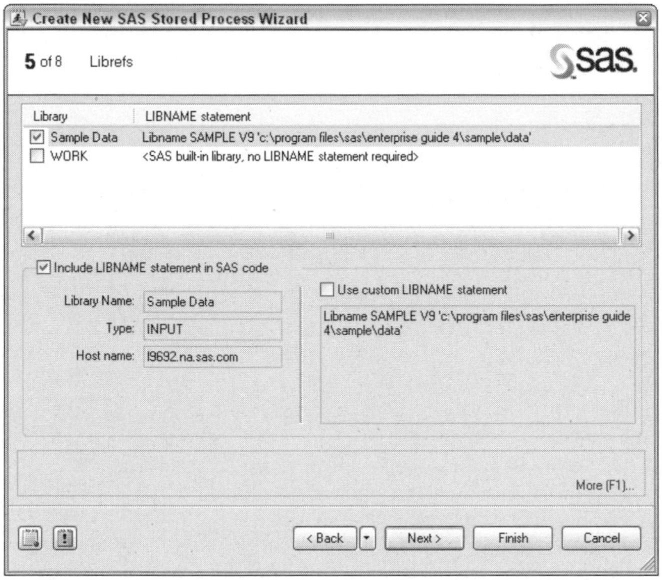

Figure 11-17: Do you know where your data comes from?

Because SAS Enterprise Guide can make it easy to access data, it's very possible that you inadvertently added data to your project that cannot be reached from the central stored process environment. This window gives you the chance to reconcile that.

8. **After you review your data references, click Next.**

The Parameters window appears, as shown in Figure 11-18. Because this project contained two parameters as part of the query step, the wizard automatically promotes those to stored process parameters, or prompts.

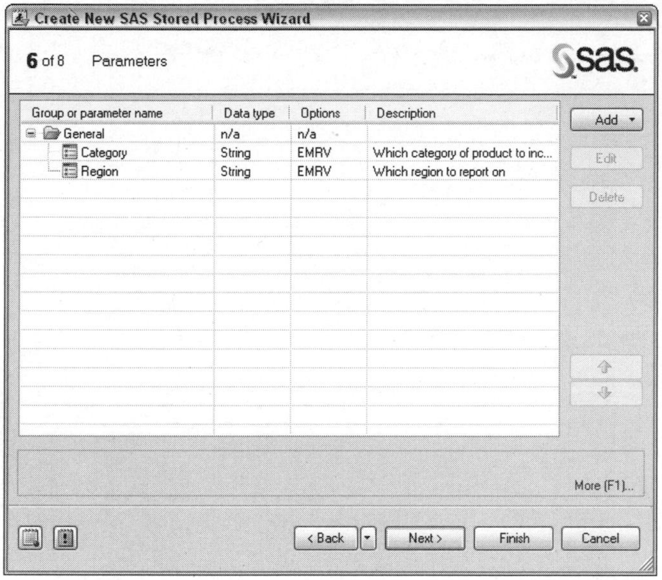
Create New SAS Stored Process Wizard
6 of 8 Parameters
sas.
Group or parameter name
Data type
Options
Description
General
n/a
n/a
Category
String
EMRV
Which category of product to inc...
Region
String
EMRV
Which region to report on
Add
Edit
Delete
More (F1)...
< Back
Next >
Finish
Cancel

Figure 11-18: Parameters now, prompted report later.

9. **Using the controls onscreen, you can add more parameters and adjust the properties of those that are already defined.**

   Stored processes with parameters are the key to supplying your audience with *prompted reports* — reports that can be customized at run time by gathering answers to simple questions. This example has two parameters: one for the product category (candy or nuts), and one for the region (East, West, and Central).

10. **Click Next to get to the output options.**

    The Output Options and Input Streams window appears, as shown in Figure 11-19. Unless you're creating a stored process to run in a special environment, you don't need to change anything in this window. The Transient Package of Files option should be selected; most of the time, you can leave it that way.

11. **Click Next to move to the final screen.**

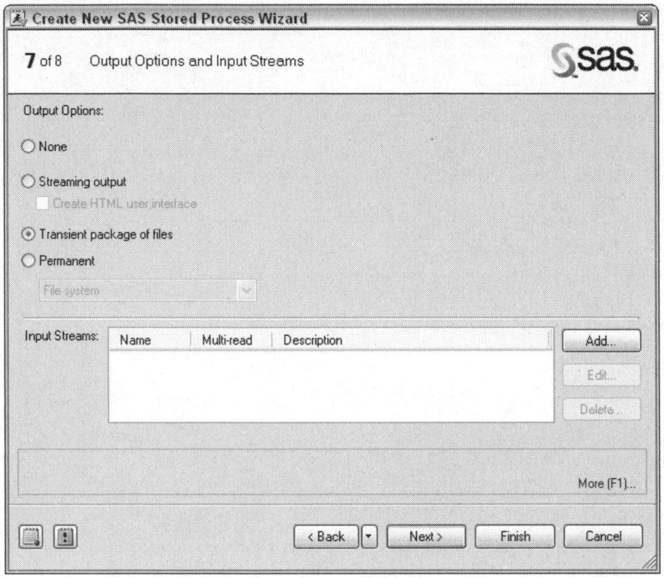

Output Options:

○ None

○ Streaming output

☐ Create HTML user interface

⊙ Transient package of files

○ Permanent

File system ▾

Input Streams: Name   Multi-read   Description   Add...

Edit...

Delete...

More (F1)...

< Back ▾   Next >   Finish   Cancel

Figure 11-19:
Just clicking
through;
nothing to
change
here.

The last screen is a summary of all the options you specified in this wizard, as shown in Figure 11-20.

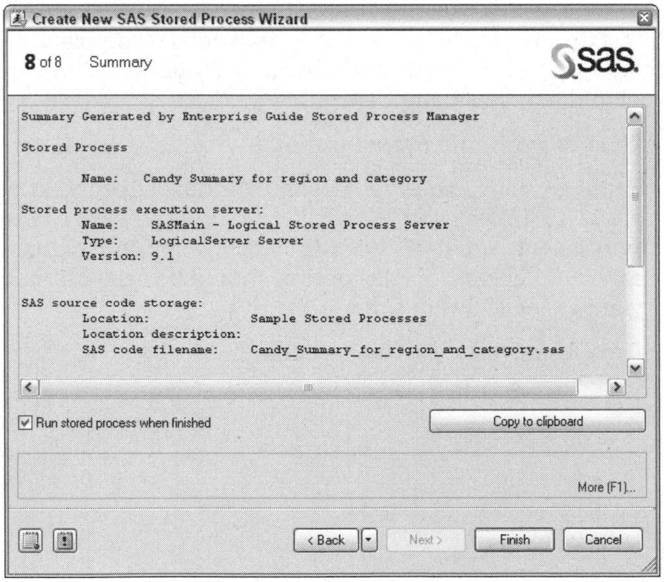

```
Summary Generated by Enterprise Guide Stored Process Manager

Stored Process

      Name:    Candy Summary for region and category

Stored process execution server:
      Name:    SASMain - Logical Stored Process Server
      Type:    LogicalServer Server
      Version: 9.1


SAS source code storage:
      Location:            Sample Stored Processes
      Location description:
      SAS code filename:   Candy_Summary_for_region_and_category.sas
```

☑ Run stored process when finished   Copy to clipboard

More (F1)...

< Back ▾   Next >   Finish   Cancel

Figure 11-20:
Finally, it's
complete!

12. **You can review the text of the summary if you want, or you can click Finish and hope for the best!**

    SAS Enterprise Guide adds the completed stored process to your project. If the Run Stored Process When Finished check box is selected, it runs immediately. If it contains any parameters, you are presented with the prompts as it runs. Figure 11-21 shows an example of the prompt window.

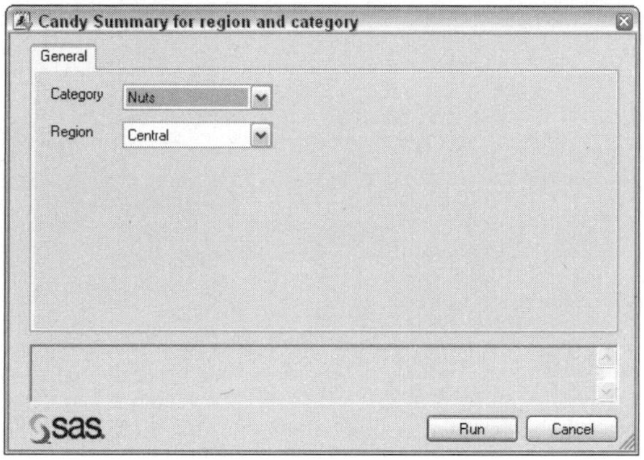

Figure 11-21: The stored process at run time.

With the stored process registered for use, other people can now use it in other applications. Congratulations on making the world a better place by sharing your brilliance!

Chapter 12

OLAP: Impressing Your Co-workers

Detailed historical or transactional data is useful for reporting and statistical analysis. In the real world, this data can grow to very large sizes with companies having millions or even billions of records on just one topic, such as sales transactions or customer history. As data grows to very large sizes, even systems like SAS can be slower than you might like, especially for data exploration where you want to ask multiple related questions of the data in quick succession.

OLAP (Online Analytic Processing) is a technology that pre-summarizes, stores, and accesses the data in a much more compact format than standard data tables (such as Microsoft Excel, Microsoft Access, or Oracle tables). With OLAP, a billion-row table that takes five minutes to access in a traditional manner can be accessed from an OLAP aggregated form in a matter of seconds. SAS provides a server for storing your data as OLAP data, appropriately named the SAS OLAP Server. SAS Enterprise Guide can leverage the powerful capabilities of the SAS OLAP Server in a variety of ways.

This chapter covers the basics of OLAP access and analysis with SAS Enterprise Guide.

Who Invited All the Cubes?

OLAP data is stored in two generic forms to enable great speed and simplicity of access: dimensions and measures.

- A *dimension* is a logical grouping of data used for the same purpose. Examples of commonly used dimensions include geography, time, and customer. Geography, as a dimension, could have multiple levels of the dimension that are available for your analysis. *Levels*, which are organized as a hierarchy of the most encompassing grouping to least encompassing grouping of the data for a given dimension, could be set as continent, country, state, and city.

- *Measures* are data attributes or facts that can be counted, added, summed, or averaged. Examples of measures include sales amount, units sold, employee compensation, or number of stores. Measures can typically have a wide range of mathematical operations performed on them such as summing, averaging, finding the range, and counting.

Similar to the way in which data stored in a standard database is called a *table*, data stored in an OLAP server is commonly referred to as a *cube*.

Using just the concepts of dimensions, hierarchical levels within the dimension, measures, and operations that can be performed on the measure, you can do a lot of amazing analysis with OLAP. Figure 12-1 shows a view of a sales OLAP cube accessed with SAS Enterprise Guide. On the left side, you can see the dimension geography displayed with three levels: Continent, Country, and Region. Values for country include Canada and United States; various regions are displayed in the United States. Across the top, you can see two measures: Cost Price Per Unit and Quantity. The measure Cost Price Per Unit has the statistic average applied and Quantity has two different statistics applied: Sum and Average.

SAS OLAP Server provides easy access to pre-summarized data that is calculated from your relational data. Someone in your organization would define the OLAP cubes that you need by subject area and build the definitions. On a periodic basis, the cube definitions are run so that your cube is built and/or updated on a regular basis.

The SAS OLAP Cube Studio application facilitates defining and building these cubes, but we don't cover this feature in this book. The manual for SAS OLAP Server covers this application.

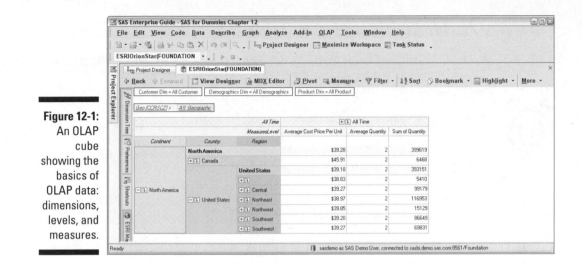

Figure 12-1:
An OLAP cube showing the basics of OLAP data: dimensions, levels, and measures.

OLAP data is so much faster than traditional relational data because although some of the detail is lost (such as detailed transactions down to the individual order lines), key information is gathered and stored very efficiently so that you can quickly explore it. Building a cube can take anywhere from minutes to hours, but rarely is access for the end user more than a few seconds per request after the cube is built.

OLAP Features

The great thing about working with OLAP data and the OLAP viewer provided in SAS Enterprise Guide is that you work interactively. You specify a new measure to view (for example, average sales amount) and it appears immediately in your viewer. Everyone likes immediate gratification, and OLAP delivers in this area. Drilling down and up enables you to move down and up the various dimensions in your table or graph (for example, you can drill down from United States to all States or from product lines to individual products). Filtering (also called *slicing*) data allows you to subset the data you are viewing. OLAP also lets you view the data in the form of various charts. You can use bar, pie, and geographic map charts to show the data — a map of sales by region for 2005, for example. Finally, you can export data from your OLAP view to a relational table form. This is useful if you want to export a view to SAS or Microsoft Excel for reporting or further statistical analysis.

OLAP table interaction

With OLAP, seeing how it works is the quickest way to become proficient, so follow along with this example (with your own cube) if you have an OLAP server. (SAS OLAP Server is available with SAS Enterprise BI Server.)

Note that SAS Enterprise Guide can access two other vendor's OLAP servers:

- **Analysis Services:** This is the SAS OLAP Server equivalent available from Microsoft SQL Server.
- **SAP BW:** SAP BW (*business information warehouse*) is the SAS OLAP Server equivalent from SAP.

Most of the functionality shown in this chapter is available with these other vendor's OLAP servers.

The first step to accessing an OLAP cube is the Open dialog box. Cubes can be opened in SAS Enterprise Guide by choosing File➪Open➪OLAP Cube.

OLAP analysis is a highly interactive activity. You can quickly add and remove the information you want from an OLAP table, like the one shown in Figure 12-2. From the Cube View Manager, shown on the left of Figure 12-2, you can add new dimensions, such as Product or Customer, to table rows or columns. You can also add new measures or existing measures (by applying a new statistic to a cell already in the table).

After you add a measure, you can easily change the statistic being applied to the measure. For example, when you add Units to a table, the default statistic for that measure might be Sum of Units Sold. After you add this, you might change the units to Average Units per Sale, Minimum Units in a Sale, or Median Units per Sale. Measure statistics available in a cube are determined by the author of your cube.

Drilling and expanding your mind

After you select the dimensions and measures for your table from Cube View Manager, you can then interact with the table directly. For example, if you drill down on the dimension North America in Figure 12-2, you see the levels below it: Canada and United States. You can drill down by clicking the down arrow icon to the left of the level. When you drill down, the level you were just at is no longer displayed but the values of the level below are now displayed. Therefore, drilling down on North America would show Canada and the United States, but not North America in the table. You can also drill up. To drill back up to the prior level, right-click the level value and choose Drill-Up.

Similar to drilling down and up is the concept of expanding and collapsing. Expanding a level displays the level below the current one while keeping the current level displayed in the table. This is actually what was done in Figure 12-2. Specifically, North America was expanded by clicking the plus symbol right next to the word North America, and United States was expanded. Conversely, collapsing is very easy to do; just click the subtraction symbol next to an expanded level to collapse it from the table.

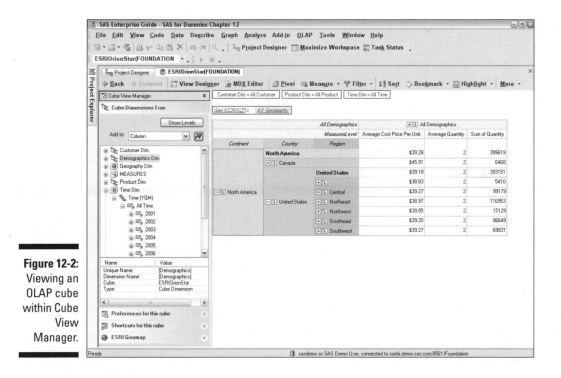

Figure 12-2:
Viewing an OLAP cube within Cube View Manager.

Filtering out the weak and member isolation

Sometimes, you just want to be left alone. This is where *member isolation* can be useful. It allows you to focus on just one or several values in the level of a dimension. By right-clicking a member (such as the Central region of the United States) and choosing Isolate (see Figure 12-3), your table automatically goes down to the next level of the dimension. Isolating shows just the values within the level selected.

The results of isolating Central are shown in Figure 12-4. (We also drilled down through Customer to the Customer Gender level.) You now see the states within the Central region. Also, note that the navigation information just above the tables shows the current location within the dimension Geography: Geo⇨All Geography⇨North America⇨United States⇨Central.

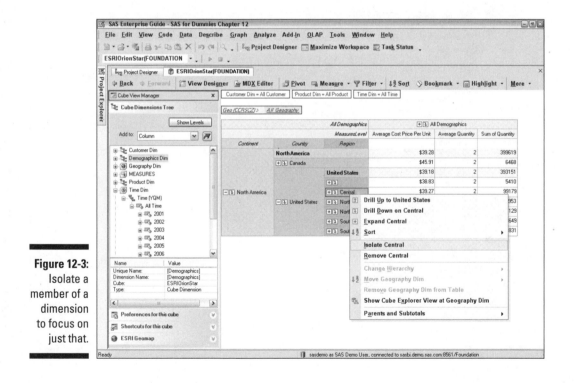

Figure 12-3:
Isolate a member of a dimension to focus on just that.

TIP

You can easily undo what you do to a table view by using the Back button on the toolbar, just below the Project Designer tab. This allows you to navigate backward in your cube actions in a manner very similar to using a Back button in most Web browsers. After you start navigating backward, the Forward button will become available to go back to where you last left off.

To filter the data on a dimension not used in the table, you can use the Slicer. The Slicer is a tool in the OLAP viewer that allows you to filter the data in your table or graphs by a dimension not in use in the table or graph. The Slicer is available right below the MDX Editor button shown in Figure 12-4 (Customer Dim, Product Dim, and Time Dim). By default, the dimensions used in the table do not show up in the Slicer at the top of the table view: in this case, Customer, Product, and Time dimensions.

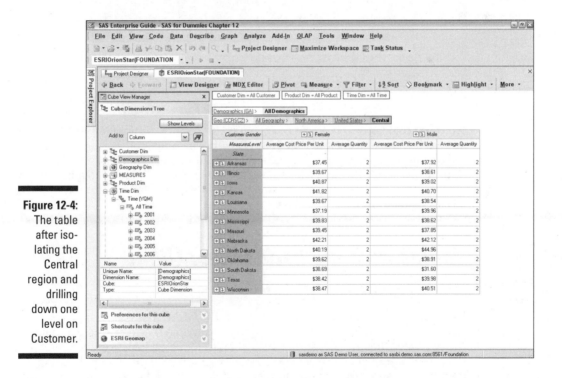

Figure 12-4:
The table after isolating the Central region and drilling down one level on Customer.

Suppose you want to keep the current table view and analyze only Jogging apparel sales. You can do this by clicking the Product dimension in the Slicer; this brings up the Change Slicer dialog box, as shown in Figure 12-5.

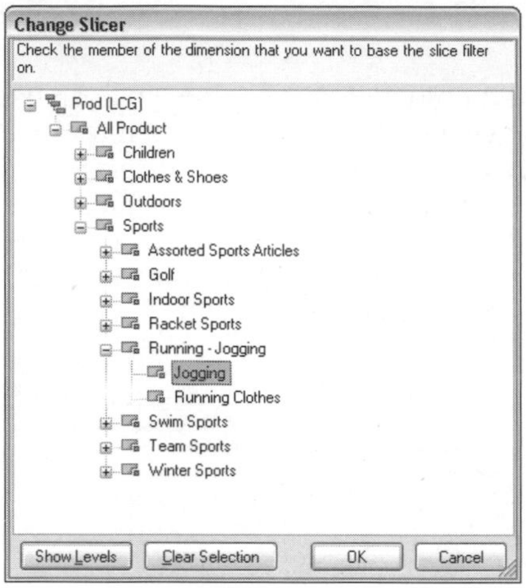

Figure 12-5: Filtering OLAP table data via the Slicer.

We expanded the levels to get to Jogging. The results of slicing by Jogging appear in Figure 12-6. Note that South Dakota has no female buyers of Jogging apparel and that the lowest average sale amount is for Male customers. Note that the Slicer for Product Dim shows the current slice value of Jogging in Figure 12-6; only Jogging data is used in this table summary (contrasting with all products shown in Figure 12-4).

Tables give me headaches: What about graphs and maps?

SAS is heavy on graphical capabilities, and the OLAP Analyzer is no exception. Graphs tend to work best with one measure, so in the example at hand, the Average Quantity measure is turned off to focus on just Average Cost Price per Unit. You can remove a measure by right-clicking it and choosing Remove Measure. To turn on the graph, click the More button at the top right of the table and select Graph.

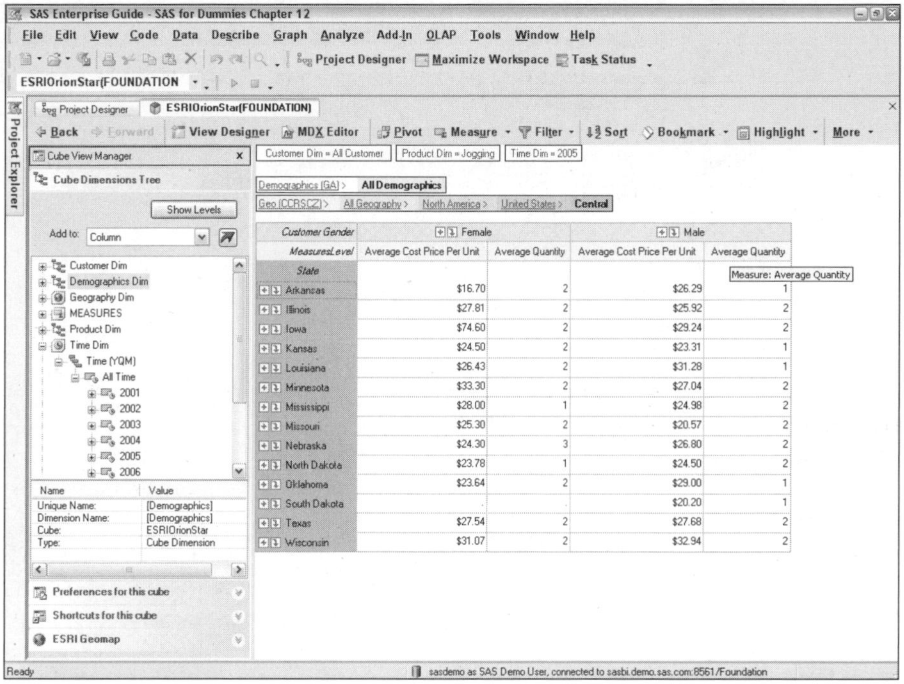

Figure 12-6:
The table
after slicing
the data for
Jogging
apparel.

The following table appears in the SAS Enterprise Guide screenshot:

State	Female		Male	
	Average Cost Price Per Unit	Average Quantity	Average Cost Price Per Unit	Average Quantity
Arkansas	$16.70	2	$26.29	1
Illinois	$27.81	2	$25.92	2
Iowa	$74.60	2	$29.24	2
Kansas	$24.50	2	$23.31	1
Louisiana	$26.43	2	$31.28	1
Minnesota	$33.30	2	$27.04	2
Mississippi	$28.00	1	$24.98	2
Missouri	$25.30	2	$20.57	2
Nebraska	$24.30	3	$26.80	2
North Dakota	$23.78	1	$24.50	2
Oklahoma	$23.64	2	$29.00	1
South Dakota			$20.20	1
Texas	$27.54	2	$27.68	2
Wisconsin	$31.07	2	$32.94	2

Figure 12-7 shows the example with the bar chart graph for the data at hand.
Note how much more obvious the outlier state for Female Cost stands out in
the graph versus the table — either Iowa females have very expensive tastes
or something else is going on here.

This is the great part about OLAP data: You can quickly zoom in on an anom-
aly that might be important to your business. Note that you can also display
other chart types such as horizontal bar, pie, plot, or area charts. Drilling up
and down and expanding the data can be done from the graph by right-clicking
the member values, as shown in Figure 12-8.

Although traditional graphs are nice, when geography is important to your
analysis, seeing the data in a map is helpful. This is possible if you use the
SAS OLAP Server in combination with ESRI ArcGIS software. ESRI ArcGIS is a
product from ESRI, which is a leader in geospatial data mapping and analysis
that has partnered with SAS.

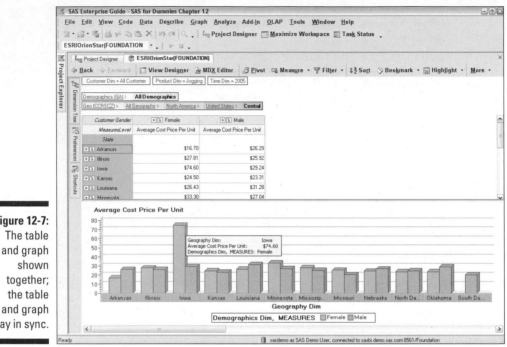

Figure 12-7:
The table and graph shown together; the table and graph stay in sync.

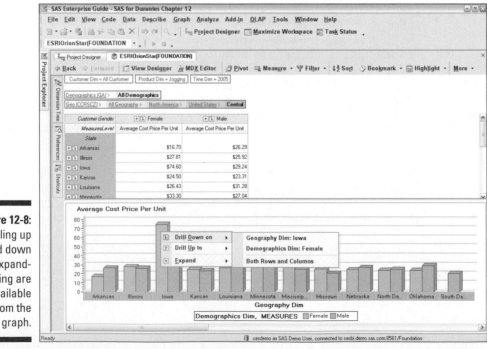

Figure 12-8:
Drilling up and down and expanding are available from the graph.

To turn on a map instead of a chart, click the More button (at the top right of the table) and choose ESRI Map. After you do this, you see something similar to Figure 12-9. Note that only the current level of the geography dimension and one of the values of other dimensions are shown in the table: in this case, Females. You can easily change which other dimension values are displayed.

It's all relative: Understanding the percentages

If you're interested in exploring the details of one dimension, especially the relative percent contribution of each value within a level, Cube Explorer is a valuable feature to use. Cube Explorer is available from the OLAP toolbar: More⇨Cube Explorer. We accessed the cube used in this chapter with the Cube Explorer in Figure 12-10 and drilled all the way down into the counties of Montana.

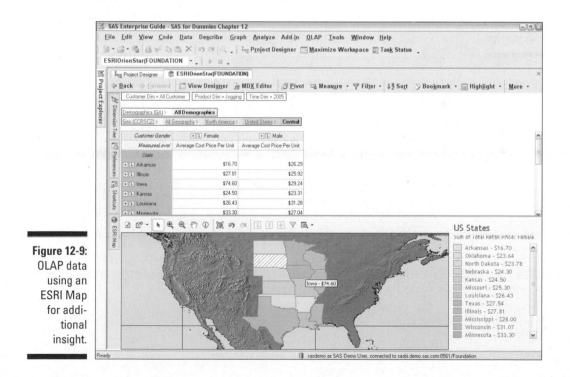

Figure 12-9: OLAP data using an ESRI Map for additional insight.

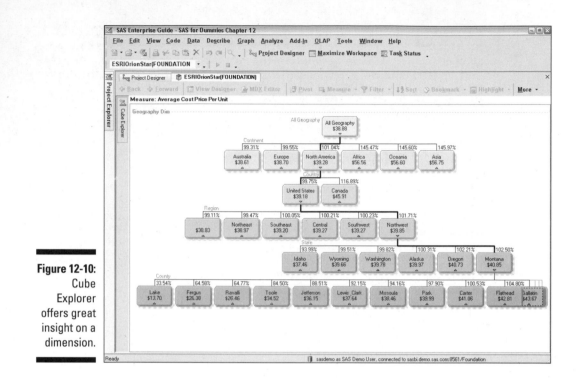

Figure 12-10:
Cube
Explorer
offers great
insight on a
dimension.

In this example, we're examining average cost across the various geography levels. Starting at the top, you can see an average cost of $38.88 worldwide. Going down one level, you see the average price for each continent, with Australia being the lowest and Asia being the highest. You also see the values as percentages of the parent level: the world, in this case. Asia is 145% of the worldwide average cost. When you double-click any value, the interface automatically goes down one level from that starting point.

When we made this view, we double-clicked All, North America, United States, Northwest, and then Montana. You might notice that the counties seem to stack up on the far right side; you can easily scroll over to see the covered up counties by clicking and holding the click while you scroll to the left. This view offers a lot of insight in the static form. It is even more valuable interactively; try it out if you have the chance!

A slice of data for further analysis

What if you find something of interest in your OLAP data, but you want to use the other SAS Enterprise Guide tasks from previous chapters with that data? Here is a solution: After you're at the level of OLAP data you want to analyze, just select the task you want to run. In Figure 12-11, we ran a Box Plot task against a view of the OLAP data. This view was based on an examination of total retail sales by county in New York State for 2001–2005. The box plot shows the distribution of total sales by county over the five years selected. Other tasks people use include forecasting tasks, reporting tasks, and other analytic techniques that might be relevant to your data.

Figure 12-12 shows the data "slice" that was automatically created in order to use the Box Plot task.

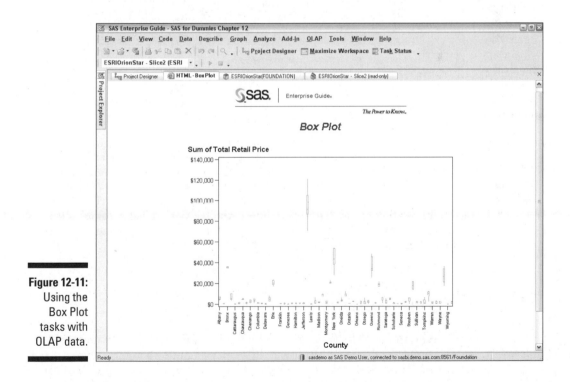

Figure 12-11: Using the Box Plot tasks with OLAP data.

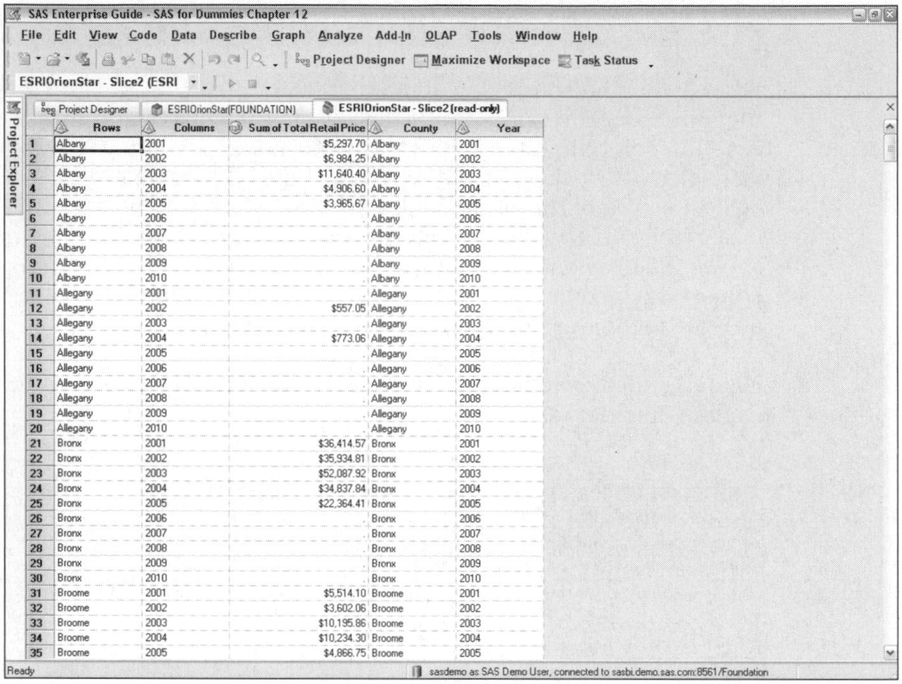

	Rows	Columns	Sum of Total Retail Price	County	Year
1	Albany	2001	$5,297.70	Albany	2001
2	Albany	2002	$6,984.25	Albany	2002
3	Albany	2003	$11,640.40	Albany	2003
4	Albany	2004	$4,906.60	Albany	2004
5	Albany	2005	$3,965.67	Albany	2005
6	Albany	2006	.	Albany	2006
7	Albany	2007	.	Albany	2007
8	Albany	2008	.	Albany	2008
9	Albany	2009	.	Albany	2009
10	Albany	2010	.	Albany	2010
11	Allegany	2001	.	Allegany	2001
12	Allegany	2002	$557.05	Allegany	2002
13	Allegany	2003	.	Allegany	2003
14	Allegany	2004	$773.06	Allegany	2004
15	Allegany	2005	.	Allegany	2005
16	Allegany	2006	.	Allegany	2006
17	Allegany	2007	.	Allegany	2007
18	Allegany	2008	.	Allegany	2008
19	Allegany	2009	.	Allegany	2009
20	Allegany	2010	.	Allegany	2010
21	Bronx	2001	$36,414.57	Bronx	2001
22	Bronx	2002	$35,934.81	Bronx	2002
23	Bronx	2003	$52,087.92	Bronx	2003
24	Bronx	2004	$34,837.84	Bronx	2004
25	Bronx	2005	$22,364.41	Bronx	2005
26	Bronx	2006	.	Bronx	2006
27	Bronx	2007	.	Bronx	2007
28	Bronx	2008	.	Bronx	2008
29	Bronx	2009	.	Bronx	2009
30	Bronx	2010	.	Bronx	2010
31	Broome	2001	$5,514.10	Broome	2001
32	Broome	2002	$3,602.06	Broome	2002
33	Broome	2003	$10,195.86	Broome	2003
34	Broome	2004	$10,234.30	Broome	2004
35	Broome	2005	$4,866.75	Broome	2005

Figure 12-12: Relational data view automatically created from the OLAP data.

Keep in mind from the analytics discussion in Chapter 8 that variance is a key to almost every type of statistical technique. OLAP, because of its summarized nature, loses this detail in order to give you greater speed. You should only use the detail data used to create your OLAP cube for any critical statistical analysis technique. Using the aggregated OLAP data is useful for a first, "dirty" pass at the data, but it is not a substitute for statistical analysis with the detailed data.

More OLAP Features

Maybe you thought the last section had it all; but no, there are even more great features with the OLAP viewer! Bookmarking allows you to save a current OLAP cube view (including layout, levels, and filters) and quickly return to it just like you do with an Internet browser bookmark. Calculated measures let you create custom measures (such as net sales) from measures available with the cube. Another great feature of OLAP is the capability to drill to the detailed transaction values behind a single number. For example, from the average sales amount for June 2006, you can drill down to all sales transactions in June 2006 with one click. Conditional formatting allows you to highlight values that are particularly good or bad so that you can quickly find anomalies, such as net profit percent above 55% or below 10%. Finally, if you are brave and really like tweaking your results, you can use the MDX editor to send the exact query you want to the OLAP server — going beyond what the point-and-click capabilities will let you do!

Bookmarking: Where was 1?

Bookmarks allow you to save a particular view of your cube, much like favorites in your Web browser. Dimensions, drilling, expanding, isolating, measures, and slices can all be preserved in a named bookmark of your choice. To bookmark a view from the OLAP toolbar, choose Bookmark⇨ Add Bookmark. To open a bookmark, click the Shortcuts for this Cube section under Cube View Manager, and then click the desired bookmark.

Using calculated measures

If the measure you wanted doesn't exist in your cube, don't despair. If you want a measure that can be based on other measures in the cube, you can add a *calculated measure.* A simple example is net sales, based on gross sales minus returns. To create a calculated measure, click Measure from the OLAP toolbar and then choose Add Measure. The Add Measure wizard can walk you through about 20 types of calculations. Here are the major categories:

- **Simple Calculations:** For example, Sum and Difference

- **Time Series Analysis:** For example, Rolling Totals, Average Over Time, and Growth

- **Trends and Forecasting:** For example, Correlation and Linear Regression

- **Count Analysis:** For example, Unique Item Count

- **Relative Contribution Analysis:** Expresses the contribution of a cell as a percentage of the overall total (such as sales for tennis balls in Ohio as a percentage of all sporting goods in the U.S.)

- **Custom Calculation:** Allows you to do complex calculations not available with the wizard

Drilling down: Just the facts, please

Maybe there is a value of interest in a table that you want to investigate. With the OLAP table, you can drill through to the detail data that was used to make the OLAP cube. For example, in Figure 12-6, you might want to see what was going on with male customers in Wisconsin to make them the highest average cost state. To drill through to detail, just click the cell of interest ($32.94), right-click, and choose Drill through Detail. A detail table opens, just like any other data table accessed with SAS Enterprise Guide. Note that not all OLAP cubes have this feature enabled, so ask your cube author to turn it on if it isn't available.

Conditional formatting: Isn't that special?

Some people just love to stand out, so they dye their hair blue or pierce various body parts. Creating conditional highlighting in your table can do the same for your table but with much less trouble and cost. *Conditional highlighting* is a feature that lets you apply specific font changes (say, bold), colors, and even special icons beside the cell value (such as a happy face or a sad face). For example, say you want sales values lower than $20 to be bold and red and sales values higher than $40 to be green and have a smiley face. You can do this with conditional highlighting from the OLAP toolbar Highlight menu.

Adding details about your values

Some OLAP cubes have extra data — member properties — about the values in their dimensional levels. *Member properties* provide the ability to add special details to a value, such as population for the state of Wisconsin or the manager name for a particular product sold. Member properties are obtained by right-clicking a member value and choosing Member Properties.

Speaking MDX with the OLAP cube

Every time a new view of the OLAP data is retrieved from the OLAP Server, a special language is used to specify the data to retrieve on your behalf. This language is MultiDimensional Expression (MDX). MDX is similar to the Structured Query Language (SQL) that you might be familiar with. The main difference is that MDX is intended for OLAP data, and SQL is intended for relational data.

If you want to use an MDX query for a given table view in another application or modify it yourself for SAS Enterprise Guide, use the MDX Editor (see Figure 12-13). Just click the MDX Editor button on the OLAP toolbar. From the MDX Editor, you can copy the query, modify it yourself, or paste in your own MDX query.

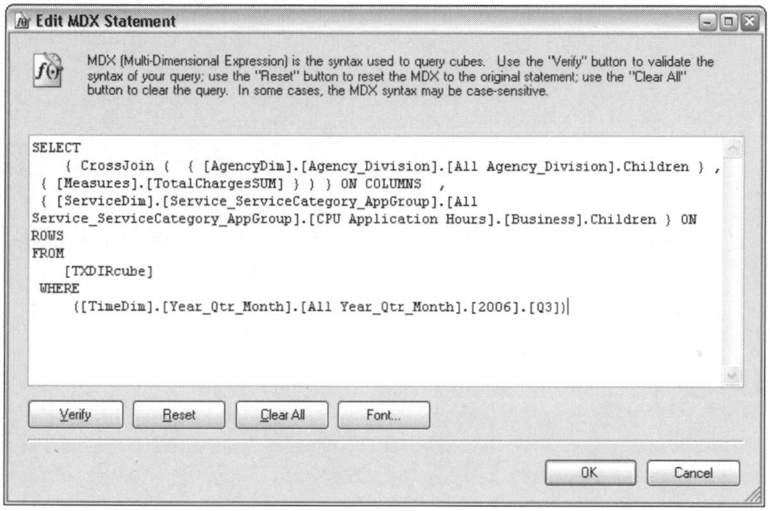

Figure 12-13:
A sample MDX query viewed from the MDX Editor.

Chapter 13

Supercharge Microsoft Office with SAS

*T*he SAS Add-In for Microsoft Office (shortened to *the add-in* in this chapter) is an application from SAS that appears inside Microsoft Office applications, both from the menu and also from toolbars in Excel, Word, and PowerPoint. The add-in is part of the SAS Enterprise BI Server and SAS BI Server offerings. The add-in relies on the architecture in Office that allows other applications to integrate in the Microsoft Office environment, called the Add-In model. Hence, the name! You can use all the Office formatting and layout features with content you create using the add-in!

This chapter shows you how the add-in provides you with an easy way to access the power of your SAS servers for data access, reporting, graphics, and analytics directly from the comfortable applications of Excel, Word, and PowerPoint. Your SAS server results are immediately available to format, lay out, print, and present just like your normal Office spreadsheets, documents, and presentations. Equally important, you can refresh your SAS content at will — whenever you need to update your analyses with the latest data or tweak your results for those revisions that managers tend to request at the last minute.

Much of what you can read in this book is directly applicable in the add-in because the add-in and SAS Enterprise Guide share a lot of functionality. The add-in has a slightly different workflow and is missing some of the more powerful capabilities of SAS Enterprise Guide, but the add-in replaces those things with additional functionality relevant to the Office environment. We have personally visited many add-in users, and they almost universally love this application and find it easy to incorporate within their familiar world of Office.

The Power of SAS from the Cozy World of Office

To start using this great wonder of modern computing, you need to have access to the SAS BI Server or SAS Enterprise BI Server at your organization. If it's not already there, ask to have the add-in installed on your PC. We show version 2.1 of the add-in in this chapter.

After it's installed, you will see something similar to Figure 13-1 when you open Excel. We focus on Excel throughout the chapter because it is the most powerful, general-purpose business analysis tool in Office as well as with the add-in. On the Standard Excel toolbar, located between the Data and Window menus, notice the new menu named *SAS*. Additionally, two additional toolbars are installed with the add-in that you can see below the Standard toolbar in Excel: SAS Data Tools and SAS Analysis Tools. To highlight the toolbars, Figure 13-2 shows them dragged away from their normal docked location to float over the Excel spreadsheet.

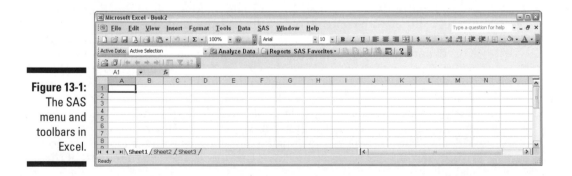

Figure 13-1: The SAS menu and toolbars in Excel.

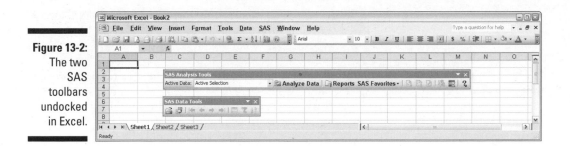

Figure 13-2:
The two
SAS
toolbars
undocked
in Excel.

SAS Data Tools provide the capability to open data from your SAS server directly into Excel. You can browse this data and even use it in combination with standard Excel functionality. SAS Analysis Tools provide you with the capability to access the many data management, reporting, graphical and analytical capabilities (via SAS Tasks) covered in earlier chapters of this book. Analysis Tools also offer you access to stored processes that can be published from SAS Enterprise Guide.

Stored processes are called *reports* in the add-in because many non-technical users are familiar with this term but not with the term *stored process.* This falls in line with specifically targeting the traditional Office power user rather than the traditional SAS power user with the add-in.

Exploring just a little bit more, you can see the items available from the SAS menu in Figure 13-3. Additional areas of functionality not mentioned in the last paragraph include

- ✔ **SAS Favorites**: Let you quickly acccss your favorite data, reports, and tasks
- ✔ **Modify:** Enables you to change the settings for a result obtained from the add-in
- ✔ **Refresh and Refresh Multiple:** Enables you to update your results with the most current data
- ✔ **Tools:** Lets you access a variety of utility functions including Server Connection information
- ✔ **Options:** Lets you set general add-in behavior options
- ✔ **Help:** Provides help specific to the add-in

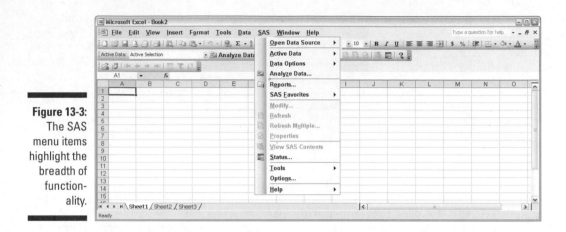

Figure 13-3:
The SAS
menu items
highlight the
breadth of
function-
ality.

SAS Add-In for Microsoft Office Options

SAS Add-In for Microsoft Office Options offer a variety of ways to control the add-in's behavior and are useful to review after using the add-in a bit. The Options dialog box is shown in Figure 13-4, available by choosing SAS➪ Options. These options let you control data browsing, results types and style, graph settings, task settings, stored process defaults, and advanced settings. Here are some of the important areas to examine:

- ✔ **The number of records to display when browsing data:** On the Data tab; the default is 500. You might want a smaller number, such as 25, for quicker data viewing.

- ✔ **Turning off the Status Window:** On the Results tab; this is on by default. If you find it distracting, you can always bring it up from the Status button on the toolbar.

- ✔ **SAS output format type:** On the Results tab; this is set for each Office application. The default is SAS Report because it offers the best flexibility for formatting, but you can specify other formats such as CSV (comma-separated values), HTML, and RTF.

Just as important as Options is configuring your SAS server connections from SAS➪Tools➪Server Connections. This allows you to set your user name, password, server name for metadata connection, and default SAS server on which to process your analysis.

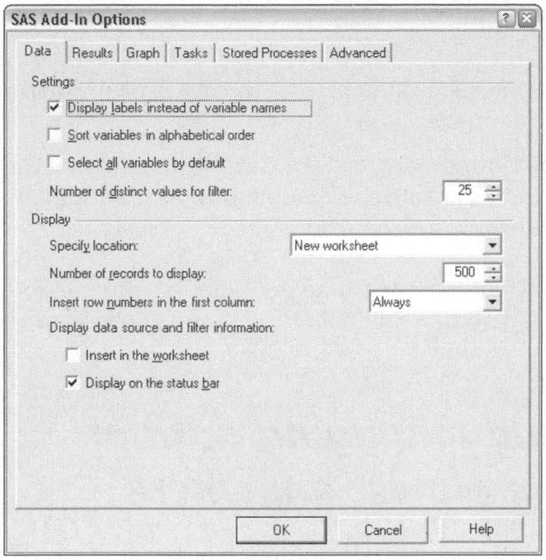

Figure 13-4:
The SAS
Add-In for
Microsoft
Office
Options.

Knowing which Office applications are supported

The add-in requires Office 2000, XP, or 2003. Older Office versions are not supported, and Office 2007 will not be supported until the add-in release slated for late 2007 (also known as version 4.2). The add-in is available from Excel, Word, and PowerPoint. Excel offers all add-in functionality. Word and PowerPoint do not have a data grid similar to Excel, so they lack the functionality on the SAS Data Tools toolbar. This primarily includes the ability to browse SAS server data. You can still use Word and PowerPoint to access the data, analyze the data, and run reports (SAS stored processes).

Using the Add-In to Get the Most Out of Office Integration

The SAS Add-In for Microsoft Office brings the power of SAS into your Office application and also lets you bring your Excel data sources to SAS for use in analysis. The main features of this integration include the capability to

✔ Access any data, of any size, from within Excel and other Microsoft Office applications

✔ Perform ad hoc analysis on this data or on any of your local Excel worksheets by using the power of SAS

✔ Run predefined SAS programs, called stored processes, within the Office environment and incorporate the results into your spreadsheet, Word document, or slideshow presentation.

After you have SAS content in your Office documents, you can easily refresh this content with the latest data and share the results with your organization.

Accessing and managing data of any size from almost anywhere

Microsoft Office applications are easy and familiar, but they generally are not very adept at dealing with data sources other than those from Microsoft (including mainframe-based data, UNIX data, Oracle databases, and DB2 databases) or large volumes of data (more than a few million rows). In particular, Excel worksheets have a limit of 65,536 rows of data with no more than 256 columns. This is fine for some applications, but many times, key data is in a remote source and/or is large, with millions or even billions of rows of data becoming commonplace in many companies.

The SAS Add-In for Microsoft Office can help you blow past this issue because SAS accesses and analyzes the data for you even though you preview and browse it in Excel. The add-in achieves this by using SAS as a caching mechanism. The add-in shows you data in small pieces — the default being 500 rows — and allows you to easily filter and browse this data at will.

Opening data with the add-in

From Microsoft Excel, you can easily open SAS data, select the relevant columns, filter the data, and browse it at will.

1. **To access the sample table Candy_Sales_Summary, choose SAS⇨ Open Data Source⇨Into Worksheet.**

   The Open Data Source dialog box appears, as shown in Figure 13-5.

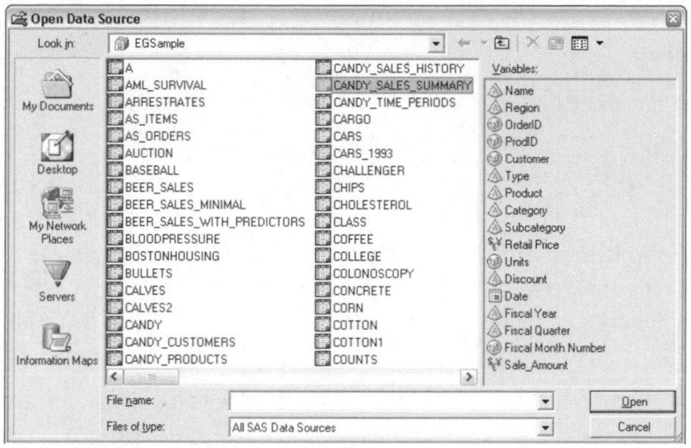

Figure 13-5:
Opening
data from
the SAS
server in
Excel.

Figure 13-5:
Opening
data from
the SAS
server in
Excel.

2. Select the Candy_Sales_Summary data set (notice that the variables are previewed on the right side of the dialog box before you actually open the data) and then click Open.

The Modify Data Source dialog box appears. Unlike with SAS Enterprise Guide, you are provided with further data access options prior to viewing the data. This dialog box has several tabs: Variables, Filter, Sort, and Output Location.

3. From the Available box on the Variables tab, choose Customer, Product, Retail_Price, and Discount and add them to the Selected box by clicking the right arrow button.

After you do this, the dialog box should look similar to Figure 13-6.

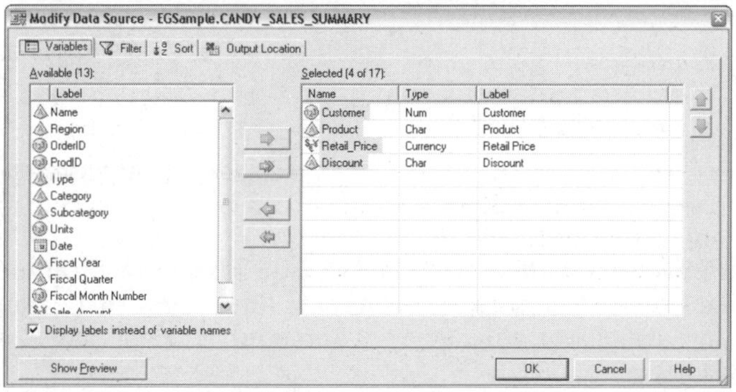

Figure 13-6:
Select
just the
variables
you want to
view in
Excel.

4. **To filter the data for the East region and the first quarter of 2004, do the following:**

   a. Click the Filter tab.

   b. Choose Region from the first drop-down list.

   c. Choose Is Equal To from the second drop-down list.

   d. Click the button with the ellipse (...) in the third drop-down list and then choose East.

   e. Choose AND from the fourth drop-down list.

5. **For the second row of filter criteria, choose**

   • Fiscal Quarter

   • Is Equal To

   • 2004Q1

   Your dialog box should be similar to Figure 13-7.

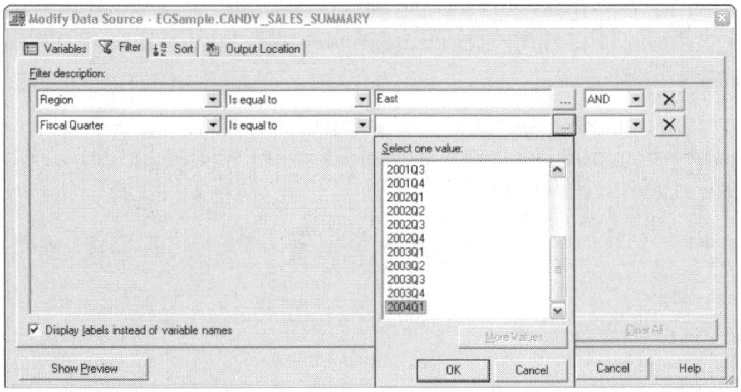

Figure 13-7:
Filter the data before you view it in Excel.

6. **Click OK.**

For more sophisticated filtering, the Advanced Expression Editor is available from this dialog box by clicking Advanced Edit. (*Note:* You can't see the Advanced Edit button in Figure 13-7 because it's hidden behind the data values list.) The same filter conditions you just defined with the standard dialog box are displayed in the Advanced Expression Editor shown in Figure 13-8.

The data appears in Excel, similar to what you see in Figure 13-9.

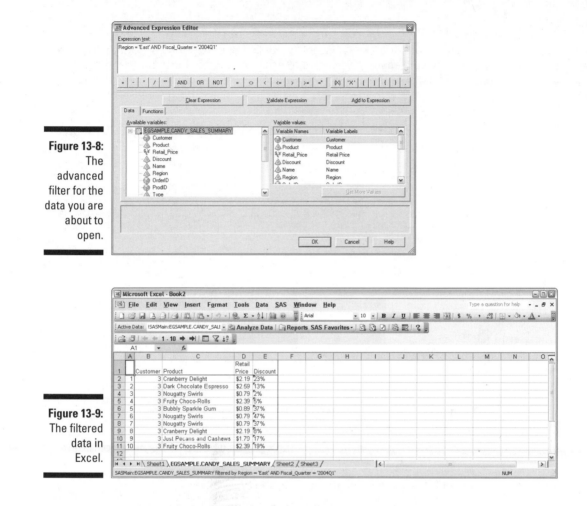

Figure 13-8: The advanced filter for the data you are about to open.

Figure 13-9: The filtered data in Excel.

Note that just the variables you selected are displayed. The number of rows accessed is shown in the SAS Data Tools toolbar: in this case, rows 1–10. Just above that information is the Active Data dialog box, which shows that we opened the data set referenced from server SASMain. (The worksheet is also named after the data you just opened.) Finally, notice that the filter conditions are shown in the Excel status bar at the bottom of the application.

The arrow icons just next to the row information allow you to page forward and backward through the data. These are available only if you cannot bring all the data into Excel at once. You can also respecify the Variable and Filter selection by clicking the icons to the far right of the SAS Data Tools toolbar.

Using the add-in to move your Excel data to SAS

Just as the add-in makes it easy to access SAS data sources from Excel, it also allows you to transfer Excel data to your SAS server for use with the SAS Tasks. To do so, follow these steps:

1. **Open your Excel data source.**

   See Figure 13-10 for the example from the SAS Enterprise Guide sample directory, `Boards.xls`.

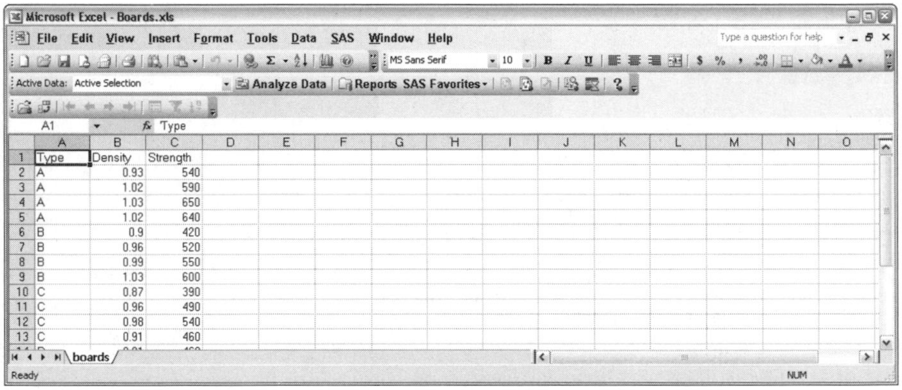

Figure 13-10: The SAS Enterprise Guide sample Excel spreadsheet.

2. **Choose SAS⇨Active Data⇨Copy to SAS Server.**

   The Copy to SAS Server dialog box appears, as in Figure 13-11. Note that the WORK library is the default, with _EXCELEXPORT the default data set name.

3. **Click OK to transfer the data to the SAS server.**

   Your data is now on the server and available for use with your SAS Tasks, which we discuss in the next section.

Ad hoc analysis: Awesome!

You can apply SAS power to your Excel or SAS data quickly with ad hoc analysis techniques, including pivot tables and built-in SAS tasks. These are tasks that end users can perform on their own with no support required from a SAS programmer or administrator.

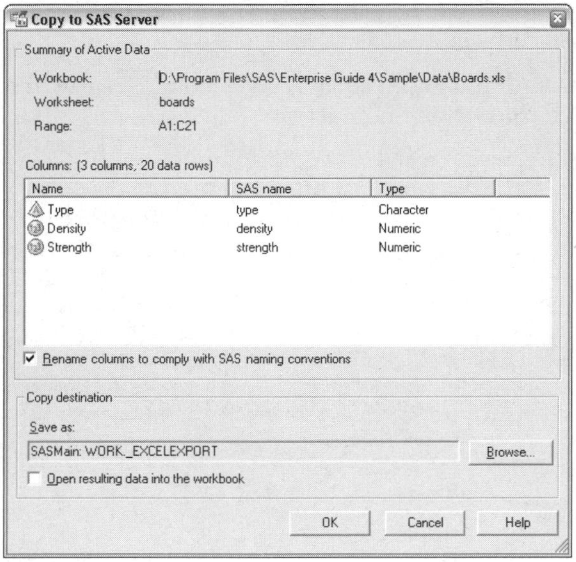

Figure 13-11:
Copying the
data to the
SAS server.

Turn, step, pivot (table)!

Many users of Microsoft Excel love the pivot table functionality. The add-in
allows you to use the power of pivot tables with SAS data sources. If you have
SAS OLAP Server or data in SAS you want to analyze in pivot tables, you can
easily open these data sources into a pivot table by choosing SAS⇨Open
Data Source⇨Into PivotTables. Figure 13-12 shows the Open into PivotTable
dialog box.

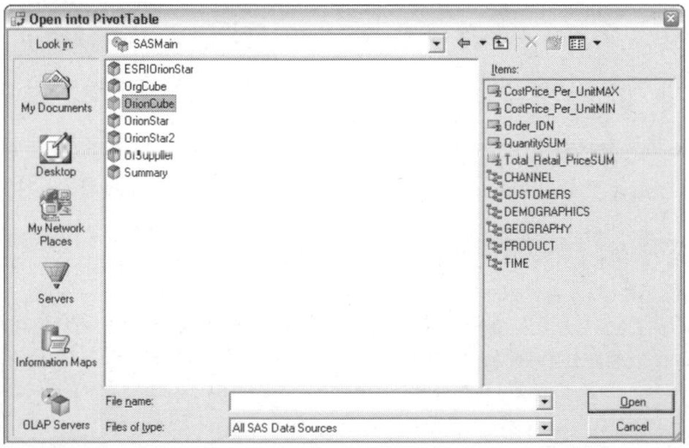

Figure 13-12:
Open OLAP
Server into
an Excel
pivot table.

Although you can open OLAP server data or any other SAS data source, note
that OLAP data will be faster — perhaps much faster — than regular data
sources. There are two reasons for this:

✔ **OLAP data is already summarized in a manner similar to how pivot tables present information.**

✔ **All the non-OLAP data must be moved to your PC for pivot tables to work.** This is a limitation of Excel pivot tables.

This second scenario means that data sources larger than a few million rows are unsuitable for opening into pivot tables.

After you open your data source into pivot tables, standard pivot table functionality is available for your use. In Figure 13-13, we opened the Candy_Sales_Summary data set and used standard pivot table functionality to analyze candy sales by category, subcategory, and fiscal year.

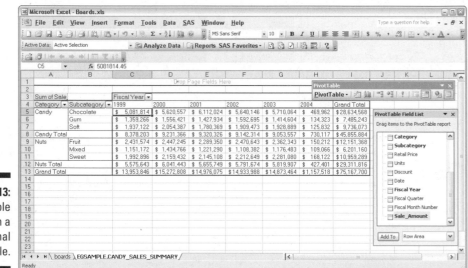

Figure 13-13: A pivot table based on a relational sample.

Using SAS Tasks from the add-in

Combining the data access provided by the add-in with the SAS Tasks (the same ones in SAS Enterprise Guide from prior chapters) offers a completely new world of possibilities for Office users. Whether you want to analyze large volumes of data or use some of the more advanced data management, graphics, or statistical capabilities SAS has to offer, the add-in really adds a lot of oomph to your Office environment.

Almost every SAS Task used in SAS Enterprise Guide is available, with a notable exception being the Filter and Query task. The Filter and Query task is replaced with the simpler Modify Data Source dialog box that appears by default whenever you open data into a worksheet.

A few tasks in the add-in are not available with SAS Enterprise Guide. SAS Forecast Server is a newer solution from SAS that offers automated forecasting straight from the add-in. SAS Forecast Server is designed to allow massive volumes of data for forecasting. It automatically optimizes your forecast models, and it even allows for manual adjustments to forecasts based on your expert opinion. Several tasks in the add-in give you access to SAS Forecast Server. Accessing the SAS Tasks from the add-in is easy; just go to SAS⇨Analyze Data.

Using the board strength data from the earlier section, you can follow this example to perform an Analysis of Variance using the add-in. Suppose your board materials supplier claims that his new Type A material is superior to your other materials, so you should pay a premium for Type A material. In this example, you will determine whether board strength is linked to the type of board material used, the board density, or both factors. Using the 20 test boards created with the various materials and board densities, you want to see whether you should pay more for Type A material. You suspect that board density with the much cheaper Type C material will still allow you to have boards that are more than strong enough for your customers:

1. **Follow the steps in the "Using the add-in to move your Excel data to SAS" section earlier in this chapter.**

2. **Choose SAS⇨Analyze Data⇨ANOVA⇨Linear Models Task.**

   The Linear Models dialog box appears, as shown in Figure 13-14.

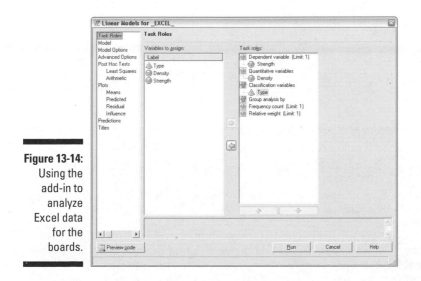

Figure 13-14:
Using the add-in to analyze Excel data for the boards.

3. **Because Strength is the variable to predict, add it to the Dependent Variable role.**

4. **Add Density and Type to the Quantitative and Classification variables roles, respectively, as shown in Figure 13-14.**

   Density and Type are the variables influencing strength.

5. **Specify the model by clicking the second pane named Model; select Density and Type and then click the Main button.**

   By doing this, you are stating that there is a simple predictive relationship for Strength as a function of Density and Type.

6. **To graphically view the differences among the Types, click Plots/ Means from the left pane, turn on the Dependent means for main effects plot, and click Run to execute the analysis.**

   The Choose Location dialog box appears, prompting you where to place the results in Excel.

7. **Select the New Worksheet radio button, as shown in Figure 13-15.**

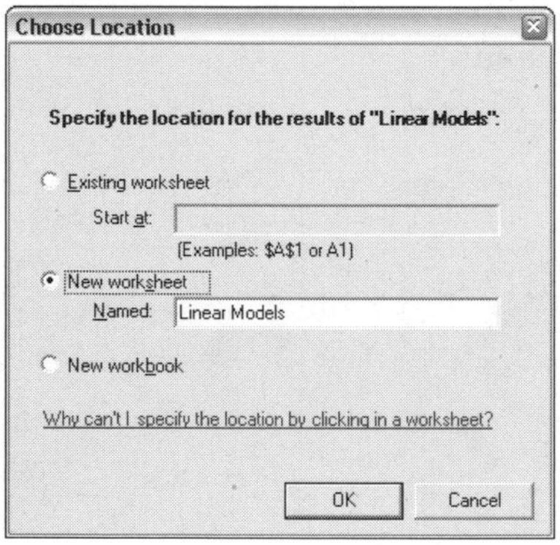

Figure 13-15:
Choose the location of your output in Excel.

The analysis shows that the strength of our test boards is 95 percent explainable with just Density and Type. Although both variables are significant predictors of strength, it appears that density is about 20 times more important than type in making a strong board. Put another way, the cheaper material with a slightly higher density than Type A material will be just as strong.

Based on your analysis, you tell the salesperson, "No." You want Type A material only if it is no more than 5 percent more expensive than Type C. The Mean Plots of Strength by Type are shown in Figure 13-16.

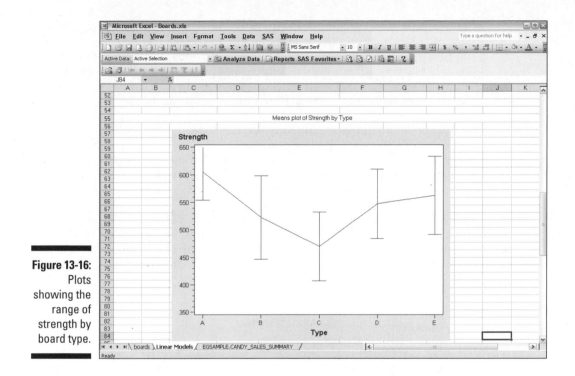

Figure 13-16:
Plots showing the range of strength by board type.

Although we used Excel in this section, do not forget that the output of SAS Tasks can also be used directly in PowerPoint and Word! The main restriction is that you can only preview the data used in your task in the Open Data Source dialog box (via the Show Preview button in Figure 13-6).

Stored processes: Leaving spreadsheet hell

You might recall from Chapter 11 the idea of stored processes. A *stored process* is a centrally stored SAS program that can have prompts for a user to specify details about the analysis. When you select the details and then run the stored process, you are presented with the results of the program based on your details. Stored processes can be run from the add-in. This section gets you up to speed on why and how you access stored processes using the add-in.

Checking out an example of how not to use data

Although Excel is indeed customizable and powerful, the details of the work done in one spreadsheet are not easy to integrate in another spreadsheet. A simple example can illustrate the problem. Peter in Sales wants to project the sales of an updated product at his company. He jumps through some hoops and finally programs a spreadsheet to create a forecast. Unknown to him, Cindy in Marketing has done the same work in her Excel spreadsheet with the same historic data. They both show up at a meeting with the CEO and tell him two very different numbers! How could they avoid this scenario?

More importantly, if Peter and Cindy had collaborated and created a forecasting stored process published by one of them, they could open it and refresh it at will with the latest data from Excel, Word, or PowerPoint. Because the stored process exists only in one place and has access to all their corporate data stores, it is one version of the truth for their forecasting problem.

This is a big deal because you can also run this stored process from the Web in SAS Web Report Studio (see Chapter 14) or from SAS Enterprise Guide. If the logic for the stored process is updated next week for some new business rules, anyone who opened it before will access this new logic the very next time he reruns a forecast estimate. To sum:

> Centralized Data Access
> Centralized Data Management
> Centralized Analysis Rules
> +   Access from the Web, Office, and SAS Enterprise Guide
> One Version of the Truth!

In addition, no more egg on Peter or Cindy's face when the CEO is presented with two very different forecasts!

Remember that almost anything SAS can do is accessible from stored processes, so go ahead and use them to simplify your life! To brush up on the basics of creating stored processes, read Chapter 11.

Accessing stored processes via the add-in

Accessing stored processes from the add-in is easy: Just go to SAS⇨Reports. When you do this, you see a dialog box similar to Figure 13-17. The Reports dialog box shows you the SAS metadata folder tree; this is the place in metadata where content like stored processes are stored. Your view will likely be different depending on the setup on your SAS server.

In this example, we browsed the tree (just like in Windows Explorer) to the Orion Stored Processes folder and then double-clicked the Forecast Stored Process in the contents pane on the right. After opening the stored process, the prompting dialog box in Figure 13-18 appears. This stored process has three parameters — or prompts — that you can make selections from to specify exactly which forecast you want to see. The drop-down selectors were used to specify a 12-month sales forecast for the USA. After clicking Run, you can see the results in Excel, as shown in Figure 13-19.

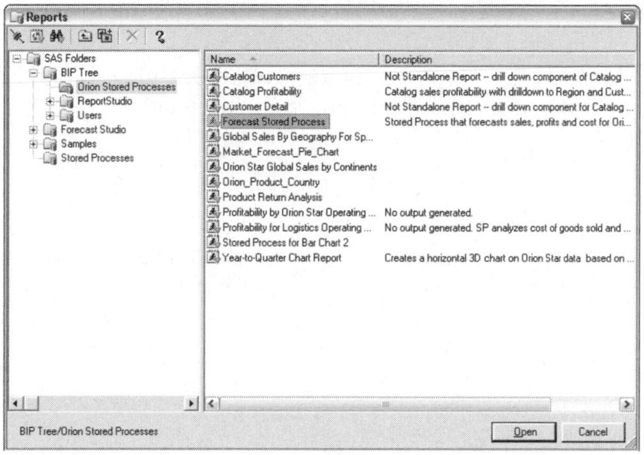

Figure 13-17: Browsing the metadata repository to open a stored process.

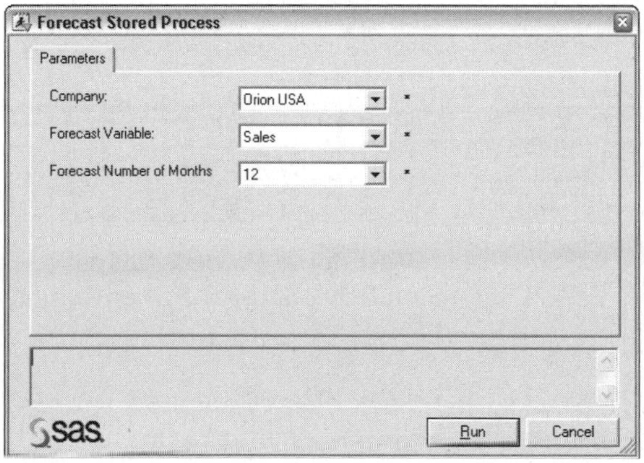

Figure 13-18: An example set of parameters for a stored process.

Just to show how widely available stored processes are, we ran the same stored process from PowerPoint and then Word. The results are shown in Figures 13-20 and 13-21. Note that in both examples, the add-in separated the table from the graph by putting them on separate slides in PowerPoint or pages in the Word document. The add-in intelligently breaks up your output onto slides or pages. Also, note that in Figure 13-20, we used the standard functionality of PowerPoint to add our own title to the second slide.

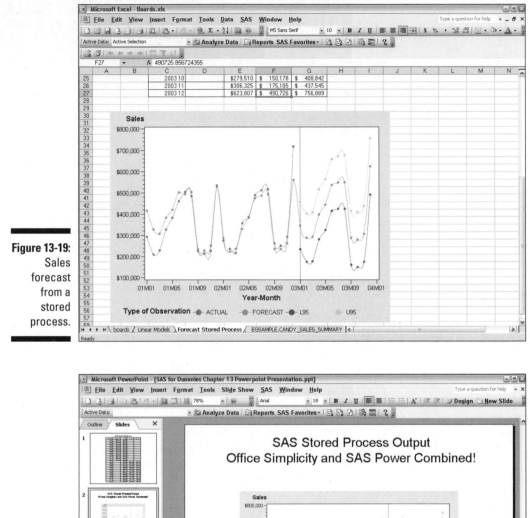

Figure 13-19:
Sales
forecast
from a
stored
process.

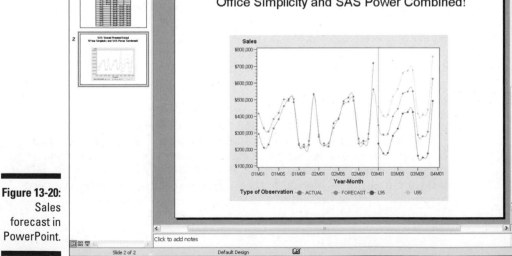

Figure 13-20:
Sales
forecast in
PowerPoint.

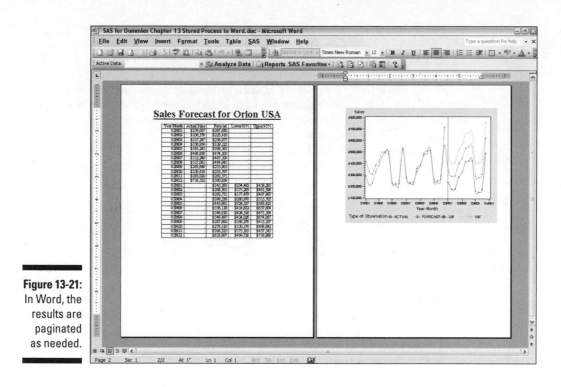

Figure 13-21:
In Word, the results are paginated as needed.

Refreshing results from the add-in

You have several options after opening data, creating some output with a SAS Task, or opening a stored process. All these results can be modified or refreshed. After clicking the SAS output in your Office document, you can choose SAS⇨Modify, Refresh, Refresh Multiple, or Properties.

Modify allows the following:

- ✔ **For data:** Modify allows you to update the Modify Data Source dialog box (Variables, Filter, and Sort).
- ✔ **For task output:** Modify takes you back to the task dialog box to update the options for that task.
- ✔ **For stored processes:** Modify allows you to respecify the parameters selected.

Refresh reruns and opens the updated data, task output, or stored process.

Note that results do not automatically update when you reopen the Office document. You must refresh them or set the property (from the Properties dialog box) to automatically update upon Office document opening.

If you want to refresh some or all of your SAS content in your document, choose *Refresh Multiple*. Refresh Multiple allows you to rerun all content or selected content, and invoke the Modify dialog boxes before rerunning if desired. See Figure 13-22 for an example Refresh Multiple dialog box. Note that this also shows where the SAS content is located in the far-right column, which is a very useful feature.

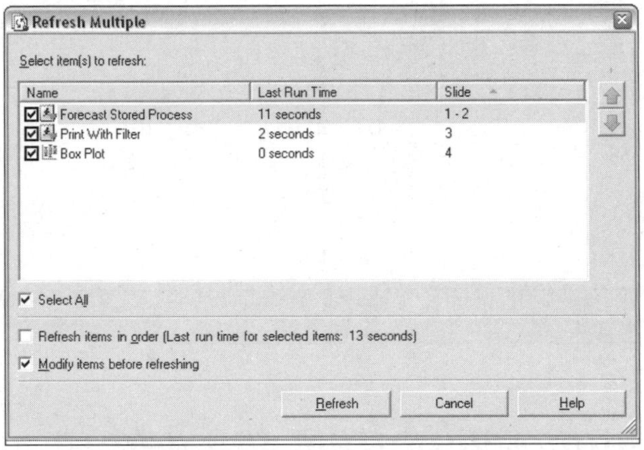

Figure 13-22:
Refresh
Multiple
SAS items
from the
add-in.

The *Properties* dialog box, as shown in Figure 13-23, allows you to view the properties of the SAS content. Information and options available include

- ✔ Date created
- ✔ Date modified
- ✔ Last run time
- ✔ Data used
- ✔ Any filters applied to the data used
- ✔ Whether to automatically refresh the item when you open the file in Office
- ✔ Various appearance settings

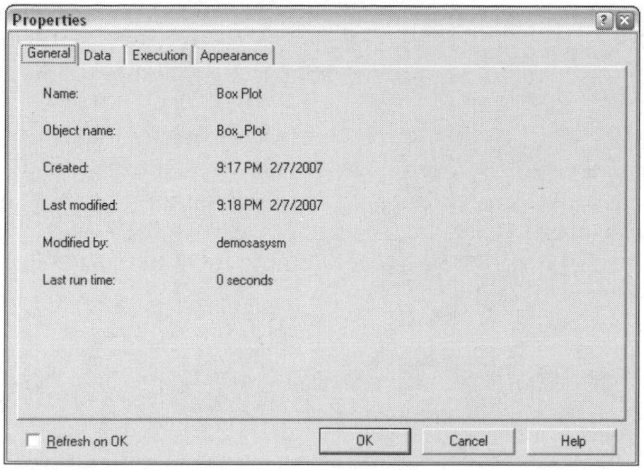

Figure 13-23:
SAS item properties from the add-in.

Sharing your work with others

The add-in adds a new possibility for sharing your content. Just like any other Office document, you can save your Office documents with SAS content in the same manner. In addition, if you e-mail your Office document to folks who do not have the add-in, they can still view and print the entire document just like you; however, they cannot refresh the results or view properties, and so on. The add-in provides true Office content. As a result, you can use all the formatting (bold, coloring, and font) and layout capabilities (multiple slides or one, moving pieces amongst various worksheets) in the Office application.

The SAS folders you navigated to access stored processes can also be used as a location to centrally save your Office document. To save your Office document to the SAS server, go to SAS⇨Tools⇨Publish. The Publish dialog box is shown in Figure 13-24. Here are the two advantages to this approach:

✔ **You centrally store your SAS/Office documents in the same folders where you access your stored processes.**

✔ **Your SAS data warehouse administrator has access to Impact Analysis data about your document.**

Impact Analysis allows your data administrator to see whether data sources are used by end users so they can understand the effect of making any significant changes or deletions to the data you use.

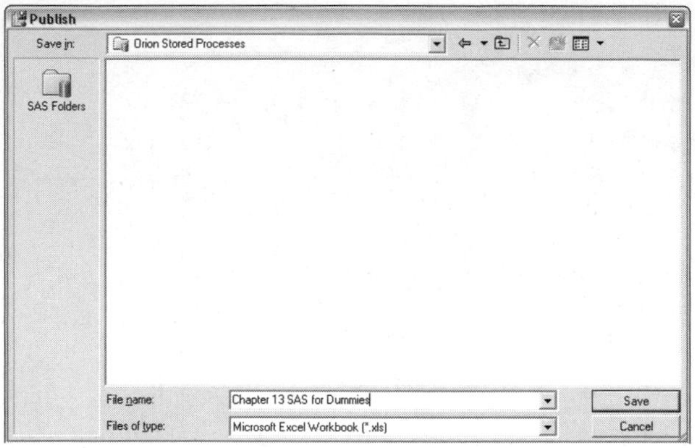

Figure 13-24:
Publish to
metadata
repository.

You can use this functionality regardless of whether SAS content is in your document. Anyone who has the add-in can open your documents via this mechanism from the same dialog box uses to open stored processes, via SAS➪Reports.

Chapter 14

Web Fever: Yeah, SAS Has That Covered

*M*any people use the Web for easy access to e-mail, searching for information, reading the daily news, accessing bank statements, or researching stocks and mutual funds. People love the Web because it makes getting to the data relevant to their needs easy and fast. Although applications such as SAS Enterprise Guide and the SAS Add-In for Microsoft Office are powerful and flexible, they require installing software and a certain amount of training before you can be proficient with them.

SAS has a great Web application to provide you with easy access to SAS reports: SAS Web Report Studio. Like other Web activities, minimal training is required to get going, and no application needs to be installed on your PC to use this application. Casual users of SAS, who aren't technical and don't view learning the SAS clients to be worth their time for their role at work, are the target audience of SAS Web Report Studio. SAS Web Report Studio offers easy

✔ Access to reports created by others for you

✔ Customizing and refreshing of reports

✔ Creation of new reports via reporting wizards

✔ Printing of your report

✔ Exporting the results to Excel

✔ Scheduling and sharing your reports with others

This chapter covers the highlights of SAS Web Report Studio functionality as highlighted in the preceding bullets.

Self-Service Reporting for Everyone

It's great that you can use SAS Web Report Studio like most other Web sites to open content someone else has created for you. Suppose, though, that you have a different question to answer than what the publicly available reports provide? Never fear, because SAS Web Report Studio makes it easy to create your own ad hoc reports with a mix of listing tables, crosstabulation tables, graphs, and stored process output.

With SAS Web Report Studio, you can easily create using just information maps and report wizards. An *information map* is a user-friendly, subject-specific view of data created by your SAS administrator. Information maps are useful because they simplify how complex data sources are presented, using terms that are meaningful to a business user of the data. Without information maps, you could end up seeing a table called S_R_Ref instead of a map called Sales Returns and Refunds, or you could see a column named N_Re_010 instead of Net Returns. The Report Wizard walks you through the report creation process in five simple steps.

The following example shows you the major steps to creating a report using the wizard. This example shows you how to use the Orion Star sample data, available from the SAS Support Web site, to create a sales report by product category, continent, and gender for calendar year 2005:

1. **After obtaining the Web address for logging into SAS Web Report Studio at your organization, go to your browser and type it in the address bar. You will be presented with the SAS Web Report Studio login screen, where you can enter your user name and password.**

2. **Start the report wizard from Report⇨New Using Wizard from the SAS Web Report Studio menu.**

   You can find this menu located below your Web browser menus in the browser window.

   The first step of the report wizard appears. This step allows you to select your information map and the items from the information map, as shown in Figure 14-1.

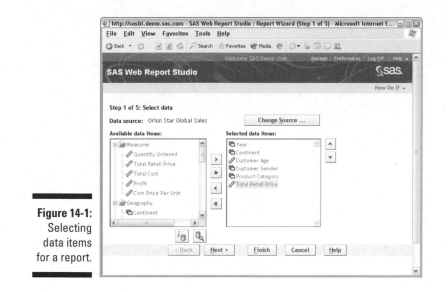

Figure 14-1:
Selecting
data items
for a report.

3. **Click the Change Source button to select the Orion Star Global Sales information map.**

4. **Add the desired data items that you want to use in your report to the Selected Data Items pane by clicking each item in the Available Data Items pane and then dragging it over to the Selected Data Items pane.**

   For this example, you should add Year, Continent, Customer Age, Customer Gender, Product Category, and Total Retail Price.

5. **Click Next to continue to Step 2 of the Report Wizard.**

   Step 2 of the Report Wizard appears, as shown in Figure 14-2. This step allows you to filter the data.

6. **For this example, click the drop-down list box for the item Year, select 2005 to use only 2005 sales data, and then click Next.**

   Step 3 of the wizard allows you to specify group breaks for your report, as shown in Figure 14-3. These allow you to order the overall report by group break variables with a separate section for each unique group break.

7. **For this example, click the Break By drop-down list, choose Product Category, and then click Next.**

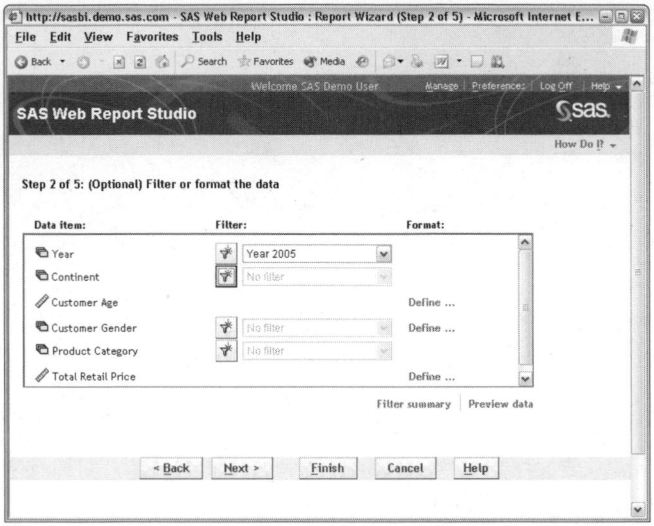

Figure 14-2:
Specify the
data filter
for your
report data.

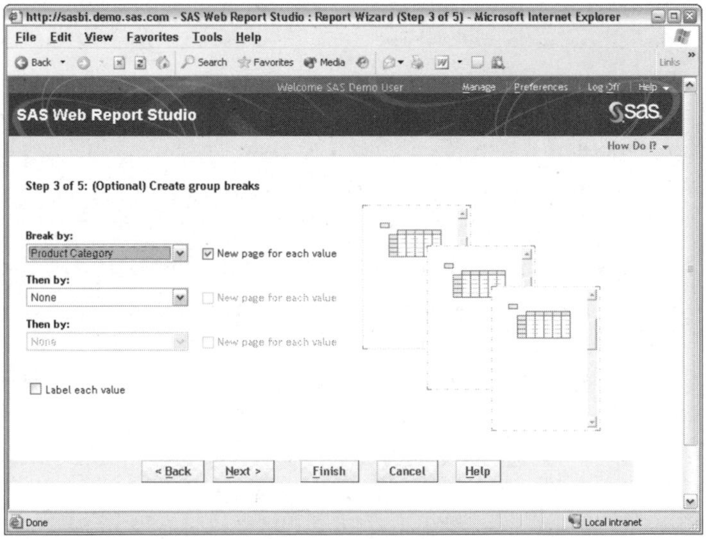

Figure 14-3:
Specify the
group
breaks for
your report.

Step 4 of the wizard appears, as shown in Figure 14-4. This step allows you to select whether you want a table, a graph, or both. You can choose between a list table or a crosstab table layout for the table, and you can also pick which columns to display. Additionally, you can also turn on a graph, select a graph type, and select the items to use for the various parts of your graph.

Figure 14-4:
Choose report table and graph details.

8. **For this example, click the Graph check box and select Total Retail Price from the Bar Height drop-down list, Continent from the Bars drop-down list, and Customer Gender from the Bar Subgroup drop-down list. Then click Finish to generate your report.**

We skipped Step 5 of the wizard here. It lets you specify the titles and footnotes for your report.

The report appears, as shown in Figure 14-5. Note that the data is grouped in the upper-left corner.

You can navigate by clicking the product category of interest to you. Each product category has a unique list table and bar chart for the category.

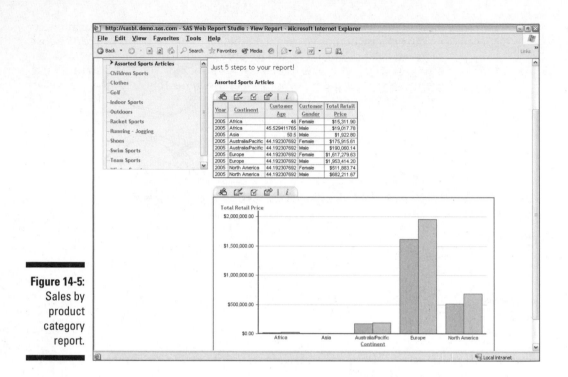

Figure 14-5:
Sales by
product
category
report.

Going beyond Basic Reporting

As you can see in the preceding section, SAS Web Report Studio makes ad hoc reporting from the Web simple, fast, and flexible. If you desire more advanced report creation and editing capabilities, you can also harness those from SAS Web Report Studio. An example of the advanced report-editing interface is shown in Figure 14-6.

Because of the extensive number of advanced features, here is a simplified overview of some of the more advanced report authoring capabilities:

✔ **Data**

- *Use OLAP (Online Analytic Processing) or relational data in a crosstabulation layout.* Much like pivot tables in Microsoft Excel, SAS Web Report Studio allows you to view relational data sources in crosstabular format.

- *Use conditional highlighting based on data values in your tables.* For example, sales greater than $1,000 are green, and less than $100 are red.

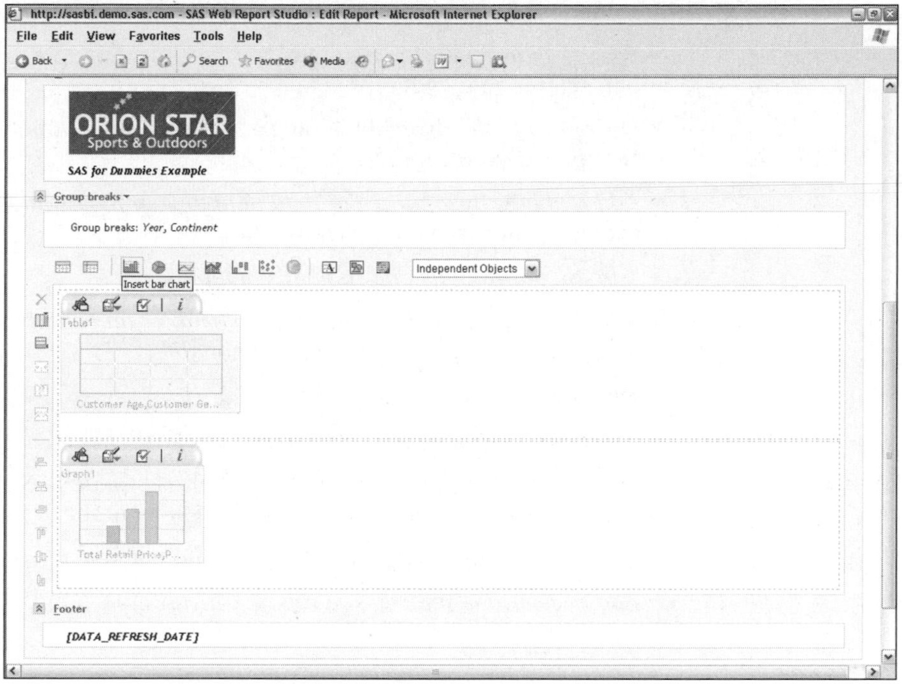

Figure 14-6:
Advanced
report
editing in
SAS Web
Report
Studio.

- *Specify whether to show detailed or summary data in list tables.* The default is summary aggregations of your data.

- *Modify the format of a data item in a report.*

- *Create new custom (calculated) data items from items in your information map.*

✔ **Interaction**

- *Users of your report can drill down, drill up, expand, and collapse your OLAP-based crosstabulation tables and charts.*

- *You can add drill-to-detail transactional data from crosstabulation reports.*

- *You can link reports so that users can drill from a high-level report (sales summary by continent and quarter) to a detailed report (sales transactions for a particular continent and a particular quarter).*

- *Add prompts to a report so that the data is automatically filtered whenever a user opens it.*

✔ **Tables and graphs**

- *Specify chart types:* for example, bar, bar-line, line, pie, progressive bar, scatter, and geographic maps of your data.

- *Customize table layout,* including adding multiple table or chart sections to your report.

- *Add rankings by a particular data item to your tables and graphs:* for example, sales ranked by continent.

- *Turn on or off totals and subtotals in tables.*

- *Add the ability to synchronize multiple tables and charts with drill down/up and expand/collapse functionality.*

✔ **Miscellaneous**

- *Leverage a stored process as a report section.*

- *Open a report published from SAS Enterprise Guide in SAS Web Report Studio.* You can also add additional content to these reports.

- *Save a report as a template for the creation of new reports.*

- *Add background images to a report:* for example, a big, bold, red *Confidential* image in the background of your report.

- *Add text objects to the body of your report.*

More Details on SAS Web Report Studio

This chapter can cover only the most commonly used features of the estimated 200 reporting features available in SAS Web Report Studio. This section presents a few examples of the advanced reports you can generate with this product. A key feature is the capability to secure reports, either for yourself or for a specific group. In addition, Web pages sometimes don't print as you might expect, so SAS Web Report Studio uses a smart system to transparently convert your report to an Adobe Acrobat file when you ask for it to print.

And what would a reporting tool be without the capability to export your data to Excel? SAS Web Report Studio also provides this functionality. Finally, it's nice to automatically schedule long-running or critical reports so that they are ready when you need them — this is another feature offered by SAS Web Report Studio.

Checking out some cool report examples

With some idea of the flexibility of SAS Web Report Studio under your belt, walk through how the average casual user of the product uses it. Many users open a report once or twice a month, view it, perhaps print or export the data in it, and that's it. To perform this simple scenario, you would log in to SAS Web Report Studio and choose Report⇨Open, at which point you would see a dialog box similar to Figure 14-7. In this example, we clicked Top 10 and Bottom 10 Customers by Spend - Single Page. After selecting the report, it automatically opened to Figure 14-8.

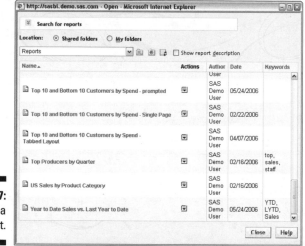

Figure 14-7:
Opening a
report.

Another example of an advanced report available from SAS Web Report Studio is shown in Figure 14-9. This report is an example of using maps and crosstabulation views of the data in one report. Users can change the measure item being mapped by clicking the drop-down list at the upper-right of the map and selecting a new measure item: for example, net profit. You can also drill down or expand into one of the continents shown by clicking it in the map and then clicking the drill or expand icon above the map.

Note that mapping functionality requires the SAS OLAP Server (available with the SAS Enterprise BI Server) and ESRI ArcGIS (something you must buy from ESRI, a partner of SAS).

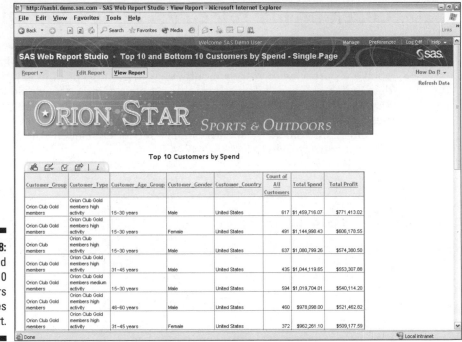

Figure 14-8:
The Top and Bottom 10 Customers Sales report.

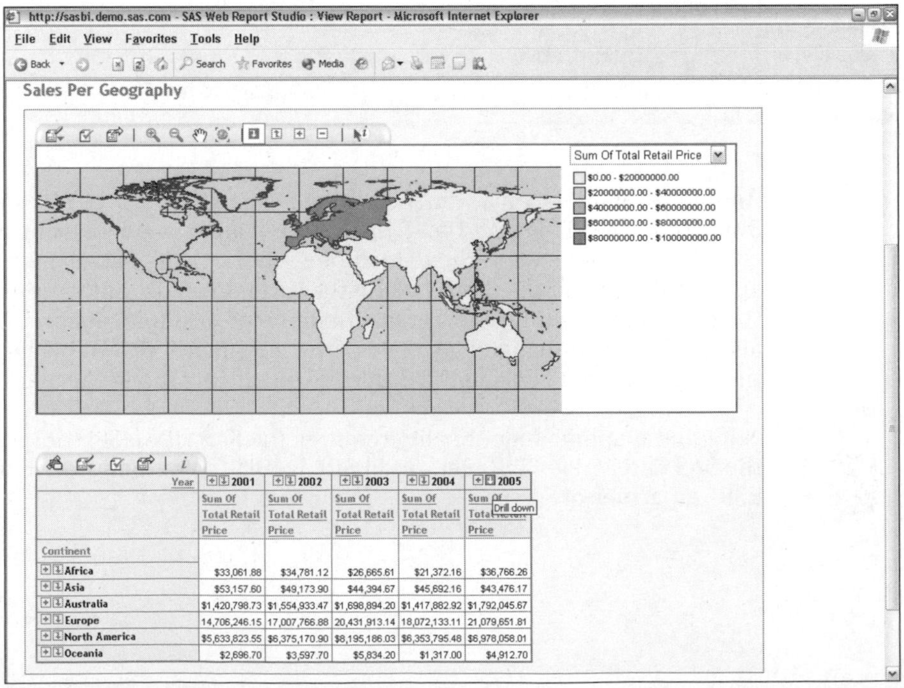

Figure 14-9:
An interactive map and crosstabulation report.

Securing reports

You can secure each report created and specify it as available for anyone who uses SAS Web Report Studio, for a specific subset of user groups based on SAS metadata, or as a report just for your own personal use.

Users of SAS Web Report Studio can also be given specific usage permissions regarding product functionality. The roles that you can assign to users range from using the full authoring capabilities to just having the ability to open and print reports. For further details, see the SAS White Paper on SAS Web Report Studio, "SAS Web Report Studio — An Introduction and Overview."

Printing smart

If you have used the Web to print important documents, you might have observed that Web pages do not always print out very well. For example, you might have pages too wide to print, missing page headers and footers, and page breaks that cut important tables or graphs in half. SAS Web Report Studio gets around these limitations by automatically converting the Web page you see into an Adobe Acrobat PDF document that you can print. This enables the product to provide you with intelligent pagination and headers/ footers, thus avoiding the typical poor printing from most Web pages. The only requirement is that you have Adobe Reader installed to print. (The vast majority of us have this. You can download it for free from www.adobe.com.) If you don't have Adobe Reader, you can simply use the standard browser-based printing, which will have some of the same problems as any other Web page.

Exporting data to Microsoft Excel

If you have the Microsoft Excel spreadsheet program, you can export the entire report view or the data behind a table a graph to Excel. When exporting the entire report, a compressed or Zip file is created that contains a spreadsheet, an HTML file, and various image files. After you save the Zip file to your PC, just open the spreadsheet inside the Zip file and say Yes to any warning prompts in Excel to view the report in Excel. Data from a table or graph can also be opened in Excel as a tab-delimited text file.

Exporting from a table has an additional option to use the report formats for the data when you open it in Excel. This is handy because you won't need to reformat fields like currency or dates.

Note that each of the export mechanism methods listed results in a static Excel spreadsheet. To update the spreadsheet, you need to re-export the contents from SAS Web Report Studio. If dynamic content in Excel is important for the task at hand, use the SAS Add-In for Microsoft Office (discussed in Chapter 13) to create your spreadsheet instead.

You can also distribute reports via e-mail as a PDF or an HTML file. You can send the report to a single person or a wide audience based on your mailing lists. To distribute a report you are viewing, just choose Report⇨Distribute.

Scheduling reports

When you're opening or viewing a report, you can decide to schedule it if you want it to run on a periodic basis. To schedule a report you are viewing, just choose Report⇨Schedule.

It's a good idea to schedule reports that take quite a while to run, especially if the report uses large data sources or if the report is used frequently by many people in your company.

You can also archive scheduled reports so that colleagues can easily compare today's report with last week's report. Figure 14-10 shows the Schedule Report dialog box, available when you choose Report⇨Schedule. You can also schedule an entire folder of reports to run with this same mechanism.

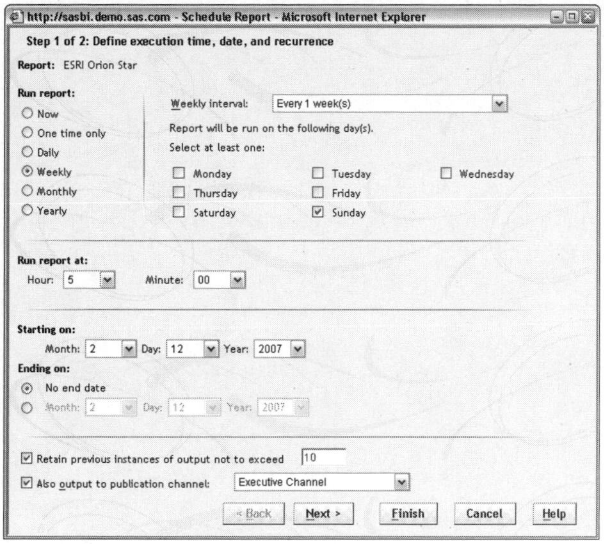

Figure 14-10:
The scheduling wizard for SAS Web Report Studio.

Part V
Getting SAS Ready to Rock and Roll

The 5th Wave   By Rich Tennant

"I started running 'what if' scenarios on my data, like, 'What if I were sick of this dirtwad job and funneled some of the company's money into an off-shore account?'"

In this part . . .

This part is where we quarantine most of the truly technical information. Software setup and configuration usually involves professional IT staff, but it's good for anyone using the software to understand how it works. For example, for those of you with enough data to fill a warehouse, we describe the concepts of categorizing and arranging that data in a repeatable process — *data warehousing*.

And no matter how much you thought you knew about SAS programming, there is always something new to master: for example, how to use SAS Enterprise Guide to get more done, faster.

Chapter 15

Setting It All Up

● ●

In This Chapter

▶ Installing SAS Enterprise Guide and SAS for Windows locally

▶ Using server-based SAS with SAS Enterprise Guide

▶ Defining data sources once and for all

● ●

*I*nstalling and configuring SAS software can be as simple as popping a few CDs into your computer and clicking a few buttons — no more difficult than loading some music on a portable music player. Or it can be more complicated, like assembling a home theater system, requiring moderate site preparation before you get started. Then again, it can be a terrific engineering and political challenge, like launching an international space station, involving months of planning and coordination among several stakeholder groups before the first button is pushed.

In this chapter, you can read about the basic configuration of SAS on a personal computer, which is the easiest to set up and use. You can also read about some of the behind-the-scenes work required to configure SAS for use in a multi-machine environment, where multiple people use a centralized SAS installation in an administered setting. Finally, you see what's involved in configuring your data sources so that nothing will stand in your way when you want to use SAS to access and analyze your data.

How Complicated? It Depends

What makes the difference between a simple, no-fuss install process and a complicated deployment is determined by your answers to questions like the following.

✔ **What type of computer hardware will you use to host and access your SAS software?** By far, SAS for Microsoft Windows is the easiest to set up. It installs similarly to most software packages that you might use at home. However, SAS is also available for use on most operating systems employed by businesses today, including Linux, various flavors of UNIX, and the IBM z/OS on mainframe systems. Installing on these server-class machines requires personnel with system administrator experience.

✔ **How many people need access to use the software, and where are they are located relative to the computer hardware?** When you have multiple people who need to access SAS on a single computer, installing SAS is only the first step. You must also install and configure the additional products and technologies that allow remote users to access SAS as a central server.

✔ **How many different SAS software products do you plan to use (and therefore configure)?** A complete SAS deployment might comprise dozens of different products. Some products are simple to install and need no additional configuration. For example, you can add the SAS/OR product to the mix, which supplies you with a collection of SAS procedures to support operations research and optimization modeling. After installation, no extra configuration is necessary.

In contrast, installing a product such as SAS Forecast Server requires that you configure the SAS Analytics Platform, which is a services layer that allows multiple people using SAS Forecast Studio to create and work with forecasting projects. SAS deployment tools attempt to make these types of additions manageable, but they can do only so much to simplify this complex process.

The Sweetest Setup: Local-Local

With SAS and SAS Enterprise Guide installed on your personal computer (running Microsoft Windows), no additional configuration is necessary. It just works.

In this setup, the SAS installation is on your PC (local to your machine). You don't need a SAS Metadata Server (discussed in the following section) because SAS Enterprise Guide can detect that SAS is available without having to "look up" where to find it. SAS support folks call this setup *local-local* because SAS is local to your machine and the metadata repository is inferred as a local installation.

Figure 15-1 shows a SAS Enterprise Guide session with this simple setup. Notice that the message in status bar on the bottom right indicates `localhost`, meaning that the metadata repository is built into this local configuration. And the only SAS server showing in the Server view is Local.

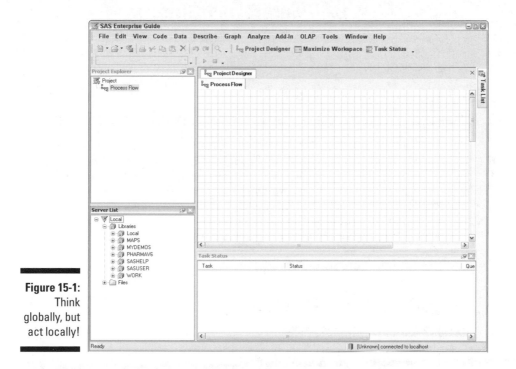

Figure 15-1:
Think globally, but act locally!

To tell whether you have SAS installed on your local PC (as well as what version), choose Help⇨About SAS Enterprise Guide. In the About SAS Enterprise Guide window, click System Information. The first few entries in the System Information window show you whether SAS is installed (SAS System Version) and, if so, which version.

Distributing SAS to the Masses

If you work in an environment where many people use SAS, chances are good that you make use of a centralized configuration. For example, you might have SAS Enterprise Guide on your desktop, but your SAS server is located somewhere else (in another room, another building, or even another state or country). If so, you're living the dream of *distributed computing,* made possible by powerful server machines and fast computer networks.

SAS Learning Edition = SAS + SAS Enterprise Guide

In fact, the local-local scenario is exactly the configuration supplied in the SAS Learning Edition. *SAS Learning Edition* is a special packaging of SAS and SAS Enterprise Guide, targeted toward students and professionals who want to learn SAS. It's a full-featured version of the software with a restricted license that simply limits the size of the data you can process.

Now, whether you *feel* like you are living a dream depends on your perspective. Many end users prefer the good old days when their SAS installation was local. However, today's IT departments use words like *total cost of ownership* and *centralized control* to justify the distributed environment. The upside of this type of arrangement is that usually more people in the organization have access to SAS because not everyone needs a personal copy installed on their machines.

Drowning in tiers: Talking across boundaries

A distributed SAS environment can have many pieces, and they all have to be able to find and talk to each other to work smoothly. The pieces are divided into *tiers,* which are logical boundary points between the various parts. Sometimes tiers are configured on separate machines; other times they are simply logical service layers that share space on a single machine. These are the main tiers in broad terms:

- **Client tier:** Usually where you are, at your desk or PC.

- **SAS server tier:** Where your SAS session runs, processing your analysis and reports and crunching the numbers. This can be a SAS workspace server or a stored process server.

- **Metadata tier**: The SAS Metadata Server, which serves as a directory for finding everything else.

✔ **Data tier:** Where your data resides. This can include database data such as Oracle, OLAP data from the SAS OLAP server, or other SAS data servers such as SAS/SHARE.

✔ **Web middle tier:** Where your Web-based applications reside, such as SAS Web Report Studio or the SAS Information Delivery Portal.

As an end user, your main interaction is with the client-tier pieces. Your client-tier applications include SAS Enterprise Guide, SAS Add-In for Microsoft Office (running in Microsoft Word or Excel, for example, as discussed in Chapter 13), and your Web browser (to access the Web-based SAS applications).

Metadata: The keys to the kingdom

The SAS Metadata Server is the central repository that directs all the pieces of the SAS environment. It contains information about how to find all the resources available at the various tiers. It also provides a central point of control for administrators to decide who can access what resources and data.

The main tool of the SAS administrator is the SAS Management Console application. Figure 15-2 shows an example of it. Notice the types of items that you can manage here, including servers, data libraries, stored processes, and much more.

Figure 15-2:
SAS Management ment Console: Not for the faint of heart.

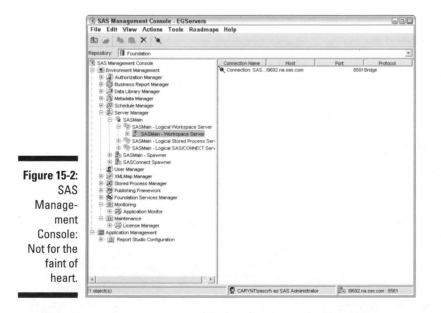

At the client tier, the main configuration activity required is to ensure that you are pointing to the correct metadata server. In many organizations with dozens or hundreds of users, a SAS administrator might have performed this step for you.

If you find that you need to adjust this configuration, you can find the settings in Tools⇨Options. At the bottom of the Options window is the Administration section. The metadata configuration is on the Repository and Server.

A *metadata configuration* consists of just a few key pieces of information:

- ✔ The name (machine host address) of the metadata server
- ✔ A port (unique address on the machine)
- ✔ A user ID and password

In addition, you might need to select from a list of logical repositories on the machine.

Figure 15-3 shows an example of the repository configuration window from SAS Enterprise Guide. The settings that you supply here will be very particular for your environment and will almost certainly be prescribed by your friendly SAS administrator.

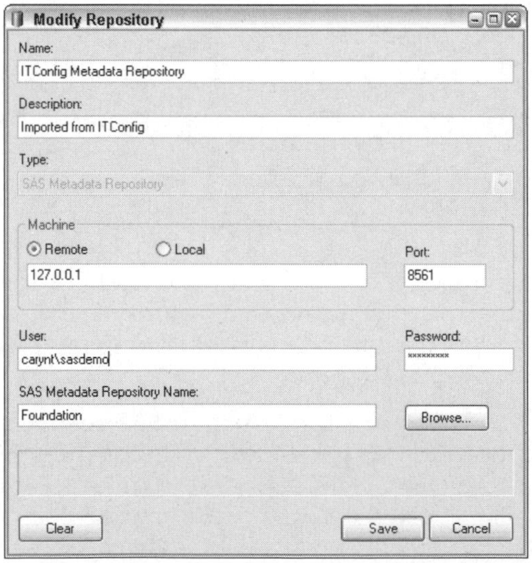

Figure 15-3: Configure your metadata to get on the correct path.

Good News Travels Fast — How about Your Data?

Data access can be mysterious, like drawing water from the kitchen sink. You can see the water come out of the tap — and touch it and taste it, which is instantly gratifying. But do you really know where the water comes from? And do you know exactly how much water there is beyond that magical water faucet? Probably not — that's something that most of us simply take for granted.

However, when you have a problem — water doesn't flow, or it flows too slowly — then you really notice. And diagnosing plumbing issues is something that most people are uncomfortable with. (If you're lucky, it's just a kink in a hose somewhere.)

Data access works the same way. When your data flows freely into your SAS Enterprise Guide session, it seems like you can do nothing wrong. You can view it in the data grid, create queries, and run tasks. However, when data access points are not defined efficiently, that data flow can feel like you're trying to suck an elephant through a straw. Everything seems to take so much longer to accomplish.

Crash course in data plumbing

Diagnosing data access issues can be easier than household plumbing chores. You simply need be able to answer three main questions:

- ✔ **Where does the data source originate?** For example, is it in a database system such as Oracle, or is it in a text file on your server file system?

- ✔ **How large is the data source?** SAS and SAS Enterprise Guide can deal with data sources that are millions or even billions of records large. However, understanding the data size is important to understanding the tradeoffs of various data configurations.

- ✔ **What route does the data travel to get to your SAS session?** Because SAS needs to process your data for analysis and reporting, your data needs to travel the shortest distance possible from its point of origin into your SAS session. Even though you might use SAS Enterprise Guide to select your data source, what counts is how many "hops" the data must make to get to the SAS session where the real work occurs.

All this leads to the golden rule of efficient data access with SAS:

Define your data sources in terms of your SAS server. Use SAS libraries to connect to your data sources, and route all of your data access through those libraries.

Passing Niagara Falls through a garden hose

Because SAS Enterprise Guide makes it easy to get to data in many ways, you can easily violate this rule (inadvertently, of course). For example, you can choose File⇨Open⇨ODBC and select a data source defined relative to your local PC. However, when you use that data within your project, SAS Enterprise Guide realizes that this data is not presently accessible to your SAS session, so it attempts to perform the great favor of copying it for you.

SAS Enterprise Guide is a great tool for many things, but it can be a bottleneck in the process of copying data. Copying data from an external source to your SAS session with SAS Enterprise Guide as the go-between is very inefficient. If the data is large, this operation can take several minutes (or longer!). In technical terms, this called "going around your elbow to get to your thumb."

SAS/ACCESS: The plumber's helper

Fortunately, it is easy to avoid moving all those data records through SAS Enterprise Guide: Simply define access to the external data source on the SAS server. SAS provides a set of data access products — SAS/ACCESS — to make this easy to do. A SAS/ACCESS module exists for just about every major database type in use today. For any that are missing, you can use SAS/ACCESS to ODBC, which can be like a universal pipe fitting to connect you to any data source.

The SAS/ACCESS products allow you to define the data sources in terms of SAS libraries. And after a data source is in a SAS library, your SAS programs can access it just as if it were a native SAS data set.

SAS libraries can be defined in your environment by a SAS administrator, or they can be defined as needed within your SAS Enterprise Guide project.

Example: Project meets data, just in time

Time to look at an example of creating a project library. In this example, pretend that you need to access a set of data tables in an Oracle database. You have a sticky note on your desk from your database administrator that tells you the schema of the data source and other important access information.

With this information and the Assign Library task within SAS Enterprise Guide, you can define a SAS library for this data source.

1. **Choose Tools⇨Assign Library.**

   The Library Wizard appears, as shown in Figure 15-4.

2. **In the Name field, type the name that you want to give to the library.**

Library Wizard

1 of 7   Enter a name and an optional description for the library.   §sas.

Name:
ORA10

Description:

Note:
This library definition will not be permanently stored with the SAS server. To use this library again in a future session, you will need to rerun this task within your project. To create a permanent library definition, use the New Library wizard in SAS Enterprise Guide Explorer.

< Back   Next >   Finish   Cancel   Help

The name must comply with SAS naming conventions, which means it must contain only letters, numbers, and underscores and also be no longer than eight characters.

3. **Click Next when complete.**

   The second page of the wizard appears, allowing you to select which SAS server to use for this library. In this example shown in Figure 15-5, only one SAS server is available (SASMain), but your environment might have more.

   Select the correct SAS server — the one that you know will have access to the database client necessary for the library you're defining.

4. **Select your server and click Next.**

   The third page of the wizard, as shown in Figure 15-6, allows you to select a library engine.

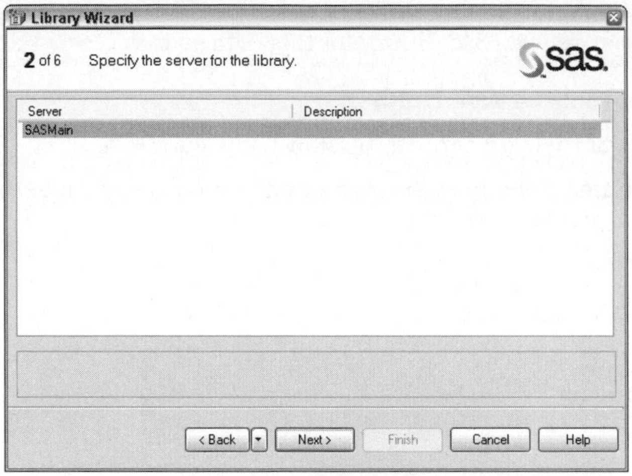

Figure 15-5:
Pick your
server.

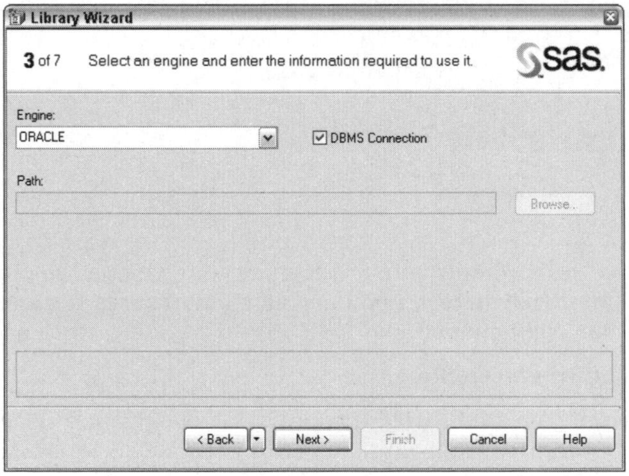

Figure 15-6:
Library
engines
make your
data go
vroom!

In SAS, *library engines* represent the protocols to talk to different
sources of data. Library engines fall mainly into two categories: file- or
path-based engines and database engines.

- *File-* or *path-based engines* map to folders or files on your server
  file system and also provide access to all the data files within those
  folders.

- *Database engines* map to database server connections, providing
  access to external databases.

In this example, you would select the ORACLE engine. When you do, the wizard automatically selects the DBMS Connection check box.

5. **Choose a library engine and then click Next.**

The fourth page of the wizard asks you for your database user ID and password, as shown in Figure 15-7. This is usually a special database account that someone has established for you, and it might not be the same as your SAS server account.

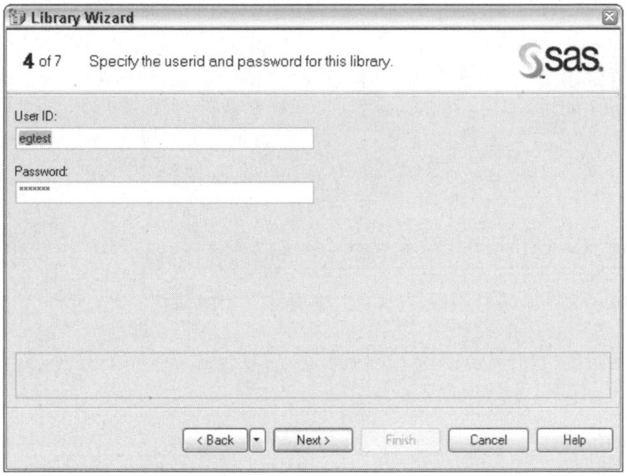

Figure 15-7:
Enter your secret codes.

6. **Enter your database user ID and password and then click Next.**

The fifth page of the wizard, as shown in Figure 15-8, provides a chance to specify any extra options that you might need to access the database. This is where that pretend sticky note mentioned earlier comes into play. Depending on the database and your particular setup, you might need to specify an option or two here. For example, the PATH option and SCHEMA option are common database options needed to make the connection.

7. **Select any desired options and then click Next.**

The sixth page of the wizard provides an optional opportunity to test your library, as shown in Figure 15-9. If you click the Start Test button, SAS Enterprise Guide connects to the SAS server and submits the library statement with the options you specified. If all goes well, the status will show as OK. If you run into a problem, click Show Log to get a hint of what might be missing or incorrect.

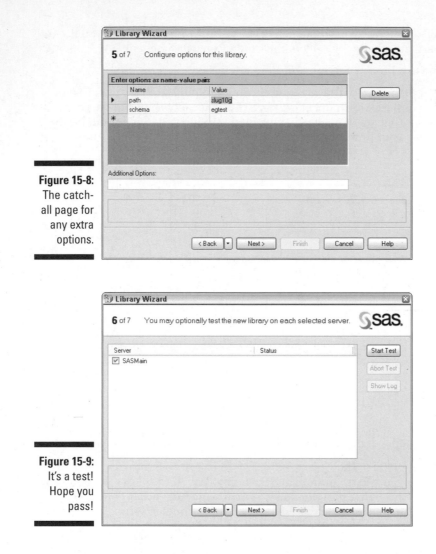

Figure 15-8:
The catch-all page for any extra options.

Figure 15-9:
It's a test! Hope you pass!

8. After testing your library (or deciding not to), click Next.

The final page of the wizard shows you the SAS LIBNAME statement that is generated on your behalf. See the example in Figure 15-10.

9. Click Finish.

The Assign Library task is added to your project and becomes part of the flow. When you choose File➪Open➪Data, the new library should appear under the SASMain server, and all the tables within are available for use in your project.

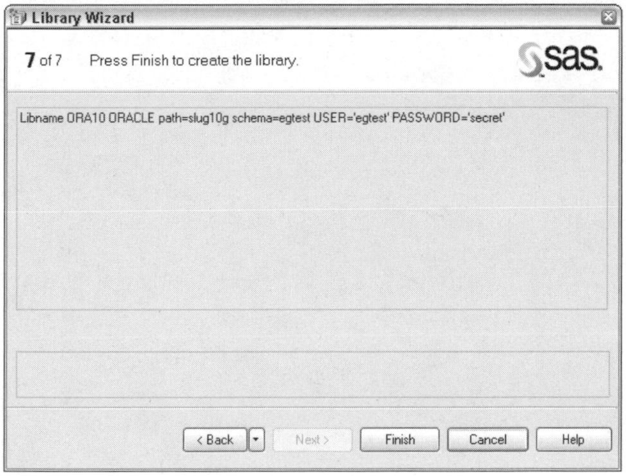

```
Library Wizard                                                    [×]

7 of 7    Press Finish to create the library.              §sas.

Libname ORA10 ORACLE path=slug10g schema=egtest USER='egtest' PASSWORD='secret'



         < Back   [▼]   Next >        Finish     Cancel      Help
```

Figure 15-10:
All that
work for
this magic
incantation.

This is a project library only. That means that it exists only within your project for the duration of your current session. The next time you use this project, you need to make sure to run the Assign Library task first before accessing any of the data that it points to.

To ensure that the Assign Library task is run ahead of any data that needs it, create a link from the task to the first reference of the library data within your project. Here's how to create the link:

1. **Select the Assign Library item in your project flow.**

2. **Right-click and choose Link Assign Library To from the contextual menu.**

   The Link window appears.

3. **Choose the data table from this library that first appears in your project and then click OK.**

   Your project now shows a direct link between the Assign Library task and the data that you need from it. Figure 15-11 shows an example of this type of link. When you re-run your flow, the Assign Library task is guaranteed to run before this data reference is used.

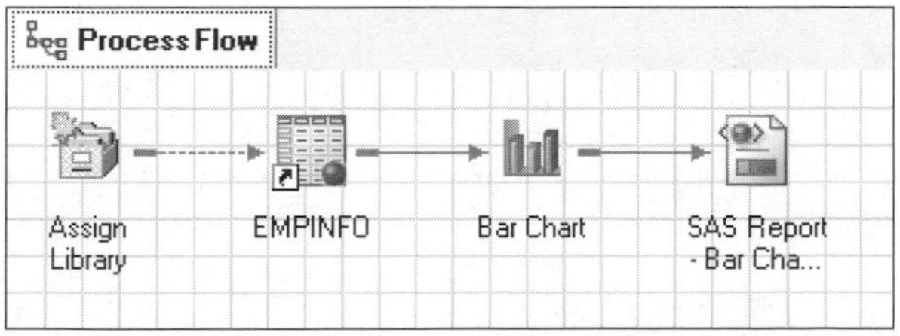

Figure 15-11:
Don't suffer
from a
missing link.

```
Process Flow

   [Assign      [EMPINFO]      [Bar Chart]      [SAS Report
    Library]                                      - Bar Cha...]
```

Chapter 16

Taming the Data Beast

*A*ccessing, massaging, cleaning up, and managing the various data sources that you need are critical to success with SAS. Well-managed data allows you to focus on creating cool analyses and graphs; in fact, it is often the overlooked key to success with SAS business intelligence and analytics. In many situations, individual data access and management work is a reasonable strategy. Comparatively, in many situations, a great deal of time could be saved and many headaches avoided by leveraging the techniques and tools of data warehousing. As a discipline, data warehousing is all about meeting the needs of many user groups (that is, you!) by providing a central data store that combines critical data needed from various systems in your company.

In this chapter, we review why data warehousing is important for everyone to understand, the basics of data warehousing, and the value of data marts (a *mini* data warehouse).

Data Warehousing: Do I Really Need to Think about This?

Consider a simple report of sales invoices, which includes data from customer, shipping, and returns systems. At many companies, the sales department maintains the customer systems, the shipping database is in operations, and returns are in finance. All these systems are often independent databases with very different rules and assumptions about the data stored in them, even though the data is describing a single process. You can use a tool like SAS Enterprise Guide to bring together the data in SAS and create the sales invoice report from all these systems.

Suppose you created 15 versions of a report in 15 different SAS Enterprise Guide projects. You have so many versions to meet the widely varying needs for various decision makers and users in your company. Now also assume that others in your company (who are, of course, not as enlightened as you) used other applications to create their own specialized forms of this report. This array of projects and systems still sounds maintainable — but only with a lot of work and coordination.

Now suppose that the data environment in which you created all these reports changes. (This happens quite often in many companies.) Suppose, too, that your company acquired a new company, adding its data sources to the scenario. Discovering poor data quality in merging companies is common: customer names, addresses, and phone numbers, in this example. (You likely have some poor data quality as well; you just haven't found them.) In addition, your company just upgraded one of the databases, which inadvertently changed the names as well as the formats of some of the variables used in this report. Finally, the same product codes that translate into product names in your company's report translate differently in the newly acquired company (for example, product code 10101 in your company is product code 20202 in the newly acquired company!). This sounds like a real headache, requiring many weeks of work to update all these reports.

In real-world companies that Stephen has worked with, there could be hundreds or thousands of reports in various tools ranging from SAS to Excel to other business intelligence (also called BI) tools from various vendors. In this scenario, someone needs to reconcile all these reports in all these tools with the new data sources, resolve the quality problems, reconcile the product codes, and adjust for the updated database variable names. If only you had used a data warehouse as your central data source, no maintenance would be required of the reports and analyses — just updates made to the central data warehouse.

Here are some of the reasons to consider the use of data warehousing at your company:

- **Simplification of end user access to a wide variety of data from a single source rather than from many systems:** Users don't need to learn all the systems providing the data — just how to use the data warehouse.

- **Simplification of long-term maintenance of reports and analyses:** You can accomplish this by isolating users from the source systems and using a consistent data structure (from the data warehouse) for reporting and analysis.

✔ **Virtual elimination of performance and maintenance impact of end users who directly access operational systems:** Your shipping team might not be very happy at 4:30 p.m. on a Friday waiting for its system to take its shipping orders because you are running a big analysis against that database!

✔ **Seamless integration of business rules used to combine data from the various systems into one process when the data warehouse is updated:** This helps avoid confusion around which report or analysis is correct. This integration also provides an easy mechanism to transparently update the underlying assumptions used in your corporate reporting and decision making. Want to change the calculation for estimated amount of returns for international customers? Just update the data warehouse rules.

✔ **Improvement of performance for end user ad hoc analysis and reporting:** Data warehouses are structured for such purposes. Most systems that feed the data warehouse aren't designed for optimal performance when reading the data; instead, they are designed for optimal performance for updating and adding new information. The shipping system was optimized to process new orders, not to run your big query accessing all ship events from 2005.

✔ **Uncovering significant quality problems in and among the various operational systems in the company:** This occurs when the various areas of the company attempt to support all their reporting and analysis needs from the centralized data warehouse and discover that they had applied different rules and assumptions to the data in the various systems.

The data warehousing and data quality tools from SAS, combined with methodologies developed over many years, can help you avoid these nightmares! If you are inspired or just plain scared by this scenario, please read on to discover the business value and effect of data warehousing.

Fundamental Principles of Data Warehousing

Before discussing data warehousing principles, read how one of the inventors of modern data warehousing defines the overall process. Bill Inmon, known as one of the founders of data warehousing, defines data warehousing as

✔ **Subject-oriented:** Data maintained in the data warehouse is organized around subject areas that are meaningful and relevant to the business users.

✔ **Time-variant:** Changes to the data and varying business rules applied to the data are captured and stored in the data warehouse.

✔ **Non-volatile:** The data is almost never overwritten or deleted but instead is maintained for long-term needs. Very large data warehouses can "collapse" or summarize older data to save on data storage space, but throwing away any historic data is generally discouraged.

✔ **Integrated:** The data warehouse maintains critical data from most of the companies' operational systems. In addition, this data is harmonized by applying the needed business rules to ensure that the data is meaningful to the business.

SAS provides the SAS Enterprise Data Integration Server solution to build and maintain your data warehouse. This solution provides a rich tool set to access your operational systems and apply data quality methods, business rules, data joining, data optimization for later access, and mapping of the data into your data warehouse. See Figure 16-1 for a process overview of data warehousing.

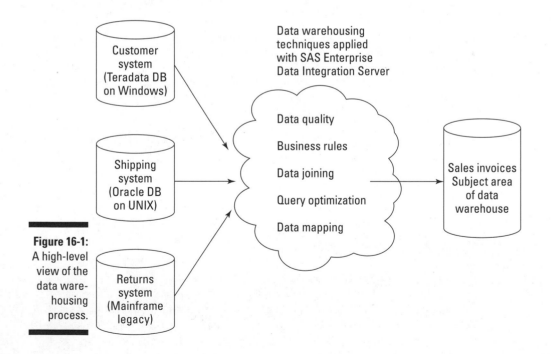

Figure 16-1:
A high-level view of the data warehousing process.

Various data storage approaches are used on the right side of Figure 16-1. These approaches are usually selected to optimize response time to your queries and to simplify updates to the data. One data structure common to data warehousing is the *star schema,* as illustrated in Figure 16-2. It's called a *star* because some clever person thought it resembled a four-pointed star that you see in cartoons and crude drawings.

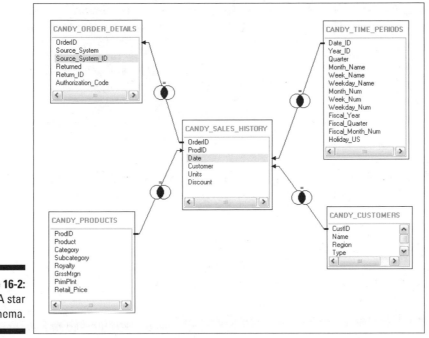

Figure 16-2:
A star
schema.

Here are the few basic ideas behind the star schema. The central table, Candy_Sales_History, is the *fact table.* A fact table is where details of an individual transaction are stored. The fact table is the focal point of a star, and it contains only measurements unique to the record of interest: in this case, units and the discount given. The fact table also contains columns to join it with the other tables; these are *foreign keys* because they allow the fact table to be joined with other ("foreign") tables.

The supporting tables in a star schema are *dimension tables.* Dimensions are tables that can be used to group or describe additional details of a record in the fact table. Product category, year, customer name, and whether it was returned are all attributes of the fact table. They typically link to the fact table via their primary keys. These keys are a unique identifier for each record in a dimension table.

The SAS Add-In for Microsoft Office and SAS Web Report Studio can access a star schema only via information maps. This avoids confronting the casual user with a star schema or the even more complicated snowflake schema! Star schemas are also frequently used as the data source input for creating SAS OLAP Server cubes (discussed in Chapter 13).

With SAS Enterprise Guide, you can join the tables in a star schema, as shown in Figure 16-2. Data warehouses could contain many subject areas and can grow to incredibly large sizes! An example of a data warehouse with multiple subject areas could include finance, sales, customer service, logistics, and employee subject areas. Typically, each of these subject areas can be linked to other areas, not just within themselves. Data warehouses can range in size from a few gigabytes (5 to 10 percent of a typical laptop hard drive) to multiple petabytes.

A *petabyte* is equal to about 50,000 to 200,000 hard drives on a typical laptop!

The Value of Well-Managed Data Marts

The simplest way to understand a *data mart* is to think of it as a subject area of the data warehouse, just without the other areas. Although data warehouses might sound like a great idea, sometimes they are impractical to implement for critical business needs — and this is where a data mart comes into the picture. From an end user viewpoint, a data mart is very similar to a data warehouse. You create and maintain it with the same tools and methodologies as a data warehouse.

Here are some reasons to consider using a data mart instead of a data warehouse:

✔ **Access to frequently needed data for areas not in your data warehouse is eased.** This is particularly true if your data warehouse group considers your subject area not in scope for future implementation in the overall data warehouse.

This doesn't mean that they can't be combined, but that they likely think your area is of interest to a small area of the company.

✔ **By using a small group of end-users as the target audience, this might lead to a much better subject-specific focus and possibly a more useful system.**

✔ **Because this is a focused system, there is often much quicker time to implementation than in an expansive data warehouse.**

Data marts might sound great, but they are not a panacea. To avoid creating silos of data and critical information in many departments, your company should consider how to integrate data mart requests into the data warehouse over time, even if doing this in the short term is not possible. Other groups will invariably find value in your data mart and want to combine it with their data mart or data from the corporate data warehouse. Synchronizing the work of your data mart with the data warehouse also helps ensure that consistent rules apply across all the data sources and that redundancy is avoided whenever possible.

Chapter 17

The New World Meets the Old: Programmers and SAS Enterprise Guide

*S*AS programmers can sometimes be . . . um (how to say this nicely?) . . . set in their ways. Although painting a whole class of people as having inflexible tendencies isn't fair, long-time SAS programmers tend to carry more legacy than folks who work in other areas of technology. After all, if the techniques you have been using to do your job for 20 years are still working, what's your incentive to change?

In this chapter, you can read about the productivity gains that you can enjoy when you add SAS Enterprise Guide to your SAS programming toolbox. You will see how to perform old tasks in a new way as well as how to accomplish some tasks that would be have been very difficult — if not impossible — without the benefit of an integrated tool like SAS Enterprise Guide.

The times, they are a-changin'

A woodworking show called "The Woodwright's Shop" airs on public television. It features an ambitious gentleman named Roy who completes woodworking projects using only turn-of-the-century tools (that is, turn-of-the-*last*-century). He is entertaining, and there is no question that he is an expert in his craft. Yet his progress in each episode is limited because he does everything by hand, the old-fashioned way. (He also occasionally has to dip into his first aid kit to patch up some minor injury.)

Another woodworking show, also on public television, is "The New Yankee Workshop." This show features a familiar personality named Norm, who works in a state-of-the-art workshop with every modern power tool and woodworking convenience. Like Roy, Norm is an expert in carpentry and all things wood. However, Norm gets so much more accomplished in a single episode. Whereas Roy might build something small, like a stool, Norm builds big projects, like a dining room set.

Experienced SAS programmers can sometimes be like Roy. They are experts in their field, and they can accomplish quite a bit by using the traditional SAS tools: for example, a plain text editor and the SAS Display Manager interface.

Tools like SAS Enterprise Guide, however, can boost the productivity of even the most experienced SAS programmer. SAS Enterprise Guide provides easy methods to perform the more tedious tasks while still allowing you to write SAS programs and integrate them into your overall processes. And SAS Enterprise Guide provides ways for you to share your work with others in new ways, making your SAS know-how more pervasive in your organization.

This is good news because many SAS programmers are finding that their old tools are becoming unavailable to them as their organizations adopt a distributed computing environment. Instead of allowing SAS to be installed on every PC, many companies install SAS in a centralized environment and supply SAS programmers with SAS Enterprise Guide as the tool to access that environment. As a result, some SAS programmers are reluctant converts to SAS Enterprise Guide. With some adjustment, these workers should enjoy increased productivity as a consolation prize.

Getting Organized with Projects

One of the biggest advantages that SAS Enterprise Guide offers is the capability to organize your work in project files. A SAS Enterprise Guide project is a great place to store related work together, including SAS programs, references to data, Output Delivery System (ODS) results such as HTML, and SAS logs. (See Chapter 10 for more details about the types of results you can work with.)

Project files do more than store all your work items, though. Project files also store the *relationships* among those work items. The process flow view of your project serves as a form of documentation for your work.

Figure 17-1 shows a sample process flow. You can read this project from left to right to easily see how it's put together. It begins with a SAS program (Make Customer Data) that builds a customer table. That table, along with two other tables, is used as input into a query task that joins the three tables together to create an output table named JoinResult. JoinResult is then used as input to a scatter plot task.

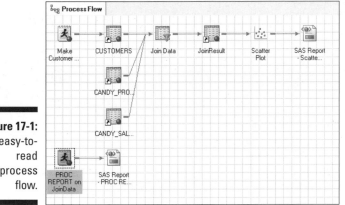

Figure 17-1: An easy-to-read process flow.

The only item that seems to be hanging out there is the SAS program at the bottom: the one labeled PROC REPORT. Although the label might be informative, seeing how it relates to the other items is difficult.

Connecting the dots with links

The relationships described in this sample project so far, as shown by the arrow links in the process flow, are *implicit*. That is, SAS Enterprise Guide detects these relationships and illustrates them in the process flow view, with no intervention needed from you. SAS Enterprise Guide also lets you define your own links among items. This adds even more readability to your project and helps enforce the sequence in which items are run.

For example, suppose that the lone SAS program with the PROC REPORT label is meant to report on the JoinResult table. To build an explicit link from the data table to the SAS program, you could do the following:

1. **Right-click the JoinResult item and choose Link JoinResult To.**

   The Link window appears, showing a list of candidate items in the project to which you can link.

2. **Choose the PROC REPORT item from the list and then click OK.**

   The process flow view updates to show the new relationship, as shown in Figure 17-2.

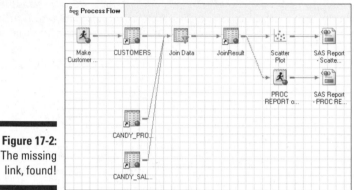

Figure 17-2:
The missing
link, found!

Another way to draw this link is to literally draw the link. You can

1. **Select an item in the flow by clicking it.**
2. **Position the mouse pointer near the edge of the item and click.**
3. **Drag an arrow to connect to another item, as if you were drawing a line segment in a paint application.**

This method is more intuitive in concept, but it can be a little tricky to master.

When you link a data item to a SAS program item as input, SAS Enterprise Guide automatically assigns the data reference to the &SYSLAST macro variable before running the SAS program. Most SAS procedures will use the &SYSLAST value as the DATA= value, if set. You can use this technique to associate data tables with generic SAS programs without having to refer to the data by name within the program.

Avoid entropy with the ordered list

The process flow ties related tasks together and makes it easy to run them all as a group, ensuring that tasks that produce output needed by other tasks are run first. But what if you want to run just a subset of the tasks in your project but still keep them in a certain sequence? The manual method would have you selecting each task one a time, running it, waiting while it completed, and repeating this for each task in order.

SAS Enterprise Guide has a hidden gem of a feature — ordered lists — which lets you build simple lists of tasks from your project that you want to run in a prescribed sequence. You can select these tasks *à la carte* from anywhere in your project, including across multiple process flows, running them in whatever order you need.

To create an ordered list

1. **Choose Tools⇨Create Ordered List.**

   The Ordered List window appears.

2. **Click Add.**

   The Add from Project window appears, presenting you a list of all the tasks within your project.

3. **Choose the tasks you want to include by clicking them; then click OK to add them to your list.**

   Press Ctrl while clicking to select multiple items at once.

   Figure 17-3 shows an example of the Ordered List window with a few tasks added.

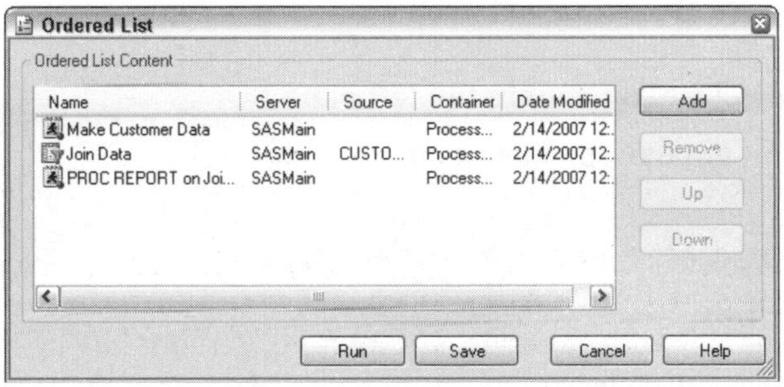

Figure 17-3:
Order SAS around with ordered lists.

At this point, the tasks might not be in the correct order for your needs.

4. **To change the sequence for a task, select it in the list and click the Up or the Down button to move it within the list.**

5. **When the list of tasks reflects the order that you want, click Save.**

6. **If you want to run the tasks immediately, click Run.**

The ordered lists that you create appear in a special Ordered Lists section of your project view. To run an ordered list after you create it, right-click the list item in the Ordered List section and choose Run Ordered List. SAS Enterprise Guide runs each task in the list in the correct order.

The project log: Your work on record

Every task and SAS program that you run in SAS Enterprise Guide generates a log file as part of its output. SAS programmers rely on log files to show what work was done, how long it took to complete, and whether any errors or warnings occurred.

The *project log* is an aggregated view of all the log files for all the tasks in your project. Every time you run your task or even the entire process flow, SAS Enterprise Guide adds the logs to the project log view. The logs accumulate across *iterations,* meaning that the project log offers a history of every task you have run in your project. When you save your project, SAS Enterprise Guide saves your project log along with it.

The project log feature is not enabled by default, so if you want to build up this project history, you should turn it on when you create your project. To enable the project log

1. **In the Project Explorer window, right-click the top node (the project name) and choose Properties from the menu.**

   The Project Properties window appears.

2. **Click the Project Log item in the left pane.**

   The window appears, similar to Figure 17-4.

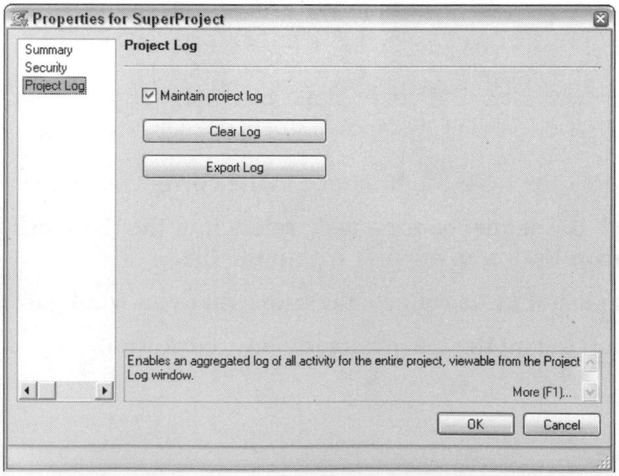

Figure 17-4:
Project
log — you
have to flip
the switch
yourself.

3. **Select the Maintain Project Log check box to turn on the project log for this project and then click OK.**

4. **To view the project log, choose View➪Project Log.**

Note that the project log won't contain any content until the first time you run tasks after turning it on.

The project log remains enabled for the life of the project. Because long-lived projects can accumulate large log files, SAS Enterprise Guide lets you clear the log as needed, saving it to an external file if you want to save it outside the project.

Letting SAS Tasks Do the Heavy Lifting

SAS Enterprise Guide supplies more than 80 tasks that generate SAS program code for you, and all you have to do is point and click. The tasks cover basic data reporting, plots and charts, and advanced statistics.

You can use these tasks as a starting point for writing SAS programs, letting SAS Enterprise Guide generate as much of the code as possible.

SAS tasks cover the most popular options for the SAS procedures. However, it doesn't take long for an experienced SAS programmer to discover that something is missing — some option or statement that hasn't surfaced in the point-and-click task interface.

There is a simple and obvious remedy: Use the SAS task to generate as many of the statements and options as possible; then take a copy of the generated code and use it as the basis for your own SAS program. The disadvantage of this approach is that after you create your own SAS program from the task-generated version, you can no longer use the task user interface to maintain the program. You are on your own with the SAS program editor.

Here's a better way: Many SAS tasks allow you to insert your own statements and options at predefined points within the task user interface. By using this feature, you can have it both ways: point-and-click for the mainstream options, with the capability to customize the generated SAS program with some extra statements.

Here are the steps to insert your own statements within a task, using the Summary Statistics task as an example.

1. **Choose Describe⟱Summary Statistics, using the data of your choice.**

   The task window appears.

2. **Use the controls on the page to select the variables to analyze and any other options that you want.**

3. **Click the Preview Code button on the bottom left of the task window.**

   The Code Preview window appears with the SAS program code that reflects your selections in the task thus far.

4. **On the top of the Code Preview window, click the Insert Code button.**

   The User Code window appears, as shown in Figure 17-5.

Figure 17-5:
Bend the SAS tasks to your will with custom code.

```
User Code                                              _ □ ⊠
Positions where user code may be inserted are indicated by the icons. Double-click on a
marked line to add user code or change existing user code.

  FOOTNOTE1 "Generated by the SAS System (&_SASSERVERNAME, &SYSSCPL) on %SYS ▲

  <double-click to insert code>
    PROC MEANS DATA=WORK.SORTTempTableSorted(
  where=(region="EAST")
  )
    FW=12
    PRINTALLTYPES
    CHARTYPE                                                    ▼
◄                          III                          ►

  [ Clear All ]            [ OK ]   [ Cancel ]   [ Help ]
```

As you scroll through this user code view, notice several lines labeled `double-click to insert code`. These are the locations within the SAS program that the task defines for you, allowing you to insert your own statements and options.

5. **To insert your own code, double-click one of the lines indicated.**

   The Enter User Code window appears with a text field.

6. **You can type your own SAS code segment into the text field.**

7. **After you add the options you want, click OK.**

8. **You can then close the User Code window, and also close the Code Preview window by clicking the button again on the task window.**

Note that whatever user code you enter is merged into the task-generated code as is. This means that you need to take special care that the code you enter is syntactically correct and makes sense at the insertion point that you selected. If you make a mistake, you will see errors in the SAS log when you run the task.

Being Flexible with Project Parameters

Like most software development, SAS programs tend to evolve over time. The first stage of any given SAS program usually consists of DATA step code and procedure statements written to perform a task against a specific source of data. Perhaps the program is required to meet a short-term goal or simply serve as a prototype or proof of concept.

If you get good results with that first version of the program, chances are good that you or someone else will want to use your program to analyze a different data source, or perhaps even a variety of data sources. It's at this point in the SAS program lifecycle that you might consider restructuring the program code to be more generic and reusable. Perhaps you would use macro variable substitution with %LET statements at the top of your program to assign values as needed, or you might devise a fancier version that contains a SAS macro program with parameters in the macro call.

SAS Enterprise Guide can integrate with your SAS programs using project parameters. You can think of parameters as SAS macro variables that SAS Enterprise Guide keeps track of, so that when you run your project, the application knows enough to prompt you for values. After gathering responses to the interactive prompts, SAS Enterprise Guide generates the %LET statements for you and submits them ahead of your program.

Where macro variables are usually simple constructs in SAS, parameters can be much more sophisticated to provide a helpful prompting experience to an end user. You can create prompts to accept text strings, numbers (with range validation), single or multiple values from a predefined list of values, date or date-time values, and even variable names for use within SAS task roles.

To get started with project parameters

1. **Choose Tools⇨Parameters (Macro Variable) Manager.**

    The Parameters (Macro Variable) Manager window appears.

2. **Click Add.**

    The Add New Parameter dialog box appears.

3. **Type a name for your parameter.**

    SAS Enterprise Guide automatically forms a valid SAS code name or macro variable name from the descriptive name you enter. You can change this code name if you want. You can also optionally add a description to help document the parameter.

4. **While still on the General page of the Add New Parameter dialog box, select the type of parameter you want to create.**

   Valid types include `string`, `float`, `integer`, `date`, and others.

5. **Click the Data Type and Values tab near the top of the window.**

   Figure 17-6 shows an example of what this dialog box might look like; its contents vary depending on the parameter type and data value type that you specify here.

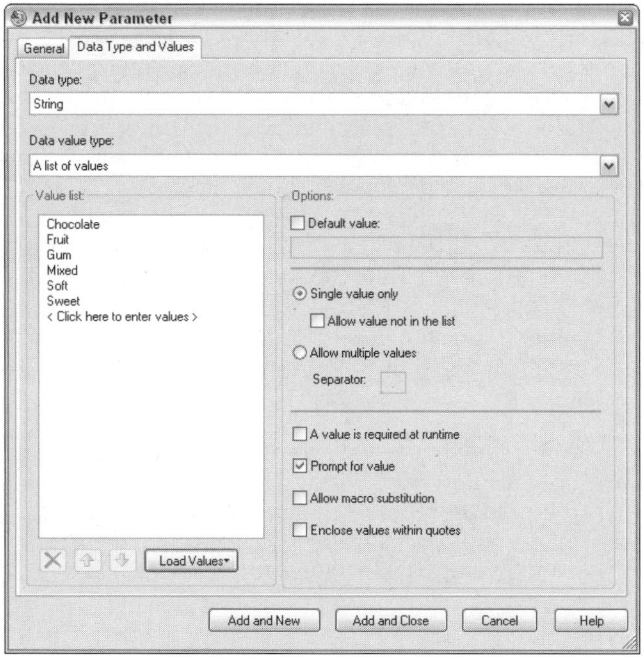

Figure 17-6:
Add a new parameter loaded with options.

In this example, the parameter type is `string`, and the data value type is `A list of values`. With this list type, you have the opportunity to specify the contents of the list to present during a prompt. The Load Values button (bottom left) offers an easy way to populate the list based on data values within a SAS data set or other data source.

Notice that the Data Type and Values tab also contains many options for how to treat this parameter. You can specify a default value, enclose the value in quotes, make it required, or even hide the parameter by clearing the Prompt for Value check box. There are too many options in this window to describe here; the feature is very flexible, and you should be able to find a combination of options to fit your needs.

6. **When you finally settle on all your options, click the Add and Close button to add the parameter to the project.**

The most natural place to use parameters in SAS Enterprise Guide is within the Query Builder. You can make a query definition much more flexible by using parameters within filters. For example, instead of creating a filter that equates to `WHERE REGION="EAST"`, you can substitute a parameter value for the literal value `"EAST"` and prompt for the valid regions. Figure 17-7 shows an example of a query that references three parameters.

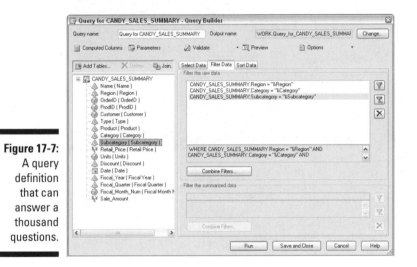

Figure 17-7:
A query definition that can answer a thousand questions.

Notice that the filter definitions simply reference SAS macro variables. The Query Builder is smart enough to recognize when you use project parameters, so SAS Enterprise Guide presents a prompt for values each time the query is run. Figure 17-8 shows an example of the prompts that you would see when this query runs.

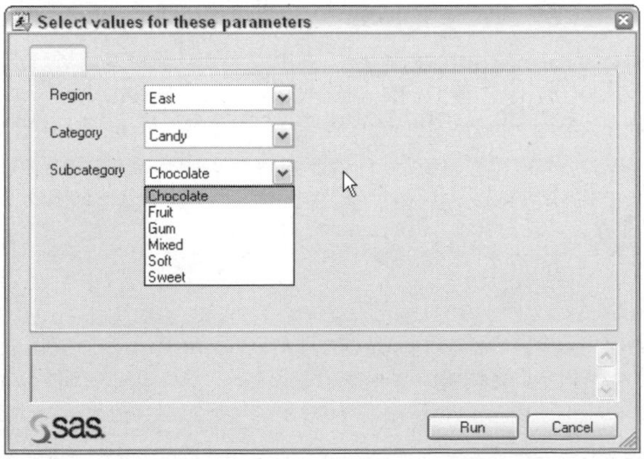

Figure 17-8:
A query that anyone can run and understand.

When you take a process flow and make it into a stored process, SAS Enterprise Guide is smart enough to promote your project parameters into stored process parameters with no extra work on your part. The prompting experience from a stored process is virtually identical to that of a process flow with project parameters.

Off-Limits: Stuff That Won't Work

Unfortunately, the world of SAS Enterprise Guide isn't completely Utopian. A handful of SAS programming practices simply won't work, at least not without a struggle.

X statements and SYSTASK (Tsk tsk)

Many SAS programs use the X statement and the SYSTASK function to escape from the SAS program and perform some work in the shell of the operating system where the program is running. For example, these techniques allow you to copy files among folders, query the contents of directories, and run batch files or shell scripts.

The default centralized SAS environment disables use of the X statement and SYSTASK function. The reason is that in a centralized environment accessed by dozens or hundreds of people, these types of shell-level commands can represent a security risk and introduce instability. SAS Enterprise Guide makes it very easy for less-experienced users to have access to your SAS environment. Perhaps it isn't a good idea for those novice users to have unfettered access to your system shell environment as well.

You can work around this limitation with the cooperation of your system administrator. You can configure your SAS environment to allow these statements again, using the ALLOWXMD system option in the SAS startup command. However, use this approach with extreme caution, ensuring that everyone involved understands the potential risks of "rogue" SAS programs.

DDE is DOA

DDE, or Dynamic Data Exchange, is a 20-year-old protocol that Microsoft Windows applications can use to send messages and commands to each other. The SAS programming language includes a FILENAME statement access method for DDE to facilitate conversations between SAS for Microsoft Windows and other applications. For years, SAS programmers have used DDE to programmatically read and write data in Microsoft Excel worksheets. When the SAS program runs, it issues commands to start a Microsoft Excel process and establish a communication link, open workbook files, and access data in particular worksheet cells. It's interesting to watch such programs in action because Microsoft Excel windows pop up and values appear in cells as if typed in by an invisible hand.

DDE technology works only under certain conditions, and these conditions often aren't met when you use SAS Enterprise Guide:

- **The two processes communicating via DDE must be running on the same machine.** In a distributed environment where SAS runs on a remote server, the version of Microsoft Excel on your local PC is inaccessible to your SAS program. Remember that the DDE link is between Microsoft Excel and SAS, not SAS Enterprise Guide. The remote SAS session might even be running on a non-Windows system, such as UNIX, where DDE isn't supported at all.

- **The SAS session must run in a windowing environment.** Even if your SAS session is running on a PC that has Microsoft Excel installed, the SAS session is running *headless,* meaning that it has no visible windows. Without this window environment in place, DDE (which relies on Windows messages) is not effective.

SAS Enterprise Guide has built-in features to import and export data to and from Microsoft Excel, and you can use those features to gain back some of the ground lost without DDE. However, SAS Enterprise Guide doesn't offer the same level of control at the cell level as DDE.

Nowhere to show: SAS/AF and %WINDOW

SAS/AF is a legacy application development environment that is built right into SAS. Using SAS/AF components, such as "frames" and screen control language (SCL), you can build applications that drive SAS processes. The user interface appears quite dated compared with most modern desktop applications and Web-based applications, but some companies continue to rely on their investment in these early full-screen applications.

Because of the client/server nature of SAS Enterprise Guide and SAS, SAS/AF applications are not accessible within SAS Enterprise Guide. These are full-screen applications hosted in SAS; and with SAS operating as a server, there is no "screen" to host these windows. In fact, any SAS language feature that would normally produce a prompt or window within an interactive SAS session is off-limits with SAS Enterprise Guide. This includes %WINDOW statements, PROMPT options on LIBNAME statements, and interactive environments such as the REPORT window and the DATA step debugger.

In general, SAS statements that require user interaction and that would not work well in a SAS batch program won't work well in SAS Enterprise Guide either.

Fortunately, SAS Enterprise Guide offers modern replacements for many of these interactive features. You can achieve much of the same experience (and more) through project parameters, the Query Builder, and built-in tasks. In fact, you can even extend SAS Enterprise Guide with custom tasks, fulfilling the needs served by SAS/AF programs for so many years.

Ending control with ENDSAS

In the world of sophisticated batch SAS programs, using the ENDSAS statement to control the program flow is common practice. The ENDSAS statement, as the name implies, ends the current SAS session. You might use this in a batch program to terminate processing when you encounter certain conditions.

However, in SAS Enterprise Guide, the SAS session is your lifeline to your results and SAS log. If your SAS program executes the ENDSAS statement, it's sort of like hanging up the phone before you've heard all the important information. Your results become disconnected and not retrievable from your SAS Enterprise Guide project.

Before you run such SAS programs with SAS Enterprise Guide, rework the logic to avoid using ENDSAS. Instead, you can change the structure, perhaps using macro statements, to conditionally execute just the code that you want instead of terminating the SAS session.

Part VI
The Part of Tens

"Your database is beyond repair, but before I tell you our backup recommendation, let me ask you a question. How many index cards do you think will fit on the walls of your computer room?"

In this part . . .

The Part of Tens is where we store those useful tips that would be pretty darn tough to figure out on your own. Even if you are an experienced SAS programmer or administrator, chances are good that you will discover something new by reading this part. We offer tips on increasing your productivity, info for admins, and some extras to boot.

Chapter 18

Ten SAS Enterprise Guide Productivity Tips

- -

In This Chapter

▶ Shortcut keys for quick action

▶ Moving data on the fast track

▶ Sniffing out your server software

▶ Fun with custom tasks

- -

SAS Enterprise Guide is a big application, sporting dozens of menu items and hundreds of windows and forms. The application is capable of so much, but many people who use it tend to spend all their time in a few focused areas related to their jobs.

This chapter offers a selection of ten helpful hints and tips to guide you while you explore SAS Enterprise Guide. Remember, it can be fun to try new things, so stray off the path occasionally to see what you discover.

The "Keys" to Success

In addition to the usual shortcut keys for copy/cut/paste and so on, here are the essential shortcut keys to quick action in your SAS Enterprise Guide session:

✔ **F4:** Takes you directly to the process flow view.

✔ **Ctrl+M:** Maximizes the view of the current document, whether showing data, code, or results. The view expands to occupy the entire SAS Enterprise Guide workspace. Use Ctrl+M again to restore the view back to normal.

✔ **F3:** When pressed with a code window active, this shortcut submits the SAS program for processing. Experienced SAS programmers will remember this key because it's the same in SAS Display Manager.

Don't Limit Yourself: Use More than One Session

SAS Enterprise Guide can open just one project file at a time, but there is nothing to stop you from opening multiple SAS Enterprise Guide sessions to work on multiple projects at once.

With multiple sessions open, you can even copy and paste content among different projects, including tasks, queries, and data references.

See What's Installed on Your Server

To see the SAS products that your site has licensed and installed on your SAS server, do the following:

1. **In the Server List, connect to your SAS server by clicking it to expand it.**
2. **Right-click the server icon and choose Properties.**
3. **In the Server Properties window that appears, click the Software tab and then click View SAS Server Products.**

   A window appears with the summary of products that were selected, showing which are licensed — and of those, which are actually installed for use.

The Switcheroo: Changing the Input Data for a Task

Most tasks in SAS Enterprise Guide require a data source for input. After you select task options and run a task for one input data source, changing the task to use a different input data source but keeping all the other options you selected is easy.

To change the input data source for a task

1. **If it isn't already referenced there, add the new input data source to your project.**
2. **Right-click the task within your process flow and choose Select Input Data.**

A cascading menu appears with a list of the other data sources within your project.

3. **From that list, choose the input data source that you want to use.**

The process flow automatically refreshes to show the new data source as flowing into the task.

One caveat: If the new data source doesn't contain all the columns referenced within the task (that might have been in the previous data), you have to open the task and fix any necessary column assignments.

Watch the Log Grow

If you're running a monster SAS program, you don't need to wait for it to complete to see its progress. Simply right-click the running task or program item in your process flow and choose Open Log. You can watch the SAS log scroll by, even as your SAS program runs on a remote SAS server.

If you open the project log (View➪Project Log), you can monitor the progress of the entire project as one task leads into the next.

Copy Data

Here's an easy way to copy data from one server to another:

1. **In the Server List view, expand the server with the source data so that you can select the data set.**

2. **Right-click the data set and choose Copy.**

3. **Expand the target server in the same way, selecting the library where you want the data to land.**

4. **Right-click the library and choose Paste.**

SAS Enterprise Guide copies the data set record-for-record over the network from one server to the other. Note that for large data, this operation can take a long time.

Another more efficient way to move data around is to use the Upload and Download SAS Data tasks. They currently don't ship with SAS Enterprise Guide "out of the box," but they are available on the SAS support Web site (http://support.sas.com) in the Software Downloads section under *U* (from the alphabetical listing). Then, look for Upload/Download SAS Data Sets — Tasks for SAS Enterprise Guide.

Expand Your Horizons with Custom Tasks

You can extend the capabilities of SAS Enterprise Guide with custom tasks. Developing new custom tasks is an advanced process requiring not only SAS programming skills but also Microsoft Windows programming skills. However, anyone can easily *use* custom tasks.

SAS provides a collection of custom task examples on the SAS support Web site, many of which are useful just as they are. For example, tasks are available to merge data, create picture formats, browse SAS catalog entries, and more. To see the available custom tasks, visit `http://support.sas.com/eguide`.

Submit a Selection

If you have a large SAS program but need to run only a bit of it (for example, a single DATA step or a macro definition), you don't need to submit the entire program in SAS Enterprise Guide. To submit just a subset of the program, highlight the statements that you want to submit in the code editor. Then, right-click and choose Submit Selection on *SAS Server,* where *SAS Server* is the name of your SAS server. SAS Enterprise Guide submits just the selected statements; the resulting log and output reflects the selected statements, not the entire program.

Don't Wait for Data to Open

When you add data to your project, SAS Enterprise Guide opens the data grid view so that you can see the first batch of records. This can take several seconds to complete, depending on the location and type of data.

If you're already familiar with your data and don't want to wait for the data view to open, you can turn this behavior off by default. To change this option

1. **Choose Tools➪Options.**

2. **In the Options window that appears, choose the Data: Data General category from the left pane.**

3. **Clear the Automatically Open Data When Added to the Project check box.**

If you also want to save time by opening results from programs and tasks, choose the Results: Results General category and then clear the Open Generated Data/Results Automatically check box.

Need Not Be Present to Win: Schedule Your Project

After you get your SAS Enterprise Guide project running just the way you want it, you can schedule it to run unattended, even when you're not logged into your computer.

To schedule a project, choose Tools⇨Schedule Project. SAS Enterprise Guide creates a script file and helps you to schedule the script through the Microsoft Windows Task Scheduler. The script, when run, automates SAS Enterprise Guide to open, run all tasks, and save your updated project.

Even though the project can run while you're not logged into your computer, your computer does need to be turned on and plugged into a network connection to have access to any remote servers and data that it needs. Also, in order for a schedule task to run unattended, you must provide your Microsoft Windows user ID and password in the Task Scheduler interface.

Chapter 19

Ten Tips for Administrators

*U*p until just a few years ago, if you were a SAS administrator, your life was relatively uncomplicated (at least where SAS software was concerned). Your main duties included keeping the SAS license — SETINIT — current for the handful of SAS users in the organization. Perhaps you served as the SAS site representative, acting as a liaison between your SAS user community and SAS technical support staff. You might also have kept one or two SAS/SHARE servers running so that multiple SAS users could access your valuable SAS data simultaneously.

Today, SAS software comes in many shapes and sizes. It's in front of more users than ever, some of whom might not even realize they are using SAS. This chapter offers a selection of ten tips for the SAS administrator. These nuggets of knowledge are not obvious or well documented elsewhere, and so might prove very useful to you.

Determining When SASUSER Isn't Usable

The SASUSER library is sort of the "My Documents" location for output that you want to save across SAS sessions. Experienced SAS programmers know that SASUSER is a user-specific location that they can rely upon for semi-permanent storage. It's not exactly an enterprise-class storage repository, but it's not a temporary scratch space, either.

In this new world of SAS within a distributed environment, two common configurations make SASUSER unusable as a storage area that persists across sessions:

- ✔ **SAS running on IBM z/OS:** The first configuration is specific to the IBM z/OS (the mainframe system formerly known as OS/390, which in turn, is formerly known as MVS). When accessing a z/OS SAS session from a client application such as SAS Enterprise Guide, the SAS session is created with the SASUSER library marked as temporary. This means that it behaves just like the WORK library; when the SAS session is over, anything stored in the library is deleted.

- ✔ **SASUSER is configured as read only:** This troublesome second configuration is very common in SAS 9 deployments. Because some types of SAS 9 servers (such as the SAS Stored Process server) typically run under an administrative server account, the SASUSER library doesn't even really make sense.

As a result, the typical SAS 9 deployment includes the RSASUSER system option in all server configuration files. The RSASUSER option tells SAS to treat the SASUSER library as read only, thereby rendering it off-limits for output from your SAS programs. Technically, you can remedy this by making sure that the configuration file used to launch your workspace servers doesn't contain the RSASUSER option. However, a better practice is to avoid use of SASUSER in the distributed environment. This helps ensure that SAS programs behave correctly in stored processes as well as within interactive SAS and SAS Enterprise Guide sessions.

Managing Logins from SAS Enterprise Guide Explorer

In most organizations, resources such as databases and servers require credentials in order for a user to access them. In SAS, credentials are managed as logins, and logins are associated with your metadata identity.

Different types of resources require different logins, spread across a variety of authentication domains. Your metadata identity is like a key ring, and each login is like a key that unlocks a different resource.

For example, the login required to connect to a SAS workspace might be different than what is needed for an Oracle database. Your SAS workspace host and the Oracle database server have different authentication domains so that you can have distinct logins for each resource.

To see what logins you have on your key ring, you can do the following in SAS Enterprise Guide:

1. **Choose Tools⇨SAS Enterprise Guide Explorer.**

   The SAS Enterprise Guide Explorer window appears.

2. **Choose File⇨Manage Logins.**

   The Login Manager window appears, as shown in Figure 19-1.

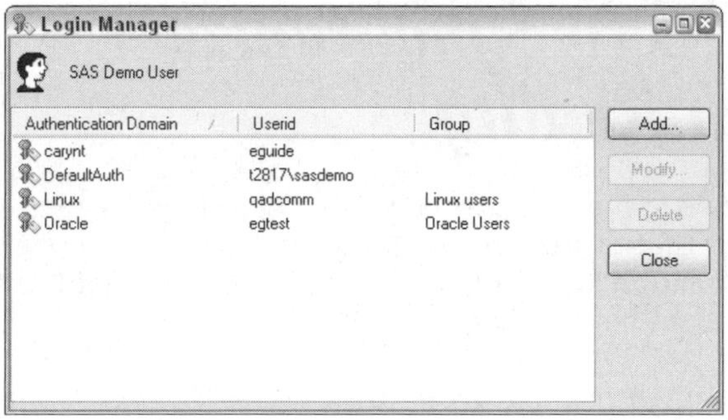

Figure 19-1:
Login
Manager
offers a key
to your keys.

This window offers a single view of the logins to which you have access. From here, you can add and delete logins, and also update the user ID and password values for the logins you already have. Some logins are inherited as group logins; you cannot delete or change those from here. However, seeing which logins might affect your ability to access protected resources can be useful.

Disarming SAS Enterprise Guide Explorer

Speaking of SAS Enterprise Guide Explorer, you might have noticed that it's an extremely useful tool to view and modify your SAS environment. Some SAS administrators might say it's *too* useful — especially the part that lets you modify library and server definitions.

When you install SAS Enterprise Guide, the install screen presents you with an option to install the administrative components of the product. The default is "yes, please install all that powerful stuff." If you or your end users installed with that option selected and you later regret it and want to take it back, the remedy is simple. Here is how to disable the administrative capabilities of SAS Enterprise Guide Explorer.

1. **Locate SAS Enterprise Guide on the end user machine (usually in `C:\Program Files\SAS\Enterprise Guide 4` by default).**

2. **In that directory, delete or rename the file named `SAS.EG.SDS.Admin.dll`.**

It's perfectly safe to remove that file — its only purpose is to enable the administrative features of the tool.

Using METALIB to Synchronize Metadata with Reality

SAS libraries defined in metadata can contain definitions for tables (SAS data sets or views) that reside in those libraries. Some SAS applications (such as SAS Information Map Studio) absolutely require that those tables be registered in metadata before they can be used.

So if you have SAS programs that create data tables that you want to use later, how can you ensure that the metadata contains the table definitions? The easiest method is to use the METALIB procedure. PROC METALIB can report on existing library contents, create a report of the differences between the physical contents of the library and metadata, and synchronize the two.

You can access full documentation for the METALIB procedure from the SAS support Web site (http://support.sas.com).

Getting Better Performance from Information Maps

SAS information maps can simplify data access for end users, but ensuring good data access performance from all environments can be tricky. Here are two reasons why SAS Enterprise Guide and SAS Add-In for Microsoft Office need special consideration when accessing information maps:

✔ **These two products allow end users to decide which SAS server to use as a default server for certain data access operations, including information maps.** This is an issue only if more than one SAS server is defined in your environment. Data access is most efficient when you open the data using the server that is closest, in relative terms, to the data source definition. Think about the structure of information maps: Maps contain columns, which originate from tables, which reside in libraries, which are associated to a SAS server. Therefore, you achieve the best performance when you access the information map using the server connects to the related library definitions.

✔ **SAS Enterprise Guide and SAS Add-In for Microsoft Office access the detail data of the information map.** The detail data is appropriate for these applications, which let you perform further ad hoc analysis with the data. Other client applications, such as SAS Web Report Studio, access an aggregated view of the data. Because the detailed data is likely to have much more volume than the aggregated view, optimized access is even more important.

Making Your Database Work for You with Implicit Pass-Through

You can use SAS Enterprise Guide to build queries that run on any database. The Query Builder generates SQL statements, and SAS/ACCESS components provide transparent access, using SAS libraries, to databases that are not part of SAS.

Every database vendor supports a different dialect of SQL and a different set of SQL functions. Still, the Query Builder in SAS Enterprise Guide generates the same SQL statements, regardless of the target database. It can get away with this apparent lazy approach because the SAS/ACCESS product has a feature called *implicit pass-through,* which optimizes the SQL for the target database before passing it on. This means that there is a better-than-even chance that the database server (instead of SAS) will process your generated query; having the database do all the work is the best scenario for optimum efficiency.

However, you can make selections in the Query Builder that preclude pass-through, forcing SAS to pull large amounts of data from the database to process within your SAS session. For example, if you select to join two tables and narrow the result set with filters, and one of those tables is a SAS data set (not in the database), SAS might have to pull the entire second table from the database, perform the join, and then filter, instead of pulling only the matching records from the database.

Another way to break pass-through is to specify a filter expression that contains a function supported only in SAS (and there are plenty of those). If the database server doesn't have a corresponding function to match what is in your expression, SAS must pull the entire table from the database and process within your SAS session.

The key to success is awareness of which query actions are database friendly. You might have to encourage some end users to break up a large complicated query into a few smaller ones, simply to ensure the database server is used for the heavy lifting. For example, it might be more efficient to upload a small table to the database before joining it with a larger table — ensuring that the join operation can happen on the database server.

Publishing Reports from SAS Enterprise Guide: What's Needed

You can use SAS Enterprise Guide to build sophisticated reports, which you can then share with SAS Web Report Studio users — if, that is, all the pieces are in place and connected. Here is a summary of how to make the planets align so that this can work:

1. **Create your output in SAS Enterprise Guide, using the SAS Report format.**

   You cannot share HTML, PDF, RTF, or listing output with SAS Web Report Studio.

2. **If you want the shared report to be dynamic (refreshed each time you access it in SAS Web Report Studio), you must create a stored process to produce it.**

3. **If you build a composite report with the built-in Report Builder (using File⬄New⬄Report), each part of the report must originate from a stored process (if you want all parts to be dynamic).**

4. **SAS Web Report Studio must be configured with Report Web Services enabled.**

   This allows SAS Enterprise Guide to communicate with SAS Web Report Studio. The instructions are included in the SAS Web Report Studio installation directory as `deployment.html`.

5. **To allow SAS Enterprise Guide to find the proper Web services connection, you must have accessed SAS Web Report Studio at least once from a Web browser by using its *external* URL (that is, not from the Web server machine with `localhost`).**

Catching and Killing a Runaway SAS Session

We've all done it — that is, made a mistake that we immediately regret. For SAS users, the mistake often takes the form of a foolhardy query that, if left unstopped, would run for days.

When you submit a query like this in SAS Enterprise Guide, you have two ways to atone for your mistake. In the task status window (accessed by choosing View➪Task Status), you can right-click the query item in the list and choose Cancel. That's a nice gesture, but it's sort of like yelling, "Stop, thief!" when the purse snatcher is already two blocks away. Usually, SAS is so busy processing your query that it doesn't take time to listen to your polite request to cancel.

Alternatively, you can right-click the item in the task status view and choose End SAS Session. That kills the SAS process, putting it out of its misery.

Killing the SAS process can have a few side effects. For example, any temporary data or results that you had in your SAS session are gone, following your SAS workspace process to the grave. Also, if your query request was accessing another database process via a SAS/ACCESS library, the database process might continue to process the request until you intervene further.

Telling One SAS.EXE from Another

The SAS Metadata Server, workspace server, OLAP server, stored process server, SAS/SHARE server, and others all have one basic thing in common: Namely, they all show up as SAS.EXE processes when running under Microsoft Windows. This can make it a challenge to determine which SAS processes are orphaned or consuming all your CPU cycles.

The *Process Explorer tool* from Sysinternals (recently acquired by Microsoft) is a Task Manager replacement that offers more detail about running processes. With this tool, you can view more details about SAS processes that are running on your server and actually discern the different SAS server processes.

Figure 19-2 shows an example of a system with several SAS processes. You can see from the command line details column that one process represents the SAS Metadata Server (running as a service), and another is the SAS stored process server (judging from the `-config` option). The other two SAS.EXE processes happen to be workspace sessions.

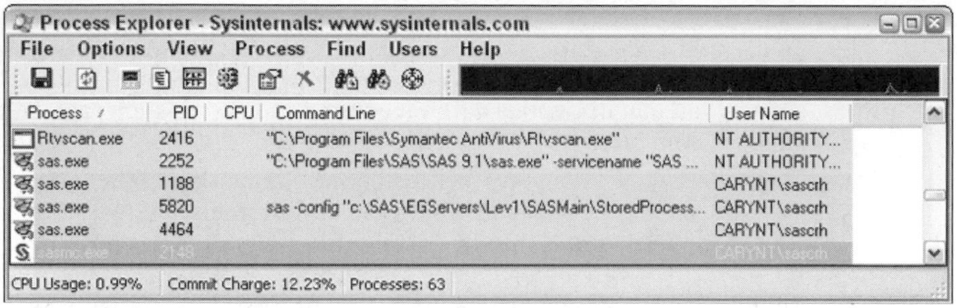

Figure 19-2:
Will the real
SAS
Metadata
Server
process
please
stand up?

You can find Process Explorer and other useful Sysinternals tools at www. sysinternals.com.

Peering under the Covers with Process Logs

SAS programmers are familiar with *SAS logs,* which provide details about what happened during their SAS programs.

SAS administrators need to become familiar with server logs. Each class of SAS server offers its style of log, providing appropriate information. Here is a summary of the popular log types:

- **SAS Metadata Server log:** Contains details of which users and processes connect to the SAS Metadata Server. It can also show when metadata is added, deleted, and modified — and by whom.

- **SAS object spawner log:** Contains initialization details for the servers that it controls. Also contains details about connections to workspace and stored process servers, how those processes were spawned (launched), who attempted to connect, whether they were successful, and error conditions if failures occurred.

- **SAS workspace server log:** Contains a snapshot of activity during a single SAS workspace session. This activity includes data access and SAS code processing. Usually, there is one workspace log file for each workspace process that is spawned. This means that the folder that contains the log files can become cluttered quickly, especially if many users are connecting to SAS sessions.

You can configure the logging activity of each server at a range of detail levels. The default is to show just the high-level activity, but you can tweak the options to get the nitty-gritty details, too. Much of the low-level details are useful only by SAS support staff to assist in diagnosing issues.

To turn on logging for these SAS servers, you need to specify the `LOG` and `LOGPARM` options on the SAS command or configuration file used to start the server. You can find more guidance about collecting such logs on the SAS support Web site.

Chapter 20

Ten (or More) Web Resources for Extra Information

· ·

Okay, we lied! It is supposed to be just ten resources, but we've given you more for your money with sixteen online resources! Read on for some helpful Web sites!

Need Some Support?

Just go to `http://support.sas.com` for technical support, online manuals, samples, user communities, software downloads (including Service Packs and Hot Fixes), and access to online and in-person training. You can search the same database that SAS tech support uses when you call in with a problem. In addition, you can submit a tech support problem online and view the status of your requests at any time. Also on this site is the home page for SAS Enterprise Guide documentation, FAQs, tutorials, and updates at `http://support.sas.com/eguide`.

What Else Does SAS Offer and How Are Others Succeeding with SAS?

Visit `www.sas.com/software/index.html` for details on SAS products and solutions by technology, by functional area, and by industry. For success stories with SAS in many industries and countries, go to `www.sas.com/success/index.html`. To attend a local, regional, national, or special interest user conference, go to `http://support.sas.com/usergroups/intro.html` and find one that would be useful for you.

Help Me Out with More Info on Making Effective Charts and Graphs

Go to http://support.sas.com/rnd/datavisualization/intro.htm and http://robslink.com/SAS/Home.htm for overviews, papers, and examples of the many graph types possible with SAS. Many of them can be used with the applications featured in this book; others require some SAS programming on your part to customize and adapt them for your needs.

For more background on charting data, see http://processtrends.com/ for a business slant and www.math.yorku.ca/SCS/Gallery/ for a more statistical bent on good and bad graphics.

Where Can I Find Out More about Business Intelligence?

For SAS specific help, see the Business Intelligence SAS Users Group at www.bisug.org/newsarchive.html or the SAS Community Forums at http://support.sas.com/forums. For general information, see the online business intelligence magazine, DM Review, at www.dmreview.com/ and the independent TDWI conferences at www.tdwi.org/.

Where Can I Discover More about Statistics and Analytics?

For analytics help that is specific to SAS, see www.sas.com/technologies/analytics/index.html and look up more specific topic papers on statistics with SAS at www.lexjansen.com/sugi/.

What about More Information That Just Did Not Fit in This Book?

The Web site for this book is at `http://support.sas.com/ sasfordummies`. The site contains many of the SAS Enterprise Guide project files used in this book as examples, as well as sample data and SAS programs that you might find useful.

Index

Notes

Notes

Notes

Notes

SPORTS, FITNESS, PARENTING, RELIGION & SPIRITUALITY

0-471-76871-5

0-7645-7841-3

Also available:
- Catholicism For Dummies
  0-7645-5391-7
- Exercise Balls For Dummies
  0-7645-5623-1
- Fitness For Dummies
  0-7645-7851-0
- Football For Dummies
  0-7645-3936-1
- Judaism For Dummies
  0-7645-5299-6
- Potty Training For Dummies
  0-7645-5417-4
- Buddhism For Dummies
  0-7645-5359-3

- Pregnancy For Dummies
  0-7645-4483-7 †
- Ten Minute Tone-Ups For Dummies
  0-7645-7207-5
- NASCAR For Dummies
  0-7645-7681-X
- Religion For Dummies
  0-7645-5264-3
- Soccer For Dummies
  0-7645-5229-5
- Women in the Bible For Dummies
  0-7645-8475-8

TRAVEL

0-7645-7749-2

0-7645-6945-7

Also available:
- Alaska For Dummies
  0-7645-7746-8
- Cruise Vacations For Dummies
  0-7645-6941-4
- England For Dummies
  0-7645-4276-1
- Europe For Dummies
  0-7645-7529-5
- Germany For Dummies
  0-7645-7823-5
- Hawaii For Dummies
  0-7645-7402-7

- Italy For Dummies
  0-7645-7386-1
- Las Vegas For Dummies
  0-7645-7382-9
- London For Dummies
  0-7645-4277-X
- Paris For Dummies
  0-7645-7630-5
- RV Vacations For Dummies
  0-7645-4442-X
- Walt Disney World & Orlando
  For Dummies
  0-7645-9660-8

GRAPHICS, DESIGN & WEB DEVELOPMENT

0-7645-8815-X

0-7645-9571-7

Also available:
- 3D Game Animation For Dummies
  0-7645-8789-7
- AutoCAD 2006 For Dummies
  0-7645-8925-3
- Building a Web Site For Dummies
  0-7645-7144-3
- Creating Web Pages For Dummies
  0-470-08030-2
- Creating Web Pages All-in-One Desk
  Reference For Dummies
  0-7645-4345-8
- Dreamweaver 8 For Dummies
  0-7645-9649-7

- InDesign CS2 For Dummies
  0-7645-9572-5
- Macromedia Flash 8 For Dummies
  0-7645-9691-8
- Photoshop CS2 and Digital
  Photography For Dummies
  0-7645-9580-6
- Photoshop Elements 4 For Dummies
  0-471-77483-9
- Syndicating Web Sites with RSS Feeds
  For Dummies
  0-7645-8848-6
- Yahoo! SiteBuilder For Dummies
  0-7645-9800-7

NETWORKING, SECURITY, PROGRAMMING & DATABASES

0-7645-7728-X

0-471-74940-0

Also available:
- Access 2007 For Dummies
  0-470-04612-0
- ASP.NET 2 For Dummies
  0-7645-7907-X
- C# 2005 For Dummies
  0-7645-9704-3
- Hacking For Dummies
  0-470-05235-X
- Hacking Wireless Networks
  For Dummies
  0-7645-9730-2
- Java For Dummies
  0-470-08716-1

- Microsoft SQL Server 2005 For Dummies
  0-7645-7755-7
- Networking All-in-One Desk Reference
  For Dummies
  0-7645-9939-9
- Preventing Identity Theft For Dummies
  0-7645-7336-5
- Telecom For Dummies
  0-471-77085-X
- Visual Studio 2005 All-in-One Desk
  Reference For Dummies
  0-7645-9775-2
- XML For Dummies
  0-7645-8845-1

HEALTH & SELF-HELP

0-7645-8450-2   0-7645-4149-8

Also available:
- Bipolar Disorder For Dummies
  0-7645-8451-0
- Chemotherapy and Radiation
  For Dummies
  0-7645-7832-4
- Controlling Cholesterol For Dummies
  0-7645-5440-9
- Diabetes For Dummies
  0-7645-6820-5* †
- Divorce For Dummies
  0-7645-8417-0 †

- Fibromyalgia For Dummies
  0-7645-5441-7
- Low-Calorie Dieting For Dummies
  0-7645-9905-4
- Meditation For Dummies
  0-471-77774-9
- Osteoporosis For Dummies
  0-7645-7621-6
- Overcoming Anxiety For Dummies
  0-7645-5447-6
- Reiki For Dummies
  0-7645-9907-0
- Stress Management For Dummies
  0-7645-5144-2

EDUCATION, HISTORY, REFERENCE & TEST PREPARATION

0-7645-8381-6   0-7645-9554-7

Also available:
- The ACT For Dummies
  0-7645-9652-7
- Algebra For Dummies
  0-7645-5325-9
- Algebra Workbook For Dummies
  0-7645-8467-7
- Astronomy For Dummies
  0-7645-8465-0
- Calculus For Dummies
  0-7645-2498-4
- Chemistry For Dummies
  0-7645-5430-1
- Forensics For Dummies
  0-7645-5580-4

- Freemasons For Dummies
  0-7645-9796-5
- French For Dummies
  0-7645-5193-0
- Geometry For Dummies
  0-7645-5324-0
- Organic Chemistry I For Dummies
  0-7645-6902-3
- The SAT I For Dummies
  0-7645-7193-1
- Spanish For Dummies
  0-7645-5194-9
- Statistics For Dummies
  0-7645-5423-9

Get smart @ dummies.com®

- **Find a full list of Dummies titles**
- **Look into loads of FREE on-site articles**
- **Sign up for FREE eTips e-mailed to you weekly**
- **See what other products carry the Dummies name**
- **Shop directly from the Dummies bookstore**
- **Enter to win new prizes every month!**

* Separate Canadian edition also available
† Separate U.K. edition also available

Available wherever books are sold. For more information or to order direct: U.S. customers visit www.dummies.com or call 1-877-762-2974.
U.K. customers visit www.wileyeurope.com or call 0800 243407. Canadian customers visit www.wiley.ca or call 1-800-567-4797.

Want to continue building your SAS® knowledge?

Visit our support Web site for training, technical support, documentation and other resources to help you continue building your SAS® skills.

support.sas.com